A Line of Sight

University of Minnesota Press
Minneapolis • London

A Line of Sight

American Avant-Garde Film since 1965

Paul Arthur

Published by the University of Minnesota Press
111 Third Avenue South, Suite 290
Minneapolis, MN 55401-2520
http://www.upress.umn.edu

Library of Congress Cataloging-in-Publication Data

Arthur, Paul, 1947–
    A line of sight : American avant-garde film since 1965 / Paul Arthur.
       p.   cm.
    Includes bibliographical references and index.
    ISBN 0-8166-4264-8 (hc : alk. paper) — ISBN 0-8166-4265-6 (pb : alk. paper)
    1. Experimental films—United States—History and criticism.   I. Title.
    PN1995.9.E96A78 2005
    794.43'611—dc22

                                                                          2004018120

Printed in the United States of America on acid-free paper

The University of Minnesota is an equal-opportunity educator and employer.

12 11 10 09 08 07 06 05   10 9 8 7 6 5 4 3 2 1

for Jarrett and Devin
and in memory of Stan Brakhage

Contents

ix   Acknowledgments

xi   Introduction

1   1. Routines of Emancipation: Jonas Mekas and Alternative Cinema in the Ideology and Politics of the Sixties

24   2. Identity and/as Moving Image

45   3. The Redemption of the City

61   4. The Resurgence of History and the Avant-Garde Essay Film

74   5. The Last of the Last Machine?

92   6. The Western Edge: Oil of LA and the Machined Image

111   7. Springing Tired Chains: African American Experimental Film and Video

132   8. Bodies, Language, and the Impeachment of Vision: The Avant-Garde at Fifty

151   9. "I Just Pass My Hands over the Surface of Things": On and off the Screen, circa 2003

169   Appendix: Lines of Sight (A Travelogue)

179   Notes

205   Permissions

207   Index

Acknowledgments

THIS BOOK HAS HAD A RATHER LENGTHY GESTATION, whose progress
was nourished at nearly every step by a host of friends, colleagues, and students.
The unflagging support for my work in the avant-garde, in various registers, by
David James has been a constant source of amazement, especially given the elegance
and categorical brilliance of his own writing. Our ongoing conversation has, in a real
sense, established the terms of my scholarly persistence. Janet Cutler is simply the best
academic colleague on the planet, and the most caring of friends; that she never tired
of my endless complaints, doling out advice with humor and sagacity, is testament to a
unique capaciousness of spirit. I have had the distinct pleasure of looking at and talking
about films with Amy Taubin for thirty years. Her knowledge of and experience in the
avant-garde scene have been a vital resource. Were it not for the generous technical
assistance of Larry Schwartz, accompanied as always by wry prodding, I would still be
in the throes of computer formatting issues. Devin Arthur accepted the role of local
computer guru with an imperturbable grace that belies her age. Susan Deul made an
early editorial intervention that helped me find the shape and trajectory of this volume,
then proceeded to offer me every form of sustenance in her considerable repertory. I
cannot recall a single tedious moment spent in the company of P. Adams Sitney, who
lent early encouragement to this project and whose scholarship has set a standard I do
not pretend here to approach.

Chuck Kleinhans, Nöel Carroll, Ivone Margulies, Tony Pipolo, Laura Mulvey, Bill
Horrigan, Mike Zyrd, and Chris Holmlund read or heard earlier versions of various

chapters; their comments proved extremely helpful during the process of revision. The redoubtable Steve Anker, Adam Hyatt, Saul Levine, and MM Serra supplied valuable information about the inner workings of avant-garde institutions; they constitute part of an unsung administrative backbone in the absence of which experimental cinema would languish. Over the years, a number of filmmakers have been kind enough to loan me prints or tapes of their films, often accompanied by frame enlargements: my thanks to Ken Jacobs, Pat O'Neill, Jonas Mekas, Phil Solomon, Lewis Klahr, Peggy Ahwesh, Saul Levine, William Greaves, Vincent Grenier, Tom Leeser, and Betzy Bromberg. Thanks as well to Robert Haller at Anthology Film Archives and Howard Guttenplan at Millennium Film Workshop for their expert guidance in selecting still images. Bruce Baillie's postcards and letters have afforded me rich insight into the creative travails of noncommercial filmmaking, and I wish him well. At the University of Minnesota Press, Andrea Kleinhuber was consistently helpful; special thanks go to Lynn Walterick for her meticulous job of copyediting.

The deaths of two friends, Warren Sonbert and Margie Keller, were incalculable losses both to me personally and to cinema. Stan Brakhage's death, during the late stages of preparing this volume, is an event of monumental significance. It is hard to imagine an avant-garde movement without him, and I feel, as he might have put it, blessed in my contact with his incomparable career.

Introduction

CANDLES WERE BURNING AND A NUDE WOMAN WRITHED on a wooden table in what looked like a fake dungeon. Lurid colors seeped into dense shadows. The film went on for a long time with very little story, rehearsing isolated fragments in an arcane sexual ritual the meaning of which a high school kid from suburban New Jersey in 1965 could scarcely surmise. Deeply infatuated with the remnants of Beat poetry, and a serious devotee of what was then called "avant-garde" jazz, I had spied a handbill in a Greenwich Village bookshop for a program of experimental films and decided to check it out. The Film-Makers' Cinematheque was located in a nondescript building on a midtown Manhattan side street so I arrived late, just in time to catch Bill Vehr's *Avocada* (1965), a nearly forgotten example of the sort of hyperbolic, subversive gloss on Hollywood dramatics then being cultivated by Jack Smith and Ron Rice. Several films on the remainder of the program, including Jonas Mekas's *Award Presentation to Andy Warhol* (1964), made strong impressions but, paradoxically, proved less difficult to assimilate than *Avocada* precisely because they had fewer conventional trappings.

The previous year I had twice gone to Antonioni's *The Red Desert* at a nearby art theater and—like the guys in Scorsese's *Mean Streets* (1972)—was a casual fan of Roger Corman's unhinged Poe adaptations, in particular *The Masque of the Red Death* and *The Tomb of Ligeia* (both 1964). Thus my perceptions of Vehr's film were mediated by a fledgling knowledge of consciously stylized alternatives to dominant movie language. It was also clear that desultory contact with "foreign" films and maverick independent productions could not elucidate either *Avocada*'s aberrant sexual undertow or its narrative-defeating method of organization. Here was a formal conundrum for which I felt starkly unprepared. Equally vivid in memory is the Cinematheque's *social* milieu, the scruffy underground theater whose denizens exuded a hip bohemian profile familiar from poetry readings and jazz clubs; in my mind, the antithesis of a homogeneous middle-class suburbia against which I was poised in incipient rebellion. Indeed, the atmosphere swirling around experimental cinema held an interest comparable to its onscreen images and were it not for a tenuous foothold in adjacent cultural scenes, return visits to the Cinematheque would have been inevitable. Alluring as it was, however, opportunities to hear Coltrane or Mingus or Allen Ginsberg took precedence over further immersions in the filmic avant-garde. Two years later, attending college in the Boston area, I started going to informal screenings of films by Stan Brakhage in the apartment of local activist and filmmaker Saul Levine, discovering within the bristling energies of the moment an urgent thread connecting personal pleasure in art to social identification with dissident movements. Like cutting-edge jazz, avant-garde film spoke forcefully, if typically not in direct or didactic fashion, to what I understood as uncorrupted expressions of resistance and transformation.

Nearly forty years after my initial encounter with *Avocada*, a sense of the importance of the avant-garde's social-historical fabric—as distinct from its aesthetic significations or its broader relation to cultural production generally—remains undiminished. A majority of essays selected for this volume attest to this concern, albeit in different registers and through disparate critical approaches. The title, *A Line of Sight*, is borrowed from poet Robert Kelly, a staunch supporter of experimental cinema, whose elliptical prose text of the same name was published in 1974.[1] The title harbors an additional homage to P. Adams Sitney's seminal history of the American movement, *Visionary Film*. It is nonetheless intended to signal a divergence from Sitney's abiding trope insofar as the notion of sight lines is directed toward external rather than internal processes of seeing—what takes place between movie screen and viewer, not simply impulses of light and their reception but an array of social and institutional networks, material exchanges, historical disruptions and continuities. During the past twenty years especially, the integral bond between vision and imaging has been repeatedly challenged. Hence the notion of a unified *line* of sight, except as it applies to the arc traced in the writings of a single observer, is slightly misleading. The portrayal offered here unfolds as a tangle of crisscrossing circuits that galvanize, but do not always terminate in, the aesthetic quiddity of discrete films or the output of pantheon artists.[2]

Although several essays perform detailed analyses of exemplary texts or, as in chapter 1, "Routines of Emancipation," chart the institutional vitality of a central figure, the bulk of this collection is made up of interlocking overviews of unheralded generic categories, neglected sectors of avant-garde production, and theoretical or pragmatic issues that have animated the movement at specific junctures. For instance, chapter 2, "Identity and/as Moving Image," scrutinizes the flowering of portraiture as vehicle for the projection of subaltern identities. The next two chapters examine a robust tradition of urban representation and the more recent elaboration of the essay form. Taken together, this cluster introduces new ways of classifying and interpreting a wide range of films usually addressed via different critical optics. On the other hand, chapter 6, "The Western Edge," and chapter 7, "Springing Tired Chains," treat the idea of regional filmmaking and African American contributions to the avant-garde, respectively—two areas receiving scant attention in previous literature. The goal is not to supplant or debunk morphologies constructed by other scholars but rather to offer a set of complementary frameworks in which the extraordinary breadth and heterogeneity of the avant-garde is reaffirmed.

There is, then, no pretense to a comprehensive history or an ordered review of paramount achievements. In some instances I have chosen to err on the side of capaciousness, assembling lists of works or filmmakers of uneven quality in order to indicate the magnitude of a heretofore recessive theme or emerging idiom. A loosely chronological arrangement of chapters proceeds from the sixties to the present, allowing for overlaps in historical trajectories and the occasional focus on a localized episode. Written over a period of twenty years for a mixture of publications, this collection admittedly lacks a single cohesive voice. My interests in and critical orientation toward the avant-garde have undergone marked revisions over time, a process inscribed in the accumulation of at times clangorous discursive methods. I managed to avoid a strong temptation to rewrite earlier pieces to reflect current critical resources. I did, however, take the opportunity to expand the historical scope of several early chapters and trim some extraneous matter from later chapters; where appropriate, endnotes have been updated to direct the reader to materials that appeared in the interim between original publication and the present writing.

To be sure, a prospectus of multiple, restive voices is not incongruous to a consideration of a cultural enclave in which key practitioners have worked across diverse formal vocabularies—Stan Brakhage, as is often the case, is a prime example—and have assumed myriad quotidian roles in the promotion and circulation of the movement's aesthetic bounty. Multiplicity is not a catchword in American avant-garde film; it is a deeply held impulse that in part accounts for its longevity and unquestioned achievement.[3] The tendency among artists to operate outside expected divisions of cultural labor, to shoulder burdens normally undertaken by nonartists, is a feature perhaps unique to avant-garde cinema; it is present only marginally in the spheres of postwar advanced painting, theater, dance, and music (there are a few parallel traditions in American poetry but, arguably, also a narrower range of pragmatic tasks).

Despite a possibly expedient commitment to editorial multiplicity, a bundle of recurring topics will be evident: the legacy of sixties counterculture; uses and theoretical implications of found footage; the allegorizing of technology; intersections of personal and social histories; the philosophical schism between poetic, expressive tropes and structural film's antisubjective, rationalist bias. Once again, the point is not that these motifs constitute the primary or sole continuities manifest in avant-garde film since 1965; they are merely one nexus of fascination. In a similar vein, my intention to annotate a body of lesser-known films and makers did not in the end forestall an urge to repeatedly cite the work of a handful of masters. While the composite essays do not argue for a crest line of aesthetic innovation, a distinct residue of subjective preferences and consensus landmarks has proven unavoidable.

Due in part to the specialized film readership of some original publication venues, *A Line of Sight* takes for granted at least a casual acquaintance with foundational principles and canonical films. If a review of such prominent issues as the status of narrative or the relationship of experimental cinema to modernist dynamics in poetry or painting would exceed the limits of this introduction, a synoptic sketch of a single dilemma—the aesthetic ramifications of sequential editing, or what Brakhage refers to as "aftering"—will be instructive. At the risk of oversimplifying a multifaceted development, in psychodramatic trance films and picaresque comedies of the forties and early fifties, loosely linear progressions of dramatic situations focalized around the waking or unconscious emotional states of a single character tended to dictate the logic of shot-to-shot connections. Subsequently, as reliance on story and enacted scenes began to fade, an ethos of direct subjective seeing mobilized montage strategies in order to express, through rhythm and metaphoric image combinations, a sensual immediacy of perception. In Sitney's teleological account, lyrical approaches to editing gave way to more ambitious, architectonic schemes that nourished dense associative skeins of symbolic meaning; Brakhage's hour-long *Dog Star Man* (1961–64) is the paradigmatic instance of formal "mythopoeia."[4]

With the advent of structural film in the late sixties, affective modes of editing were discarded in favor of global sequencing ordered by mathematical formulas or otherwise predetermined patterns. A small faction of filmmakers, of which Brakhage was the most vocal and eloquent member, viewed this antisubjectivist stance as an affront to imaginative and sensual possibilities of the medium.[5] In fact, as I contend in chapter 5, "The Last of the Last Machine?," structural film did not so much expunge as conveniently displace the sovereign artistic ego as principal signifier in the articulation of images. For roughly a decade, polarities of expressivist/rationalist, maximalist/minimalist bracketed the available options for filmic structure.

By the 1980s, a generation of younger makers—buoyed by established figures like Yvonne Rainer and George Kuchar—began to exert an influence on the experimental scene. Steeped in the rude energies of punk music (and film), equally enthralled by the commercial detritus of television and the high-cultural imperatives of European critical theory, these de jure or de facto postmodern ironists repudiated artistic pretenses to monumentality as surely as they deflated rhetorics of sincerity, authenticity, and didactic reflexivity. Attempting to move beyond existing styles, they inherited a crisis in editing for which neither poetic nor structural derivatives were viable. The past twenty years have witnessed an accelerating repertoire of solutions to the previous stalemate, discussed at greater length in chapter 9. Revisiting the dynamics of storytelling, as both spontaneous vocal performance and rough-hewn literary adaptation, served to deflect twin shibboleths of subjective and antisubjective sequencing. Another generative avenue has been the gathering of strictly additive, aleatory, or processual units in which the imprint of individual, intellectualized shaping is noticeably flattened or eliminated altogether. A third approach entails variants of quotation and recontextualization of extant images. These strategies are not mutually exclusive and may be found in combination or in successive works by the same artist.

Ultimately, the films and (sporadic) videos discussed in the following essays merit the epithet "avant-garde" not because of reciprocal or contrasting attitudes toward cinema, as evidenced in themes and formal designs, and not because of telling interventions in, or dialogues with, the tidal flow of avant-garde stylistics. From a contemporary perspective, this activity is defined by the system through which projects are financed, completed, exhibited, and promoted. Exactly sixty years after Maya Deren made *Meshes of the Afternoon* in collaboration with Alexander Hammid—the quasi-official inauguration of the American avant-garde—her efforts "off the screen," in terms of securing opportunities for screening, delivering lectures, writing articles, and engendering alternative channels of distribution, appear inseparable from the radiant images she conjured on screen.[6] The same can be said, I believe, of Mekas, Brakhage, Jacobs, younger adherents like Peggy Ahwesh and Brian Frye, and many others.

Indeed, even for filmmakers disinclined to engage in overt cultural or political struggle, the significance of their work is refracted by conditions of access and reception. Viewed from afar, *Avocada* is a minor film and Bill Vehr was always better known as an actor and playwright in Charles Ludlum's beloved troupe, Theatre of the Ridiculous Company. It acquired, however, a quite revealing niche in the wider cultural controversies of the period. Following initial screening at the Cinematheque, Jonas Mekas seized the film as a pretext to publicly defend the integrity of "pervert art" from assaults in the press against Andy Warhol, Jack Smith, and queer filmmaking in general. Four years later, Mekas reprinted a letter from Vehr in his *Village Voice* column describing the confiscation of Vehr's original film materials by U.S. customs officials upon his return from a gig in Canada. Listing Vehr's home address, Mekas solicited free legal counsel on Vehr's behalf to represent him at an upcoming obscenity hearing.[7] Mekas was and is an ardent opponent of censorship while Vehr, who died from complications of AIDS in 1988, just wanted to be left alone to pursue his outré fantasies.

Needless to say, a lot has changed in the precinct of avant-garde film since 1969. Yet a number of issues embedded in this slight narrative illuminate our understanding of the movement's current position. The identification of alternative cinema with aberrant sexuality, forged in the public imagination during the sixties, returned to prominence in the early nineties in the heat of so-called culture wars over public funding of nonmainstream art. The avant-garde continues to be a welcoming haven for gay and lesbian perspectives and the movement has, in various guises, flaunted a badge of sexual license. Moreover, the self-conscious exercise and/or analysis of gendered codes of performance remains a compelling premise for a spate of recent work.

Mekas no longer writes a weekly newspaper column and, despite increased critical coverage of the avant-garde, the sort of regular publicity afforded by "Movie Journal" no longer exists. Nonetheless, his gesture in circulating Vehr's legal problems and making a direct appeal for outside professional assistance reverberates across growing grassroots initiatives in exhibition and production practices, epitomized by "microcinemas" and collaborative film performance. In the wake of intensive institutionalization of

An audience at Millennium Film Workshop, circa 1972. Photograph by Lloyd Eby; courtesy of Millennium Film Workshop. Copyright 2003 Millennium Film Workshop.

avant-garde practices in the 1970s, an antibureaucratic, communitarian ethos has been revived among a strong contingent of younger film- and video makers.

The tradition of in-person screenings—a tenuous source of income for a perennially underemployed cultural sector, and an ongoing source of internal political friction—continues to be a staple of experimental cinema. Although it has been a while since a work was embroiled in an obscenity case, stories about the vicissitudes of travel and far-flung presentation are both a fact of life and a mechanism of subcultural bonding. To be sure, avant-garde cinema, regardless of format or theme or style, is a blatantly, often proudly, anachronistic system grounded in the display of time-bound moving images before a live audience in a public space. This distinguishes the movement both from the rampant use of projected images in art galleries and museums— where viewers come and go as they please and frequently do not, or cannot, watch an entire piece from beginning to end—and from various domestic-based digital technologies of image transmission and consumption. To put it bluntly, the avant-garde in its essential outlines still conforms to *cinematic* modalities put in place at the time of Lumière and Melies. As if in testimony to that obdurate conclusion, and to the avant-garde's penchant for ingeniously improvised alliances, a print of Bill Vehr's *Avocada* was posthumously restored and returned to circulation in 1989 through the efforts of friends, public funding, a sympathetic film lab (Du Art), and the New York Gay and Lesbian Experimental Film Festival. It is available for rental from the Film-Makers' Cooperative in New York.

1 | Routines of Emancipation: Jonas Mekas and Alternative Cinema in the Ideology and Politics of the Sixties

The combination of centralized authority and direct democracy
is subject to infinite variations.
—*Herbert Marcuse*, One-Dimensional Man

I prayed to be relieved of all routines.
—*Jonas Mekas, Diaries, 1964*

Seizing the Time

Archaic as it may seem, cinema was once imagined as an emblem, harbinger, and social vehicle of the transfiguration of time, heralding a phenomenology of an eternal present made image. To whatever degree this utopian conviction is already inscribed in the work of Vertov, Epstein, and others, its consummate expression and true home is in the American culture of the 1960s. In the broadest terms, an elaborated myth of "presentness"—empowering the new while repudiating the old—was held in multiple arenas of social struggle as a precondition as well as a consequence of change. Few recognized, or cared about, the paradox that this promise cast the period in the same rhetorical cloak as countless other moments of historical upheaval. Directives aimed at the discovery of new, nonalienated modes of conducting everyday life in a subjectively foregrounded present were issued in a barrage of ethical, political, and aesthetic versions from practically every station on the compass of opposition. Recall in passing such slogans as "Today is the first day of the rest of your life," "Be here now," "If you feel it, do it," or in the deathless lyric of the Chambers Brothers, "Time has *come* today."

Within the self-legitimating coils of this philosophy, the movies were a perfect setup. They embody a process whereby material is converted into fleeting stencils of light, and hence they served as a hub around which metaphors of temporality, consciousness (collective and individual), motion, and representation would accumulate and then be redeployed in a calculus of politicized rhetoric and direct experience. Although it was never supposed that film could be a principal agent of social transformation, it was granted a supporting role by many rebels and a vanguard role by some. In a state of charged reciprocity between art and life, movies were held to suffuse reality, which in turn acquired a distinctly cinematic gloss. Events unspooled on a mental screen, movies were a journey in time, actual or spiritual journeys conjured or became occasions for motion pictures (every automobile windshield a wide screen),[1] and although the revolution might be theater, as Robert Brustein had it, it was clearly scripted with the optics and cadences of Soviet montage.

Behind the visionary vernacular lurked a cluster of theoretical ideas about film just then surfacing in academic discourse. What appeared onscreen was said to have an undeniable immediacy of impact and enunciative address continuously couched in the present tense. The physical scale and fluidity of the image beckoned a fantastical dream world, transcending the banal limits of the everyday, while its surface registered an exacting, "indexical" correspondence to reality. Direct and oblique, familiar and strange—these terms rotated passionately across a discourse that sketched abstract problems as the shadow play of a new historical subject. More concretely, recognition of commercial cinema's complex machinery of desire and ideological interpellation was counterbalanced by prospects for a domesticated technology universally available to personal needs and spontaneous framing of commonplace, "inconsequential" activities. In a tactical maneuver aimed squarely, if inaccurately, at the obliteration of authority, immutable distinctions between amateur recording and commodity production were blurred in the romance of film's liberatory potential.

Unprecedented affluence in white middle-class society helped secure a privileged association of movies with the space of subjectivity. The same economic conditions that fueled the emergence of student protest and counterculture movements sanctioned a perception of filmmaking as a heady amalgam of work and play. For the first time an entire generation—trailed by images of a childhood already preserved on homey celluloid—was consciously and realistically primed to harbor the ambition of becoming "moviemakers," believing this epithet to be both inherently progressive and open to myriad redefinitions.[2] Implicitly adopting a stance in league with Marcuse's notation of "everyone a producer," a broad sociological cohort made cinema a touchstone because of its presumed accessibility and demonstrable public reach.

To many observers, film's radical potential was embodied precisely in the promise of a highly visible, collective, noncommercial mastery of the apparatus. The process of witnessing, of recording *as* a means of political representation, persons, attitudes, and events traditionally excluded from commercial channels was not simply propedeutic but virtually commensurate with social empowerment.[3] Even a staunch defender of the status quo opposed to ideals of cinematic democratization as a social practice found it hard to resist exaggerated claims of effectivity. Excoriating *Easy Rider* (1969) for its celebration of drugs, Diana Trilling concluded that "no art exerts more moral influence than the films, and for the present generation . . . more than personal character is being formed by our film-makers: a culture, a society, even a polity."[4]

Trilling is speaking of and for mass culture, not the utopian designs of an alternative system. But if Hollywood was identified during the sixties as an armature of social and economic regulation, a dominant vehicle of bourgeois values, the capacity of movies as a *ritual experience* to induce antiauthoritarian attitudes is equally evident. An adolescent mark of group solidarity, movies were consumed outside the home (unlike, for example, recorded music), were the site of erotic adventures, broke down territorial barriers of class and race, and offered a battery of dramatic characters and plots easily recoded into subcultural axioms (the cultist misreading of *Casablanca* as a parable of radical individualism is a case in point). Here it was less the idea of cinema itself than specific patterns of consumption that served to undercut established values.

The ways in which moviegoing, as the flip side of amateur recording, was threaded into the routines of daily life helped nurture a twin aspiration: a desire to reform Hollywood from the inside, replacing its repressive structures and social address with a "New Hollywood"; and the desire to challenge its status as popular commodity on its own turf through a loose network of independent production. These two projects, finally untenable yet never totally abandoned, constantly intersect a third possibility: radical disengagement from the pressures and rewards of commercial cinema in the form of avant-garde and documentary practices. These divergent approaches, each packed with internal contradictions, were in fact interdependent or interpenetrated by the other.

The biographical legend "Jonas Mekas" weaves its way through the multitextured landscape of sixties cinema like a taut sinew touching every fold, every recess. There is no single vantage from which to discern its fluid embrace. Different witnesses have couched the legend in the tireless zeal and obstinacy of a religious seer or the makeshift ferocity of a guerrilla leader operating on many fronts at once. The sheer scope of Mekas's headlong activism, the number of dimensions within film culture with which he was engaged, is matched only by the range of voices and roles he assumed for himself—proselytizer, organizer, producer, publisher, documentarist, polemicist, friend and enemy, potentate and madman. It was, he says, in his "nature to do 10 things at the same time and work on 100 levels" (Diaries, 23 August 1964). And the conviction, at least initially, that everything was possible, that in the utopian tradition the good society could be created here and now through the exercise of individual and collective will, intrinsically aligned his enterprise with the philosophical currents animating the period.

Mekas was an unlikely candidate for the mantle of counterculture hero. A practically middle-aged Lithuanian émigré and fervent nationalist with a heavy accent, trumpeting a deep and abiding attachment to family virtues in an agrarian society, he was far from the fabled person "of this generation, bred in at least modest comfort, housed now in universities, looking uncomfortably to the world we inherit" adduced as the vanguard in the 1962 "Port Huron Statement" of the Students for a Democratic Society (SDS).[5] Having digested relatively little of American mass culture and the values it transmits, he lacked the sense of betrayal shaping the activism of a younger generation. The felt burdens of alienation and the measures Mekas took to alleviate them took on meanings and implications not shared by even his closest collaborators. For instance, he harbored a flickering residue of orthodox religious faith that militated against the support of certain types of lifestyle experimentation swirling around him. His equal revulsion toward liberalism—sealed for him by the Allies' sellout of Lithuania at Yalta—and communism was necessarily of a different order from that of the New Left. "You don't have to be a communist to be anti-capitalist," he concluded, "It's enough to be a poet" (Diaries, 30 March 1960).

Despite unbridgeable gaps in personal history, especially the direct experience of political oppression, statements like the above hint at a common ground with diffuse cadres of sixties rebellion. Tensions between personal authenticity and commitment to social change, the slippery tactics of aestheticizing struggle, form a partial lingua franca. Given the mandate here to chart the "100 levels" on which Mekas contributed to and was influenced by the forces of opposition, it is necessary to sound a double warning at the outset. First, Mekas's career in the sixties cannot be reduced to an unbroken aesthetic or political profile. Its determining features are complex and often avowedly self-contradictory. No knee-jerk model of increasing radicalization or radicalization followed by disillusionment is appropriate. For one thing, the well-known roster of historical events proclaimed as catalysts for protest or creative innovation—including the so-called Summer of Love, the 1967 march on the Pentagon—rarely coincide with shifts or intensifications in Mekas's clamorous campaigns. Moreover, different arenas of struggle such as filmmaking, organization building, and public discourse evince varying degrees of energy and commitment at any given juncture. Second, the temptation to establish concrete points of solidarity or mutual accord with other figures and oppositional movements cannot mask wide disparities in purpose and method; indeed, outright conflicts annotate a more general correspondence between countercultural and political sectors of film as well as other practices.

Mekas remarks that his burgeoning interest in filmmaking in the late 1940s was forged from the notion of a universal language, cinema as a "tongue in which we could reach everybody."[6] Although he and his brother Adolfas wrote fictional scripts both before and after their flight from German displaced-persons camps to New York City, Jonas's progression from documentarist to feature director to avant-garde diarist— traced diegetically in his greatest work, *Lost, Lost, Lost* (1976)—can be read as a gradual repudiation of film's universalistic mandate and the advocacy of small communities of interest, in essence taking the shape of a gyrating fall from one type of village to another. In a climate in which to "be of one's time" was virtually synonymous with "living in the moment," this evolution subtends an additional, personal process. Taking an active role in the social turmoil around film meant for Mekas the possibility of "forgetting," of subduing the past as painful memory, and inventing a new identity. As David James asserts, "as the independent cinema became the vehicle of his psychic, artistic, social, and professional lives, it enabled him to integrate them all, assuage his alienation, and eventually find a second homeland."[7]

If we consider the signature style he developed for the film diary, we see that Mekas inscribes a structural tension between preservation and erasure, a clinging to and a repudiation of the past that inevitably colors the terms by which the immediate present is captured. This dialectic is, if not unique to Mekas's artistic project in the sixties, the more powerful for its origins in an extreme succession of social displacements. In his method of production, principal labor is displaced from the reservoir of memory—enacting of prescribed events, dialogues, themes, camera placements—to rapid and direct accumulation of quotidian fragments that all but freeze the play of retrospection.

Previously he had dismissed this form of recording as "sketches," camera exercises performed *in between* feature opportunities. But when he discovered the personal efficacy of the diary, it authorized a shift in visual language that complicated memory in the throes of recording, and, likewise, in spectatorship. The standard language of scenes and takes, the image fixed in time and held in place by conventions of narrative coherence, are detonated by short single-frame bursts and twitches of handheld movement. Events and objects are constituted for the viewer as much by what is elided, what happens between frames, as by what is offered briefly for perception. Fragmentation and incompleteness, then, emerge in his work as stylistic tokens of commitment to the present and its consequent forging of a new social identity. This mode of capturing events implies an open-endedness, a willingness to abandon preconceptions and to court irresolution, reformulating the signs of a unified self as camera gesture and a shuddering trace of physical idiosyncrasy.

In the spoken narration at the start of *Reminiscences of a Journey to Lithuania* (1971–72), over footage of a stroll through the woods in 1959, Mekas recalls with pleasure not having to think about the previous decade, about the war and its aftermath. It was, he says, a new beginning, the dawning process of assimilation: "There was a moment when I forgot my home." And then: "Hey, I escaped the ropes of time once more" (accompanied by a shot of a nooselike strand of rope dangling from a tree). An entry in his 1961 diary about a group of recent films strikes a note that reverberates constantly in his public pronouncements: "New is moral, it liberates, it frees. Today all old is corrupt, it drags man down, and I am putting my bets on the young and the new" (12 July). Don't look back! Democracy is in the streets! Admittedly, this was a well-worn line in sixties radicalism of every stripe, yet it suggests one route by which Mekas found his biographical particularities and aesthetic inklings reflected in the emerging counterculture.

The past imposes itself in various guises. What was sacrificed by leaving the discipline of feature-film directing, apart from the slim prospect of affluence and a mass audience, rehearses in a minor register an initial and far greater loss. The self-contained interactions of the movie set, with its specific though not ironclad jobs, its loose hierarchy, can evoke an extended family or ad hoc village. This sense of affiliation would later be rediscovered, not in filmmaking but in its ancillary networks. During much of the ensuing decade Mekas would complain of never finding time to edit growing stacks of film footage. Having shifted his central focus decisively and on multiple levels to the public sphere, the solitary regime of editing and avant-garde postproduction must have stirred in him a raw ambivalence. Letting it all hang unfinished on the walls of various apartments protected his images from the "ropes of time," and in a sense insulated him from existential isolation. It follows that in the completed diary films, aspects of memory (labeling, explanation, ironic comparison) are vested in procedures added after the "socialized" stratum of recording: collation of footage, intertitling, voice-over narration, music.

For the "man who never wanted to leave his home"—the invocation to *Lost, Lost, Lost*—a glorious interval is spent careening between polarities of past and present, public and private, popular and elite, control and disengagement, consolidation and direct action. The dilemmas addressed here are summarized by Todd Gitlin as a typically sixties dynamic of "strategic" versus "expressive" political ends.[8] Like the incursions of a younger, and in many ways alien, generation, Mekas fought a constant battle over how to turn the ecstatic moment into historical reality.

"Let's Remain Disorganizedly Organized"

Toward the end of 1966, Mekas placed in his written diaries a neatly drafted diagram resembling the flowchart of a major corporation, a "family tree" illustrating with their dates of inception the various parent and subsidiary branches of independent cinema then under his control. The chart includes the New American Cinema Group (1960), Film-Makers' Cooperative (1962), Film Culture Non-Profit Corporation (1963), Film-Makers' Cinematheque (1964), Film-Makers' Workshop (1964), Film-Makers' Lecture Bureau (1964), friends of the New American Cinema (1964), and Film-Makers' Distribution Center (1966). It is an impressive list and a testament to the common political tactic by which simply naming a group or event validated its existence while disguising its actual clout in numbers or funding.

Yet Mekas's account is far from inclusive. It would have required more vectors and

Jonas Mekas and Adolfas Mekas in *Lost, Lost, Lost*. Photograph courtesy of Anthology Film Archives.

proliferating boxes to encompass *Film Culture* magazine, founded in 1955, the Anti-Censorship Fund (a short-lived response to repeated police busts in 1964 of *Flaming Creatures* and other "obscenities"), and the New American Cinema Exposition (a series of programs that toured Europe in 1964 and 1967 under the stewardship of P. Adams Sitney and Barbara Rubin). Another branch could have been added for a host of failed proposals such as "Shoot Your Way Out with a Camera," a scheme to train two hundred minority children to make "diary-like, journalistic, or poetic films about their own lives, how they feel, how they live, what they see . . . Make your film frames into bullets of truth" (Diaries, 2 October 1967). There would need to be space for countless alliances with commercial movie theaters and museums hosting the Film-Makers' Showcase and other avant-garde series (eighteen different venues between 1961 and 1969). Absent as well are traces of close collaborations with groups such as the Poets' Theater, the Living Theater (with whom Mekas filmed *The Brig* in 1964, ceding to them all subsequent profits), and Newsreel, the radical documentary collective whose organization he helped facilitate, publicize, and provide with film stock. Nor is there mention of the dozen or so distribution cooperatives that sprouted around the United States, Canada, and Europe, fertilized and partially supported by the New York Co-op. Finally, he provides no hint of the project that would consume the bulk of his energies at the tail end of the decade, Anthology Film Archives (1969)—the repertory "museum" that grew directly out of the Cinematheque's division in programming between avant-garde classics and new work. Extrapolating from this expanded chart, the concentric circles of Mekas's engagement cover an ever-greater arena of sixties cultural activism. Emerson said that "an institution is the lengthened shadow of one man." In this case the shadow is long indeed.

In the second report of the New American Cinema Group (1962), Mekas declares, "Let's remain disorganizedly organized"—a tactic intended both to guarantee maximum personal freedom and to disguise the real fragility of the network. It was, to borrow an oft-repeated mantra, "organizing with mirrors." Virtually the same tiny roster of participants appears at the core of every group, every public initiative. What needs to be explained is how this outline of marginalized empire actually functioned in the realm of concrete social and economic realities, and to which other tendencies and movements in infrastructural patterns it can be correlated. Precious few of the energies enumerated above have found their way into official histories of American avant-garde film. Ironically, the best source of information remains Mekas's private, unpublished diaries—some fifteen hundred pages for the years 1960–70. They are in many respects a textual complement of his diary films, a heterogeneous mixture comprising not only private musings, moral declarations, descriptions, and ideas for movies but also newspaper clippings, quotations, memorandums, and an immense body of correspondence often averaging three or four letters per day.

Appropriately, the relationship between diary materials and public manifestations is quite intricate. A diary entry might serve as a draft for, or be recycled almost verbatim in, the "Movie Journal" column he wrote for the *Village Voice* between 1958 and 1971.

Shards of insight about current trends were then expanded in articles penned for *Film Culture*. Filmed images of individual diary pages, or Jonas pecking away at his typewriter, show up in various projects, while quotations cited in the diaries get transferred into movie intertitles. Certain revelatory passages even return, years later, as voice-over narrations. For instance, *In Between: 1964–68* (1978) incorporates with slight alterations this moving assessment: "Again I thought about my splintered, fragmented single-framed world, with all monolithic ideas disappearing; a replica, a reflection of my own self, ego, as it slowly disappears, the consciousness that is becoming more and more open, with many centers" (Diaries, 21 April 1966). Last, and perhaps most germane, idealized versions of projects are mapped out in private, revised then annotated around day-to-day clashes with authority. The diaries record the interaction between private imagination and attempts to realize its goals through a praxis of improvised organization.

Like other self-created activists of the period, Mekas stepped into a vacuum of public advocacy armed only with the ambition and resilience to create a visible "image" and then use that image to bind a loose skein of collaborators and attract new recruits. The social precepts to which he responded or with which he helped shape the burgeoning avant-garde movement required little true consensus and even less strict adherence. A bohemian individualism, an abiding faith in face-to-face negotiation and directly participatory decision making, governed both the policies of and the labor performed within denoted groups. An ambiance of voluntary, decentralized power briefly allowed, as it did for political organizations such as the Student Nonviolent Coordinating Committee (SNCC) and the SDS, a suppression of conflicts between individual and group objectives. With greater numbers and widening public visibility, such harmony proved increasingly hard to sustain.

Economically, the small amounts of cash flowing into and out of various institutions under Mekas's purview seem to have been treated roughly as communal largesse. No one, aside from theater managers and the secretary of the Co-op, collected a regular—make that irregular—salary. Monies collected from rentals or theater admissions were routinely plowed back into other ventures or given to filmmakers on the basis of immediate need (often to pay lab fees on a new film), a mechanism that eventually resulted in interpersonal misunderstandings and charges of favoritism. Mekas relied on several "angels" such as Jerome Hill and publisher Harry Gant to underwrite the costs of commercial space or the printing of *Film Culture*, but virtually all outside funding was garnered on an ad hoc basis. And given his strongly antibureaucratic, antigovernment bias, there was little effort to secure public funds or foundation grants. In a 1964 diatribe against the "sad state" of European experimental film, Mekas implored, "Let's keep our art free of any sponsorship, whoever the sponsor may be" (*Movie Journal*, 114). Years later a pragmatic concession would be made to the changing cultural climate, but for the bulk of the decade an obsession with autonomy and direct personal communication shaped fiscal policy, such as it was.

This approach shared with its politically motivated kin the advantages (and obvious disadvantages) of a constantly renewed sense of crisis, whereby demands for labor or for money were masked as individual and essentially ethical choices. Mekas's instinct for creating what C. Wright Mills had called "primary publics" was unerring, affording loosely composed groups the political undertone of classic democracy practiced in the face of "giant technology, monopoly capitalism, and the behemoth state."[9] It became at once a master organizing strategy and its own program for social rectification. In fact there existed few viable alternatives to this organizational model. If the aspiration subtending independent film was to create social as well as economic options in production, distribution, and exhibition, the inscription of a personal stake in each maneuver and the concomitant of a fluid, responsive chain of command was essential. In an angry retort to rival Amos Vogel's accusations of irresponsible permissiveness, Mekas declared, "The policy of NO POLICY is also a policy" (Diaries, 25 August 1966). A familiar theme across the range of sixties radicalism, Wright's "metaphysics of participation" functioned in a positive if fleeting manner to deflect increasing centralization of authority and its public expression.

To understand how power as the precipitate of social and economic structures was exercised through Mekas's advocacy of independent cinema and how its terms overlapped with strategies in parallel precincts, it is useful to examine the development and operations of the Film-Makers' Cooperative, the lodestar and most significant legacy of the avant-garde movement.[10] The formation of the New American Cinema Group in 1960 laid the groundwork for the Co-op in its strident rejection of the putatively corrupt "Product Film" and the systems it enforced. The Group's first manifesto rails against censorship and state licensing of films and stresses the need for new organs of distribution and exhibition: "It is time to blow the whole thing up" (Diaries, 28 September 1960). Despite sundry allegiances to the traditions of narrative and social documentary held by the majority of its founders, the Group dedicated its rebellious spirit to the freeing of "personal expression" as the highest ideal of cinema.

By the early sixties, Mekas's antagonism to the "adolescent character" of American experimental film had been supplanted by a desire to merge the social awareness and spontaneity of the documentary, the popular appeal of dramatic narrative, and the solitary vision and formal boldness of the "film poem."[11] Institutional patterns would have to mirror the potential convergences of many practices: the Film-Makers' Cinematheque was advanced as a "place where all factions of cinema will meet" (Diaries, 1 December 1965); and while *Film Culture* would decisively shift its focus after 1963 to the celebration of the avant-garde, it never totally reneged on a commitment to mainstream concerns. The prospect of reconciliation and of cross-fertilization of aesthetic methods remained lodged in Mekas's sensibility even as he fully entered the experimental film orbit. Frustration at the disabling ordeal of feature production, the corrosive infighting among, and accelerating defections by, Group members, and the positive creative outburst of unfettered modes of expression would bring him to the front lines of anticommercial revolt. Nonetheless, the failure to achieve a semblance of integration echoes along the path of avant-garde organization and is rehearsed (and to some extent recuperated) within the formal antinomies of Mekas's mature films.

The Film-Makers' Cooperative was founded shortly after the death of Maya Deren, who had pioneered direct involvement of film artists in the circulation of their work. At first, films were to be selected for inclusion by a panel of members, but this stipulation was quickly dropped in favor of open submissions. Despite some unspoken guidelines, filmmakers were free to set their own rental prices, draft their own promotional materials, and control overall policy through direct vote of the membership. No special treatment was accorded any work regardless of style, content, or rentability. Only in 1966, after a spurt of growth, did the Co-op elect a representative board, and even then it functioned more like a casual, and fractious, advisory body. In five years, membership expanded from roughly twenty to 234 artists (the 1989 catalogue lists 638 filmmakers). Initially, members and their films were a diverse lot: narratives and documentaries (including early examples of direct cinema), experimental "shorts," animation, and glorified home movies. There was a scattering of women and several African Americans among the participants.

By mid-decade, Mekas's diaries indicate that the Co-op's small commercial offices rocked with the ecstatic, multifocused energy of an urban commune or a militant party headquarters. In addition to the business of rentals, *Film Culture* was edited in one corner while artists like Gregory Markopoulos, Ron Rice, and Naomi Levine spliced footage at an adjacent table. At night the offices served as a crash pad, dining hall, and impromptu screening room. Visiting filmmakers adopted it as a hub for the exchange of information, equipment, and subcultural gossip. Aside from constant monetary privation, the first real emergency erupted in 1964 over the issue of censorship. Anticipating a massive influx of tourists for the New York World's Fair, the city government decided to burnish its cultural image by harassing or closing down strip clubs, coffeehouses, and porn theaters. Jack Smith's *Flaming Creatures*—along with Jean Genet's *Un Chant d'amour* and, later, other films—was caught in the net. Projectors and box-office receipts were seized and Mekas and theater staff members were arrested, jailed, and roughed up.

This generated a long series of skirmishes conducted in newspapers and journals, at the Third International Experimental Film Festival in Belgium (where Mekas and Barbara Rubin took over a projection booth to screen Smith's film), and finally in the courts. After several appeals, the U.S. Supreme Court voted narrowly not to hear the case, but the following year it handed down its infamous obscenity ruling pegged to "community standards."[12] In the interval, the Co-op office was recruited as a private exhibition venue and clearinghouse for information and public protest. With its cachet of sexual deviancy, the *Flaming Creatures* affair briefly placed avant-garde film on the cultural map, stimulating support from quarters previously oblivious or even hostile to the movement.

Coincidentally, this was the same moment in which the Berkeley Free Speech Movement gained national attention for its insistence on the right to disseminate political materials on campus. Mining a deep vein in American political philosophy, the early New Left discovered in the confrontation with administrative censorship a volatile issue, a set of tactics, a channel for publicity, and the trigger for an analysis of wider social injustices. The suppression of Smith's languorous demolition of Hollywood-epic sexuality provided Mekas and his colleagues with a similar manual of arms. In personal terms, the experience of censorship and police harassment dredged up the specter of his and brother Adolfas's flight from their village under threat of Gestapo arrest—for publishing a clandestine newsletter—and the continuing oppression of his homeland under Stalinism. More recently, police had stopped Jonas repeatedly during the filming of *Guns of the Trees* (1962) and censorship constituted a minor theme in the earliest issues of *Film Culture*. Mekas even describes a hilarious 1961 encounter with an FBI agent eager to determine his financial support from Soviet citizens (*Movie Journal*, 41–45). Resistance to government authority fostered a binding in-group paranoia about police surveillance that later emerged as a dominant chord in Left activism. The need to "travel light," to submerge one's activities in an "underground," reverberates through Mekas's sixties diaries and surfaces publicly in a number of newspaper columns.

Like other mentors of the counterculture, such as his friends Allen Ginsberg and Julian Beck, whose first instincts were aesthetic rather than political, Mekas was forced to navigate between the promotion of independently produced art as replete experience and its functions as an instrument of information, polemic, and agitation. Through the Co-op, his writings, and related screening activities, Mekas championed documentary or satirical "protest films," as he called them, by Stan Vanderbeek, Richard Preston, John Korty, Bruce Baillie, Edward Bland, and Mark Kennedy. His friendship with activist Judith Malina prompted him to film the antimilitarist vigils of the Mothers' Strike for Peace in the late fifties (footage appears in *Walden* [1968–69] and *Lost, Lost, Lost*) just as close associations with Mailer, Ginsberg, and filmmaker-politicos Barbara Rubin and Naomi Levine provided a rationale for shooting antiwar demonstrations in the mid-sixties. Mekas was thus frequently an indirect participant in political protest, his active support of militancy deflected by the roles of observer or entrepreneur.

Nonetheless, his ambivalence would be set aside in the turmoil of specific incidents. After the 1968 police riot at the Democratic Convention, he argued for the appropriation of video technology to scrutinize and expose the venality of public officials.[13] His role in promulgating the radical Newsreel movement can be seen as a logical extension of repeated calls for the formation of politicized, noncommercial newsreel networks: "With our 8mm cameras we can record the KKK and the life in prisons, the cruelty of man to man in Vietnam, the genocides and follicides and bring it all to the public consciousness" (Diaries, 19 April 1966). "There was," Mekas often maintained, "no disagreement between the avant-garde, experimental line and the political documentary line."

In the late sixties, protest films were programmed alongside avant-garde works for theatrical and college audiences. The Co-op lent films for benefits held by the New York Civil Liberties Union and other organizations and endorsed in word and deed several antiwar strikes. Although Mekas's nourishment of overtly political filmmaking provoked friction with a number of prominent avant-gardists, the *Flaming Creatures* episode clearly demonstrated that the lines between creative expression and political resistance could be breached by official malfeasance or inventively eroded for strategic purposes.

Instances of unalloyed solidarity are, however, counterbalanced by deep-seated mistrust of mass movements, of organized protest, and the bureaucratic process. Like other convergences between political groups and countercultural activities—rock music, experimental theater, and the underground press ducked in and out of collaboration with SDS, National Mobilization, and other entities—divergent ideologies advocating societal change through the liberation of individual consciousness or through mass action coexisted uneasily. During anticensorship battles Mekas advocated mass picketing of commercial theaters showing licensed movies, but such efforts were not generally conducive to a style built on what Hawthorne refers to as "the magnetic chain of humanity." Responding to published criticism of the avant-garde for its lack of social commitment, he characteristically declared, "Down with barriers, borders, national interests, national parties, national movements" (Diaries, 18 October 1967); when Barbara Rubin and Shirley Clarke got arrested at the Pentagon in 1967, he noted, "I am no longer with it, or with them" (Diaries, November 1967).

Fear of being swallowed up by large organizations beyond his—or beyond informal group—control, of having to adopt a measure of ideological discipline, kept Mekas from completely throwing his organizational and rhetorical weight behind the rising culture of dissent. The sort of argument he used to prop up ideals of autonomy applied equally to alliances with the New Left and opportunities to steer avant-garde film to a wider and more diverse audience: "Once you use established channels you have to embrace their techniques of promotion and that will eventually affect the kinds of films you make. There is no end. You end up with a product everyone else makes" (Mekas, 1990 interview). With Marcusean insight he saw the lurking dangers of cooptation, and it mattered little whether the danger came from Left institutions or from the mass culture industry.

Yet the lure of thrusting alternative cinema into public view, and by so doing enlarging its role in the socially redemptive transformation of consciousness, remained strong even after Mekas repudiated the independent feature. He would preach disengagement in one newspaper column: "Artists shouldn't waste a single drop of their lives fighting the old: we should continue and concentrate on the creation of the new, because the old will die by itself" (*Movie Journal,* 181); and then a week later argue that "the balance must be restored. There should be three or four theaters in Times Square playing *Normal Love,* Brakhage, Markopoulos, etc."

On several occasions he explored the possibility of placing 8mm film prints in bookstores and, in 1970, considered a proposal from ESP Records (an innovative promoter of the most progressive black jazz music of the sixties) to distribute videotape copies of films in record stores (Diaries, 6 March 1970).[14] Mekas could nurture the vision of an alternative system while at the same time, and without apparent contradiction, challenge entrenched power in the commercial industry. International film festivals were a persistent target of avant-garde infiltration, and daily movie reviewers were berated in print and privately for their lack of coverage. Perhaps taking a page from Mao's Cultural Revolution, Mekas humorously proposed that student strikers "take over" the

New York Times and Time-Life buildings and "demand a complete revamping of their cultural coverage, policies, and staffs" (*Movie Journal*, 340).

As avant-garde film pressed closer to the sources of (mostly local) notoriety and power, Mekas's principled support of democratic access—in the Co-op, in "Movie Journal," and in showcase screenings—was strained by his own penchant for publicity and his contrary ambition to preserve the movement's historic aesthetic achievements, a tension movingly inscribed in the dynamics of the diary films. The spread of institutional connections with all their incumbent responsibilities widened the gap between what one can call the structural position of leadership and the rank and file. Because of his skill at and willingness to perform the mundane practical chores that kept institutions from dying, he accepted the curious bind of trying to order the resolutely, if fruitfully, disordered. Memorandums to the Co-op are playfully signed "Minister of Defense," "Minister of Propaganda," and "Minister of Finance," indicating his cognizance of a perceived dictatorial role. He was aware as well that his public image conferred an invidious privilege, yet knew that without a greater measure of regulation, the organs he had helped sustain could collapse. There is in the diaries a genuine perplexity about how to balance personal freedom with the demands of increasing authority. There is occasionally raw anger—"I am sick of playing the money father to all" (Diaries, 20 October 1963)—and the temptation to abdicate his lumpy throne: "I am a fanatic and I can do much. But it is my fanaticism that is also my danger. I have become a force, a leader, even a saint. It is time to dissolve all forces and all illusions and all saints. Even art can enslave men, take them over, take away their freedom . . . It is so easy to think that what you are doing is needed to serve the cause" (Diaries, June 1964).

Activist and key New York Newsreel member Norm Fruchter offers a salient analysis of the dilemma shared by Mekas and reluctant leaders of the New Left:

> Often [the] refusal to play responsible roles at the center of the organization was based on . . . genuine humility, the fear of authoritarian roles and the perpetuation of hierarchy . . . But just as often it was based on a sense that such roles would alter the necessary balance between political work and personal experience, a balance intuited as crucial to the new life styles being developed . . . The contradictions between SDS's articulated values and SDS's traditional organizational structures thus reflected and perpetuated ambivalences within the SDS leadership itself.[15]

The lessons of overdiscipline and bureaucratization gleaned by Mekas, as by sixties militants, from the failure of established progressive and socialist movements of the 1930s resulted in a constant cycle of hostility and self-denial. As the stakes grew higher and management more complex, accusations of egotism, "revisionism," and selling out grew more vocal.

The popular thesis in texts such as Abbie Hoffman's *Revolution for the Hell of It* is that celebrity status in a media-dominated age is a necessary tool of organizing and the concomitant of responsible leadership.[16] Mekas was never accorded the kind of access given to image-savvy radicals, but this did not prevent intrafraternal ruptures. The symptomatic tone of betrayal is captured in Amos Vogel's mean-spirited attack: "There are really two Jonases—one very dedicated, the other a Machiavellian maneuverer, a history rewriter, an attempted pope. He has two passions: film and power. His greatest talent is to make people—some people—believe that he is what he is not."[17] Mekas's close friend Ken Jacobs accused him of revoking the purity and buoyant freedom of underground film by making the avant-garde "fashionable," by "promoting a star system" in *Film Culture* and "Movie Journal";[18] and Susan Sontag found his public pronouncements "shrill and often positively alienating."[19] What appears to have happened is that for a variety of reasons—personal, principled, and otherwise—trusted associates as well as outside adversaries bought the rhetoric of imperious authority likely intended as media, or in-house, charade. There is no way of knowing, however, how much that rhetoric galvanized its author.

Mekas's longstanding feud with Jack Smith is perhaps the most bizarre yet illuminating illustration of the onus of leadership that was faced in parallel predicaments by Mekas and the New Left. Mekas claims he has never understood why Smith "turned against" him (Mekas interview, 1990). But the bases of the conflict are readily apparent: money and social power, the friction of directing a community adamantly opposed to the potential corruptions of commerce and centralized authority. In 1965 Smith accused Mekas of expropriating his Co-op rental fees and siphoning them into other accounts.[20] Several years later Smith charged Mekas with the theft of the negative to *Flaming Creatures* in order to keep the film in circulation and under his surrogate control.[21]

Jonas Mekas in the Film-Makers' Cooperative, circa 1963. Photograph courtesy of Anthology Film Archives.

Although Smith then allowed Mekas on several occasions to program work in progress, Smith lashed out in a 1972 *Village Voice* article, comparing the generosity of programming at the Elgin Theater with Mekas's "stingy" policies. Smith called Mekas a "praying mantis" and claimed that the Co-op had been transformed into a "pawn-shop."[22] Less than a year later, Smith escalated his attack in another *Village Voice* piece, referring to Mekas as a "Golden Brassiere Publicity Mummy" who had "sponged off the baby-vomit of art, while taking the opportunity to slip the museum price tag of death around the neck of each."[23] Vicious references to Mekas in the guise of "Uncle Fishhook" and other vaguely anti-Semitic characters appeared in performance pieces by Smith, and a final salvo was launched during a 1978 interview with Sylvere Lotringer in the high-theory journal *Semiotext(e)*. On the subject of Mekas's defense of *Flaming Creatures,* Smith asserts that "Uncle Fishhook wanted to have something in court at the time, it being so fashionable . . . he could be made to look like a saint . . . when he was really kicking it to death."[24] Smith says that "it made his career; I ended up supporting him." And with not entirely specious logic, he concludes, "What you do with it economically is what the meaning is."[25]

The problem for Smith is that the Co-op became a "grotesque parody of Hollywood" with Mekas as its "capitalist" purveyor while he remained an "anarchist" ("anarchy is the giving part of politics"). His "roomful" of completed films was being denied exhibition due to Mekas's restrictive agenda. As for his brief bout with celebrity, "I couldn't live with it . . . This was the golden gift of Uncle Fishhook to me. Please let him keep the blessings of publicity." Refusing to accept Lotringer's proposal that Mekas was only a representative of a more pervasive system of power, he declares: "Usually in life nothing is ever clear-cut. How many people are lucky enough to have an archetypal villain for an adversary?"[26]

Smith's outbursts bring to mind William Blake's complaint, "Where any view of Money exists Art cannot be carried on, but War only." Mekas was supposedly befouled by commerce; his ambition to preserve not only his own career but the creative possibilities of a marginal culture through publicizing and constructing institutions[27] had somehow purloined the "freedom" of those who rejected absolutely the snares of organized leadership.[28] This was in truth a family squabble, and Smith turned on the patriarchal figure most invested in succession. Thus the prophet of the personal and spontaneous in film was outflanked on the very terrain he had publicly delineated, flayed in his vision of social change as requiring material forms of perpetuation. Defending himself from a different but related attack, Mekas would exclaim, "My dogmatism is larger than their permissiveness" (Diaries, July 1970).

While the Smith feud is an extreme case, there were clashes of a similar nature with Jacobs, Barbara Rubin, and others in what could be called the "anarchist" wing of the avant-garde. Conflicts erupted in turn with an opposing camp, those who favored greater selectivity, consolidation, or focus on popular (as opposed to populist) endeavors. In 1967, Stan Brakhage briefly withdrew his films from the Co-op precisely because it refused selection and, in his view, too many works "advertised violence, hatred, dope, self-centered love, nihilism" (Diaries, 2 August 1967). Brakhage too referred to the

Co-op as a "mini-Hollywood," this time representing the avatar of "antiart." Mekas clung to the principle of open access but later worried that Brakhage's argument for the promotion of a "select few" had merit after all (Diaries, 2 April 1968). It was in this period that plans for an "academy" of independent film were given serious attention, and after the usual dire tribulations Anthology Film Archives was founded in 1970. In typical fashion, Mekas would work toward the incorporation of radical art into stable institutions while trying to uphold the theme of permanent cultural transformation.

Rhetorics of Liberation

One year after the publication of the *Communist Manifesto,* Thoreau wrote his essay "Civil Disobedience," originally entitled "Resistance to Civil Government." Mekas does not recall when he first read this piece, but the importance of Thoreau—along with Whitman, Emerson, and other nineteenth-century American thinkers—in his writing, filmmaking, and moral sensibility can hardly be overstated. A privileged text in the political philosophy of Martin Luther King as well as early factions of the New Left, "Civil Disobedience" offers a wealth of clues to the development of Mekas's political assumptions and their manner of articulation.

Thoreau's argument, consistent with his other texts, is that unjust laws should be fought less through the abstractions of petitions or mass protests than through individual confrontation: "It is, after all, with men not parchment that I quarrel." A single citizen suffering the consequences of public refusal becomes, for him, the founding "definition of a peaceable revolution, if any such is possible." Any government authority not totally respectful of the individual must be rejected. Freedom, the "obligation . . . to do at any time what I think right," rather than democracy, directs the individual's course of action.

Addressed in the first person, Thoreau's essay carries the cadences of an oral lecture. The language is direct, employing patterns of repeated words and phrases and the figure of chiasmus, a crisscrossing relationship of key terms: "Under a government which imprisons any unjustly, the true place for a just man is also a prison." As in his journals, Thoreau's argument is set off by passages of detailed visual description of nature; for example, the view of a mud puddle from his jail cell window gives the idea of spiritual freedom perceptual specificity. Without suggesting that a given text or rhetorical style can adequately encompass Mekas's political-aesthetic articulations, his assumption of the voice and prerogatives of radical individualism is grounded in a set of features analogous to those of Thoreau, hinged as always on a shifting interdependency of private and public.

Mekas's discourse about film in the sixties is exemplary in part because it shares what Stanley Aronowitz identifies as the period's leading ideological theme: "The attempt to infuse life with a secular spiritual and moral content, to fill the quotidian with personal meaning and purpose."[29] This entailed, among other things, the fashioning of a language that could integrate subjective feelings with an analysis of social ills, an appropriately indigenous speech woven from diverse strands of pragmatism, transcendentalism, utopian religious thought, and apocalyptic and "outsider" literary traditions.[30] The reformation of diction would, by this measure, lay the groundwork for a new political and social identity.

In a sweeping gesture, groups such as the SDS abjured concepts associated with Old Left or "European" thought; for instance, terms like "revolution" or "the proletariat" barely appear in *The Port Huron Statement*. There was in this omission something of a mistrust of rational argument, of language itself, and a corresponding belief in experience as an ideological benchmark.[31] Organizer Keith Lampe voiced a characteristic bias: "We emancipated primitives are free to do what we *feel* now because we understand that logic and proportion and consistency and even perspective are part of the old control system."[32] Or as Tom Hayden put it in an early dispute with the Old Left: "They *had* politics. We *were* politics."[33] Since "politics" in the inherited wisdom stood for all that was premeditated and rigid, it must be replaced by a faith in intuitive action. In a similar vein, Mekas would contend: "We want to liberate cinema from politics by putting it in the hands of the people"; "It's my soul that is my politics" (Diaries, October 1967, July 1968).[34]

Adopting a posture toward authority commensurate with that of the New Left, Mekas rejected the provenance of European culture for its complicity in two world wars and the consequent erasure of cultural entities such as Lithuania (Diaries, 10 October 1960). He says he was "taken in" during the fifties by the orthodox Marxism of collaborator Eduardo de Laurot, but abandoned this influence, and its aesthetic requisite of social realism, when the relationship collapsed in 1962 and Mekas edged closer to the avant-garde (Diaries, 12 July 1963). Nevertheless, he regularly employed political metaphors in framing the project of independent film: "What I want to achieve ideally with my film *[Guns of the Trees]*: is to overthrow the government. All governments. So we can start from the beginning" (Diaries, 11 August 1960). And both early and late he resorted to antipodes such as "capitalist" versus "revolutionary" as attitudes about art.

Such terms proved especially useful in response to those who spurned experimental film for its lack of social engagement while devoting their journalistic attention to bankrupt commercial movies (Diaries, May 1967, May 1970).[35] A general tendency to link the counterculture with resistance to capitalism was augmented by a desultory identification with the struggles of Third World countries for self-determination, a romantic self-justification figured in a rhetoric of guerrilla warfare, liberation, and underground cadres. Here as well Mekas blended into the cultural landscape by offering parallels between Third World revolutionary practice and the incursions of alternative cinema (Diaries, 1 June 1962).[36] If he grudgingly lent support to militant protests, he also wielded similar slogans and tactics of polarization. He even wrote a "New American Cinema Agit-Prop Notebook," a somewhat satirical version of the revolutionary instructional manuals flaunted by the underground press. Given sufficient common cause, such as the trashing of the New York Film Festival, he could turn over a "Movie Journal" column to the unfailingly angry voice of cadres like the New York Motherfuckers: "Up against the wall, bourgeois institutions, bourgeois culture, bourgeois life" (*Movie Journal*, 317).

The willingness to create homologies with sixties radicalism oscillates in Mekas's writings, partly in response to the trajectory of escalating claims in adjacent arenas. The pressure of relentless social upheaval forged within avant-garde film a tension between assertions of autonomy, of distance from the organized political sphere, and the expectation of a mutually enhancing solidarity. To take one issue, Mekas joined with other film activists in opposing the impersonal, hierarchal power emblematized by the Hollywood industry. While this went against both his affection for certain auteurist spectacles and his sense of absolute alterity—"Hollywood is a cow, the avant-garde is a sheep. There can be no competition between them" (Mekas interview, 1990)—he seemed to anticipate, yet rarely receive, reciprocal endorsement of avant-garde film from Left cultural organs.

One reason experimental film has been written out of the official history of sixties radicalism may be an unspoken fealty to childhood memories of commercial cinema, and to a machinery disavowed by Mekas and his cohort. As early as 1960 he began to connect the excitement of new cinematic forms with a repudiation of "professionalism" and economic domination. The impoverishment of the avant-garde's means and techniques was calibrated as a sign of a cinematic rebirth that augured a more sweeping revolt against visual convention (Diaries, 28 July 1960). Filmmakers were lauded for working through "ignorance and confusion," having freed themselves from a "trust in clarity, in pre-planning where everything is predictable" (Diaries, 5 September 1960). His comments on Lionel Rogosin's *Come Back Africa* (1960) set the tone for subsequent appraisals: "The very amateurism of the cast becomes part of the movie's truth and authenticity" (*Movie Journal*, 19). Since American cinéma vérité was found to contain the same liberating marks of rawness as avant-garde work, the crucial distinction was not in theme or narrative approach but in the ability of unfettered technique to register a passionate, subjective confrontation with reality.[37]

The valorization of spontaneous, untutored performance over clarity, structural elegance, or programmatic meaning is tied to an investment in sensory engagement, which in the sixties ran the gamut from the drug culture to rock concerts to guerrilla theater to spoken poetry. For Mekas, almost any attempt to reduce the separation between image and viewer—and by extension, between art and life—seemed worthy of praise. He was an early and ardent supporter of "expanded cinema," of film-performance fusions, and he promoted the custom of filmmakers appearing in public with their work. Immediacy was held to be the single most important criterion of not only aesthetic truth but also social effectiveness.

"This generation," he declared, "is by a dialectical necessity a generation of irresponsibility, disobedience . . . and these 'negative' characteristics should be encouraged" (Diaries, 4 August 1960). It is difficult at times to distinguish Mekas's sympathy for outlaw disobedience from his notion of political resistance. He celebrated Edward Bland's *Cry of Jazz* (1958) in its justified anger at white society (*Movie Journal*, 13), and eight years later he announced that "the students of Columbia are the only ones in this city doing anything that can be called human" (Diaries, 4 June 1968). Harlem street gangs could be seen as embodying the same "independent spirit" as emerging film-

makers: "Some disrespect for officialdom, parenthood. Society without thieves, rob-
bers, hooligans, is a dying worthless society in which all theft and murder is legalized,
done from above" (Diaries, 8 August 1960).

Increasingly explicit in the doctrine of the personal and the spontaneous was the
repudiation of private property and its legal trappings. In a seven-page manifesto, "On
Art and Politics," summarizing ten years of thinking about the avant-garde's place in
the landscape of liberation, Mekas attacks the shortsightedness of "radicals who speak
against art [but should] really speak against the property and ownership of works
of art" (Diaries, July 1970). Alternative film is crucially important because it works
toward "the destruction of the phony privacy walls" (*Movie Journal*, 281). Hollywood,
newspapers, the New York Film Festival were all on the side of property. Maintaining
the nonexclusivity of an organization such as the Co-op was by this standard a blow
against property relations (as, incidentally, was the decision by the SDS never to turn
down a request for a local charter).

Like Jack Smith, Mekas viewed himself as a brand of anarchist, and he wielded
anarchy's inflammatory appeal in the promotion of independent film. A characteristic stance was that "through anarchy filmmaking has gained a new freedom" (*Movie
Journal*, 185). Since he equated anarchism with the vicissitudes of the outcast and the
marginalized, anarchism assumes in his writings the status of simply that which sus-
tains individual liberty against demands for collective order. This offhanded appropriation of anarchism as aesthetic quality, as personal praxis, and as social design further
complicated an already complex ambivalence toward violence. More than once Mekas
decried the tactics of civil disobedience. He deemed counterproductive the propect of
serving a jail term in defense of *Flaming Creatures*. Witnessing a protest over the building of Polaris submarines, he reported: "I think all those pacifists are schmucks. I wish
they would do something violent instead. You cannot fight businessmen with passivity.
Hit them on the head" (Diaries, 26 November 1960).

Yet alongside arguments for the necessity of direct rather than symbolic action,
even when it courted physical confrontation, are stinging condemnations of destructive
impulses in both film and mass politics. Following an avant-garde screening he wrote
to the Sisters and students of Sacred Heart College that "those who will be part of the
destruction, they are helpless fools" (Diaries, January 1968). On a host of occasions
he reminded himself and implored other filmmakers not to "add to the ugliness" of
society by making works that conveyed anger or divisiveness, recommending "celebration" of love and beauty over "angry protest" (*Movie Journal*, 318). The residue of a
Christian ethics bleeds into pronouncements of militancy, and one frequently finds
demands for action nestled alongside the credo of Saint Teresa of Avila that "however
great the good, one may never do anything wrong, however small, to bring it about"
(Diaries, November 1966). A long letter published in the hippie-oriented newspaper
Avatar proposed spiritual solutions to questions of whether to enter the army or drop
out, resist, and so on (Diaries, November 1967).

Ideological crosscurrents engendered by Mekas's effort to clarify the functions of
advanced art in the juggernaut of rebellion point to wider uneasiness within sixties

counterculture. How is it possible to reconcile the self-affirming, redemptive thrust of a creative process with an unavoidable obligation to dismantle existing structures of individual domination? Should subjective transmission of immediate responses, regardless of their source or import, *always* take precedence over long-range goals? Jerry Rubin, in a famous 1967 article in the *Berkley Barb*, addressed this issue in directives that could rally cultural and political radicals alike, a proposed fusion of the "I am" with the "I protest."[38] For Mekas such unsettled, and ultimately insoluble, questions at once bracketed and fueled everyday conflicts between leadership and egalitarianism, between conducting campaigns for the public acceptance of the avant-garde and nurturing a communal spirit built around antiauthoritarian assertions of personal vision.

Marcuse postulated that "the imagination has become an instrument of progress" and that "to liberate the imagination . . . presupposes the repression of much that is now free and that perpetuates a repressive society."[39] Coexisting with utopian designs for an alternative system was the omnipresent awareness of limits to the exercise of imagination, especially within a medium defined by its technological-industrial scaffolding. The formulation of an ideological position through which to advance social options for the individual in cinema virtually compelled the collision in Mekas's writings of a critique of liberal society and an insatiable desire for withdrawal. Every gesture toward consensus, toward tactical solidarity, was chastened by the moral requisites of independence. Saint Teresa met the Motherfuckers on the barren plain of social estrangement.

Communitas

According to Fredric Jameson, it is a "social *symptom* that in the mid-60s, people felt it necessary to express their sense of the situation and their projected praxis in a reified political language of power, domination, authority, and antiauthoritarianism."[40] For all his dedication to the fluid *gemeinschaft* tenets of social interaction, Mekas was fond of applying clear, if self-consciously fanciful, labels to those on the side of grace versus those in league with corruption. People were "angels," "monks," "saints," or in an alternate idiom, "heroes," "Viet Cong," "fanatics." The rest were "devils," "bureaucrats," "capitalists." That such labels might be inverted on short notice is of less significance than their manner of dispensation, the philosophical dualism that underscores, and at time subverts, Mekas's imbrication with motifs of the period's rebellion. Indeed, alternative film and the movements with which it conspired shared more than tactics, goals, or social practices.

With historical distance it is possible to extrapolate from documents and often de facto policies at least some of the terms that for Mekas held in place the promise, and in specific areas the realization, of community: a redemptive body strung between moral and political exigencies, between personal codes of authenticity and "doing good for others" (a litany that permeates the diaries). Certain elements of this secular religion are obvious. The enactment of life as an aesthetic adventure conducted for its own sake secured the celebration of idiosyncrasy among subcultural outcasts. Doing one's own thing was an inviolate measure of opposition, of antistructure, even when it threatened to disrupt the precarious unity of group aims. The principle of permissiveness accounts for, among other things, Mekas's swift recanting in the early sixties of his distaste for homosexuality and its impact on sexual representation in the avant-garde:[41] "First I thought I'd like to see all homosexuality and lesbianism go . . . Now I understand that really it's our culture that has to go" (Diaries, January 1966).[42]

In accord with his rather ambivalent stance toward sexual license, he rejected the institution of marriage because it limited personal freedom and interfered with the commitment of the artist to his or her work (Diaries, 19 August 1960). Equally important was an implicit vow of voluntary poverty. Being on the cultural margins almost inevitably meant being on the economic margins, and while Mekas continually complained about material deprivations in his own life and that of his immediate circle, he was deeply suspicious of nearly every sign of affluence and tended to regard poverty as an index of virtue. In a similar vein, while it could be said that he himself bore symptoms of a public logorrhea, he rationalized verbal inarticulacy or circumspection in certain filmmakers as a natural result of heightened contact with the "truth" of the image. The appropriate arena for excess was that of hands-on shaping, the collapse of social style into aesthetic production.

Unquestionably, much of what Mekas admired and attempted to consolidate was a direct inheritance of the Beat ethos.[43] Pursuit of spontaneous creative explosion was fiercely maintained as a critical gauge of authenticity even as the stakes of public institutions began to expand. The model of disaffection proffered by the Beats had a corresponding effect on the development of the radical politics and sixties music. It is said that Tom Hayden tried, with others in his circle, to infuse the SDS program for social change with Beat values of "spontaneity, imagination, passion, playfulness . . . the sensation of being on edge, at the limits of freedom."[44] Simon Frith, analyzing the decisive clash in rock music between "pop" and "art," asserts that San Francisco acid rock—in fact the entire thrust of Romantic individualism exemplified by Jim Morrison and the Doors—"was the sound of the Beatniks."[45]

In both cases, the key to identification with a previous generation of social dissidents was the imagined reconciliation of individual with communal needs under the aegis of what Dick Hebdige defines as the "subcultural." Anticipating the denizens of avant-garde film, the initial activism of the SDS, and the first glimmerings of sixties rock, the Beats "expressed a magical relation to a poverty which constructed . . . a divine essence, a state of grace, a sanctuary."[46] The presumed relation between the gesture of material disavowal and personal or social redemption came under increasing pressure as challenges to the established order produced new opportunities for legitimation. But the theme of bohemian emancipation reverberates across a variety of efforts to attach vanguard political significance to marginal group activities. Beat refugee Gary Snyder delivered this message of accommodation:

The joyous and voluntary poverty of Buddhism becomes a positive force . . .
The belief in a serene and generous fulfillment of natural loving impulses

destroys ideologies which blind, maim, and repress points on the way to a kind of community which would amaze "moralists." . . . The mercy of the West has been social revolution; the mercy of the East has been individual insight into the basic self/void. We need both.[47]

Recognition of the impossibility of reforming liberal society and the consequent utopian desire to construct an alternative arrangement that would *spontaneously* substitute a new set of values for a hopelessly corrupt regime was not confined to white youth culture and politics.[48] But for organizations such as SDS, the promise of a "sanctuary" was direct and often highly conscious. Todd Gitlin testifies that the movement was, more than anything else, "a living protest against isolation and fragmentation . . . The SDS circle had founded a surrogate family, where for long stretches of time horizontal relations of trust replaced vertical relations of authority."[49] Another SDS leader, Paul Booth, refers to the tenor of a national convention as "group marriage": "We all got together and functioned as the priest."[50] Gitlin closes the circle of communitarian themes by suggesting that through feelings of solidarity with peoples trying to repossess their homelands, "we were straining to overcome our own sense of homelessness."[51]

Correlations between Mekas's personal involvement in and visionary guidance of avant-garde film and the communitarian ideals of adjacent movements permit a final observation drawn from a slightly different perspective. Anthropologist Victor Turner examined, over the course of his long brilliant career, the concept of *communitas* as a counterweight or antinomy to "social structure," the highly ordered and hierarchal set of symbols and events governing interactions in tribal societies. In the late sixties he proposed links between his notion of communitas and the evolution of mendicant religious sects during the Middle Ages.[52] A few years later, he extended this analysis to aspects of sixties counterculture. For hippies, as for monks and participants in tribal rituals, there is an attempt to establish "a timeless condition, an eternal now," in which structural adherence to segmented temporality is inapplicable, in which restrictive social roles are cast off and imagination reigns as the measure of knowledge and power. It is a modern attempt to duplicate, to make permanent, the freedoms mandated in rites of passage, especially in liminal stages of transformation in social identities.

Adducing a text on rock music published in the underground press, Turner isolated elements that align sixties culture with tribal and religious groups: the rejection of marriage; the endorsement of sexual license ("polymorphous perversity"); improvisation and abstraction; the mobilization and union of discrete sensory experiences; the enforcement of face-to-face interaction; the leveling of conventional indicators of sexual difference through dress, ornamentation, and behavior.[53] He further asserts that the work of communitas as an "aesthetic of discovery" was inherent under conditions of rapid, tumultuous change in American society. He links commitment to voluntary poverty with feelings of religious love; "cease to have and you are." The yearning for authenticity in individual existence feeds the potential power of the self-confirmed exile by casting separation as a critique of normative social order. "The difficulty," Turner

Jonas Mekas in front of Anthology Film Archives, 1987. Photograph by Hollis Melton; courtesy of Anthology Film Archives.

concludes, "with these Edenic prescriptions is that men have to organize structurally in order to exist materially at all."[54]

It is tempting to see in Mekas, self-proclaimed "monk" of avant-garde cinema, the modality of religious aspiration outlined by Turner as a common thread among otherwise disparate social phenomena. Its compensatory functions for "a man who never wanted to leave his country" cannot adequately be sounded. Yet by immersing himself in the openings created by the social ruptures of the sixties, by translating constant pressures of estrangement into a manifold form of praxis, he was able to implant a spirit of community in a field where only ragged individualism had flourished before.

(1992)

2 | Identity and/as Moving Image

> When this device is made available to the public, everyone
> will be able to photograph those dear to them, not just in their
> immobile form but in their movement, in their action, and with
> speech on their lips; then death will no longer be absolute.
> —La Poste *(Paris), 30 December 1895*

From Lumière to Woodstock

Of approximately a dozen tiny films presented by the Lumière brothers at their inaugural program on 28 December 1895, *Le Déjeuner de bébé* stands out as at once visually distinct and remarkably prescient. Lasting less than a minute, it shows a mother and father in medium shot plying their seated toddler with bits of food. Compared to vignettes featuring more widespread activities, this scene has a centered, unhurried development. The greater visual proximity of its subjects, along with their relatively subdued movements, their clothing, and physical setting, allows viewers hints of the family's affluent social position. It is for this reason the only scene from the early roster of Lumière films whose aura of familiarity deflects the clinical chill of historical distance. Where other scenes are populated by indistinct, albeit highly animated, figures, the family in *Le Déjeuner* creates an impression of particularized identity grounded in corporeal fullness and immediacy. At one point the child thrusts a piece of biscuit toward the camera, a gesture inscribing not only the unseen locus of observation but the inchoate fact of complicity between social actors and recording process. We know that the person behind the camera is her uncle Louis, his role in the profilmic reality fixed by familial, as well as economic, bonds. Thus in its narrative anecdote, as well as in the performative exchange between observer and observed, this fleeting glimpse of domestic life can be regarded as film history's primal "home movie."[1] Not coincidentally, it stamps the origins of the portrait film, a fairly recent practice that is latent from the beginning through a confluence of recording impulse, social desideratum, and pictorial inheritance from nineteenth-century painting.

In fact, the technohistorical development of home movies parallels that of the portrait film in several important respects. In both practices, conditions of aesthetic possibility have been shaped by innovations in recording devices, especially the advent of 16mm semiprofessional equipment in the 1930s and the refinement of lightweight sync-sound camera rigs in the late 1950s. Similarly, the emergence in the sixties of distinctively avant-garde approaches to portraiture closely mirrors an indigenous explosion of amateur, domestic film production.[2] Like home movies, portraits tend to be short, intimate, present-tense studies of individuals or small groups produced by autonomous makers. However, while home movies are usually created for localized consumption, the self-conscious production of both avant-garde and documentary portraits relies on at least a rudimentary network of distribution, exhibition, and promotion. Indeed, there is a strong connection between the initiation of new bases of institutional support for independent media in the sixties and the growth of portraiture as a mode of filmic organization and as a cultural—or rather, countercultural—litmus test.

Forty years after its inception, the existence of portraiture as a filmic category and, through myriad televisual extensions, a locus of popular entertainment is scarcely in doubt. Nonetheless, despite its longevity and remarkable body of achievement, there has been almost no attempt to describe, theorize, or historicize the genre as such. My purpose here is to begin to redress this oversight by providing a general account of portraiture's aesthetic, thematic, and social dynamics during the period of its initial flowering, accompanied by detailed analyses of exemplary films and leading portrait exponents. Although discussion is limited primarily to the sixties, the range of prominent idioms and the epistemological questions they raise continue to activate a rich vein of contemporary portraiture. Regrettably, there is little attention devoted here to relations between avant-garde portraiture and adjacent styles such as the psychodrama, or to the reciprocity between avant-garde and documentary portraits. Nor does the entwining of film portraiture in trajectories of American painting and photography receive the scrutiny it deserves.[3]

Bearing in mind the mercurial nature of portrait styles in general, a set of provisional formal elements and motifs can be advanced at the outset. As if following the lead of *Le Déjeuner de bébé* (which itself borrows a camera framing common to late-nineteenth-century paintings), film portraits often favor frontal midrange compositions in which a subject's face and hands are privileged bearers of expression. Subjects are typically posed in vernacular settings—rather than against neutral or blatantly symbolic backgrounds—with key objects or landscape features sometimes contributing to the rendering of personality. Portraiture is among the most literal, or nontropic, of genres yet there are numerous instances of metonymies forged by the interchange of subject and surrounding space. Perhaps not unexpectedly, there are fewer instances of radically disjunctive editing or denaturing of the image than in other avant-garde idioms. Indeed, editing patterns tend toward linear or additive structures in which strict temporal arrangement of shots equally suppresses dramatic development and poly-rhythmic articulation.

The emphasis in film portraiture on tropes of immediacy and the triangulation of observer, subject, and viewer requires a closer, theoretically inflected examination, but for now it is useful to note an ur-sixties conflation of "presence," as an effect of intimate camera handling, and the overwhelmingly youthful choice of portrait subjects. The idea of living in the moment, with its concomitant celebration of creative spontaneity and its rejection of the assumed authority of History, became a potent shibboleth in sixties art and countercultural activities. Happenings, be-ins, multimedia performance art, antiwar protests, improvised music, spoken poetry were all manifestations of an insistence on "unmediated," communally shared experience—and portraiture found a receptive niche within this wider rubric.

Personal or biological time as registered by the film portrait is highly flexible; it might encompass a single "real time" exposure, a sequence of temporally disjunctive shots, or a series of scenes recorded over several months. Despite popular confusion between the portrait form and biography or memoir—a confusion generated in part by practices of titling and commercial marketing[4]—portraits do not as a rule rehearse a subject's past life; hence, unlike standard documentary biographies, there is little use of still photos, archival footage, or ancillary verbal testimony. One obvious division between the period's avant-garde and documentary portraits is the latter's absolute reliance on sync-sound recording. The majority of experimental portraits are either silent or limited to voice-over narration and/or musical accompaniment. A landmark work bridging the prerogatives of sixties documentary and avant-garde modes, Shirley Clarke's *Portrait of Jason* (1967) features lengthy first-person recounting of past events yet it directs our attention to how stories are *performed* in the present rather than illustrated through diachronic past-tense exposition. The long-take, closely cropped format adopted by Clarke owes a considerable debt to Warhol's "underground" phase, even as its *demimonde* subject and feature-length format suggest strong affinities with contemporaneous cinéma vérité studies.

A further implication of portraiture's contribution to the era's cult of presentness concerns the tension evidenced between self-reflexive artifice and unvarnished depiction, egalitarian access and allegorical or recondite meanings. The ostensible transparency of the genre casts the issue of self-reflexiveness into high relief. Indeed, Wendy Steiner argues that portraiture—literary as well as iconographic—"epitomizes many of the problems posed in modernist art," including the function of mimesis and the inevitability of the subjective.[5] The dominant subjects in *vérité* or Direct Cinema portraits are performers, politicians, celebrities, or persons thrust briefly into the public spotlight by news stories—in short, people already identified with a particular public image or iconic code. Aside from family and friends, avant-garde portraits are largely of artists and assorted bohemian figures: poets, painters, dancers, musicians, and of course other filmmakers. There are as well a number of instances of self-portraiture and, as is true of the modernist portrait from Picasso onward, images of an Other must perforce take the measure of a perceiving self. Further, avant-garde films frequently bring to the surface a reciprocity between the act of filming (or editing) and a subject's enactment of self before the camera.[6] More precisely, the period's close encounters with individuals honor a particular type whose inferred sociocultural status refracts, enters into productive exchange with, the vocation of filmmaking. However, it is not *cinema* as a medium or entertainment industry that is granted privileged standing in the representation of personal identity but a marginalized, defiantly impoverished cultural sector dedicated in one fashion or another to challenging conventional movie expectations.

In the course, then, of valorizing an outsiders' social network through aberrant visual strategies and self-generated modes of exhibition, avant-garde portraits incorporate the terms of a parochial agenda keyed by historically grounded visions of cinematic renewal. At the same time, the avant-garde enhanced its cultural prestige by forging associations with more established art forms, an onscreen imaginary community in which experimental filmmakers occupy the same platform as advanced artists from other mediums. The internal valorization in and through film of an unassimilated cadre of moviemakers is fully consonant with the sort of utopian energies unleashed by various creative factions in the midst of generational upheavals. Hence portraits functioned as de facto advertisements and recruiting posters for an insurgent movement of cinema.

Staring Life in the Face

In 1945 André Bazin declared that photography had freed modern painting from the burdens of naturalistic representation, an idea that had already circulated through the European artworld of Picasso and his cohort.[7] Although Bazin fails to address the implications of this transformation either for cinema or for specific modes of painting—portraiture was unquestionably the pictorial genre most deeply and irrevocably transformed by mechanical reproduction[8]—his contemporaneous writings on Italian Neorealism prize exactly the sort of linear, present-tense staging of quotidian events that a decade later would galvanize the emergence of portrait films. Cesare Zavattini, a leading Neorealist practitioner and theorist, famously described a project that would show for ninety minutes the unexceptional routine of an ordinary person: "I want to meet the real protagonist of everyday life, I want to see how he is made, if he has a moustache or not, if he is tall or short, I want to see his eyes, and I want to speak to him."[9] In this unrealized chronicle, Zavattini anticipates an underlying philosophy in numerous examples of sixties portraiture, despite Neorealism's divergent aesthetic and political assumptions.

While the European art film did not lack for sources of funding or outlets for completed works, the advent of film portraiture in the United States was abetted by the development of freshly minted institutional supports and, to a lesser extent, by increased availability of inexpensive movie equipment. Artist-administered networks for distributing and showing short nontheatrical films blossomed in New York and San Francisco in 1961–63 at the same time that cinéma vérité was developing a crucial alliance with network TV, taking advantage of improvements in sync-sound recording to meet popular demands for extended celebrity profiles. If unsounded possibilities for nonmainstream production and consumption provided a material foothold for the emergence of portraiture, burgeoning public discourses and cultural ideologies mobilized against authoritarian, top-down exercises of power emphasized the liberatory potential attached to self-selected, performative markers of social identity. In both cultural and political arenas, the desire to create new historical subjects entailed a putative dissolution of boundaries between reality and artifice, public image and private behavior, the personal and the political. Convening a theater of everyday life geared to direct democratic participation in social change—as opposed to tacit "representation"—an array of political factions proclaimed the necessity of ordinary individuals "speaking for themselves," and doing so through grassroots channels erected just to the side of corporately controlled media enterprises (underground comics and street theater are two obvious manifestations of this desire). In this sense, film portraiture can be understood as a byproduct of sixties resistance, even if some of its important practitioners disavowed the aims of radical politics.

In contrast to the history of American documentary, there is no discernible impulse to portraiture prior to the sixties. It might be possible to argue that the Trance films made by Maya Deren, Kenneth Anger, and Curtis Harrington in the 1940s, in which filmmakers themselves appeared as principal actors, constitute de facto dramatized self-portraits. However, the avant-garde's aesthetic inheritance from poetry and music, steeped in the expression of abstract or inner states of consciousness, virtually precluded the kind of close observation of immediate reality necessary for full-blown portraiture.[10] A striking dissonance of means is evident in Stan Brakhage's characterization of his early film *In Between* (1955): "portrait of Jesse Collins: a daydream nightmare in the surrealist tradition." Without denying the efficacy of "surrealist" portraits, the invocation of unconscious strata of being is clearly anathema to Zavattini's prospectus for capturing the microelements of identity. Thus it is only when experimental film begins to direct its vision outward, divesting itself of the trappings of narrativized drama, that Brakhage's celebrated "adventures of perception" find common cause with the descriptive aims of portraiture. Put another way, the portrait helped solve the problem of how to film the human figure in a manner devoid of the baggage of storytelling, however loosely defined, including presumptions of formal closure, intensifying action, and so on.

In what might be the earliest example of a genuine avant-garde portrait, *Mr. Hayashi* (1961), Bruce Baillie blends poetic syntax with oddly instrumental ends. According to Baillie, the film was made as a short, silent, in-camera "newsreel" advertising the gardening services of an unemployed friend to be shown before screenings at the fledgling Canyon Cinema. Its haikulike editing of shots of Hayashi strolling along a hillside path fit with shots of scruffy foliage to signify a casual subjectivity. As an emblematic, real-time glimpse of an "everyday protagonist," it simultaneously borrows from an antiquated documentary tradition as it upends the newsreel's smug facticity. It can be said that film portraits are by nature a form of *advertisement*, visual banners touting the quiddity and in some sense the worthiness, if not necessarily the desired commodification, of their subjects.

In a 1963 interview, Richard Leacock proposed a working definition for the kind of documentaries he wanted to make: "A film about a person who is interesting, who is involved in a situation he cares deeply about, which comes to a conclusion within a limited period of time, where we have access to what goes on . . . yeah, that's about it."[11] At nearly the exact moment vérité portraits were achieving intial public visibility, another portraitist was engaged in a radically different approach underwritten by a nearly identical rationale: "I only wanted to find great people and let them be themselves and talk about what they usually talked about and I'd film them for a certain length of time and that would be the movie."[12] The disconnected observer is of course Andy Warhol and the body of work he produced in the mid-sixties stands as perhaps the signal accomplishment in avant-garde portraiture.

On the surface, Warhol's films recast aesthetic concerns endemic to modernist readings of his serial silkscreens of movie stars and artworld luminaries: variation within repetition; the face as landscape; material flatness and the illusion of depth. However, in breadth as well as formal diversity, his black-and-white portrait films rival if not exceed the impact and internal complexity of the paintings. Leaving aside the tendency to embed portrait sequences in longer narrative projects—e.g., an entire reel of singer Nico primping her hair in *The Chelsea Girls* (1966)—Warhol's exhaustive mobilization of the portrait form was dispersed among a myriad of catalogue films and individual studies whose contents were occasionally repackaged into new combinations. In size and shape the portraits range from minimalist fixed-frame recordings of a single figure to wildly improvised, seemingly interminable interviews provoked by offscreen interrogators, from internecine japes to anonymous cryptonarrative sketches like *Blow Job* (1964). Most are silent but there are examples of sync-sound monologues and dialogues and at least one densely layered image/sound *mise-en-abime, Outer and Inner Space* (1965). *Kiss* (1963) is made up of de facto portraits of couples directed to perform a single activity, while the huge series known as "Screen Tests" (1964–66) focuses on tightly framed individuals ordered to "do nothing." In temporal scale, they range from three-minute single rolls to feature-length "chamber" epics.

Jonas Mekas was the first to proclaim that "Andy Warhol is taking cinema back to its origins, to the days of Lumière, for a rejuvenation and a cleansing."[13] Considered in relation to his portraits, this insight does not go far enough; in truth, Warhol took cinema back to the dawn of still photography. Beginning in 1964 he asked visitors, as a rite of passage into the heady Factory scene, to sit for a three-minute silent "screen test." The subject was told to stare into the camera, not to "act" or even blink, until the film ran out.[14] More than *five hundred* of these rolls have been recently restored by the Museum of Modern Art and the Warhol Foundation under the meticulous guidance of Callie Angell. Shown to denizens of the Factory on a regular basis, singly or in aleatory clusters, unlike other serial projects they were never assembled into longer sequences for purposes of exhibition. In recent theatrical screenings, they were arranged onto forty-five-minute reels in roughly the chronological order in which they were made (it is unclear whether any significant aesthetic development occurred between the earliest and the last of these studies). If they function as an ironic twist on Hollywood studios'

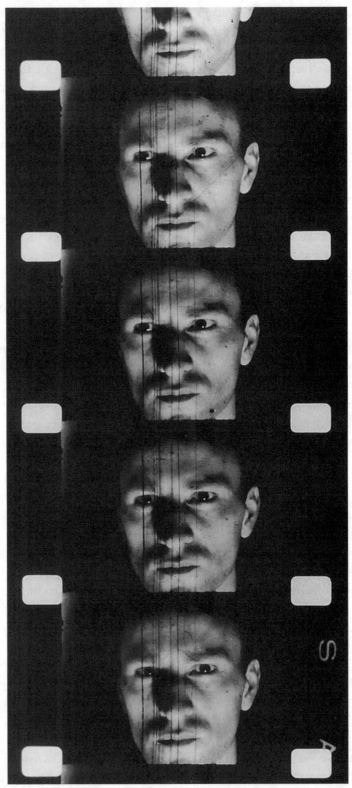

A self-portrait of Jonas Mekas in *Lost, Lost, Lost*. Photograph courtesy of Anthology Film Archives.

notorious auditions for scripted roles, they are also among the most comprehensive, and witty, documentary records of a vital New York subculture.

Equally significant, the "Screen Tests" constitute a modernist revision of an archaic photographic practice, the mid-nineteenth-century *carte-de-visite*. In 1853 Nadar opened a portrait studio frequented first by his friends in the Parisian intellectual elite and later by government officials as well.[15] As several commentators have noted, Warhol's Factory resembled a traditional artist's studio but geared to the (parodic) codes of standardized, mass media production. Following Nadar, André Disderi began in 1854 to market small mounted photos for use as calling cards. Not unlike the auto-mated photomat strips cherished by Warhol as pictorial models and image sources for his silkscreen paintings, the multi-pose cartes-de-visites were hastily made, with little attention to lighting or other aesthetic effects, and became a necessary accoutrement for bohemian stage performers. While camera technology had reduced exposure time from a grueling twenty minutes to several minutes, the sitter was still required to remain frozen in place during the recording process.

Nineteenth-century photographic portraits effectively democratized a genre previ-ously reserved for the rich and powerful as affirmation of their social status. Warhol's impromptu head shots served his urban community as indices of subcultural valida-tion, a catalogue or in-house publicity organ for budding underground "stars" in which the act of being filmed already confers a measure of notoriety. Reabsorbing a photographic tradition in which symbolic representations of power gave way to simple "likeness," Warhol's three-minute exposures at the same time limn a "withdrawal of authenticity" that demolishes humanist claims—including claims made by the cinéma vérité camp—for the portrait's ability to illuminate recondite, psychologically telling essences.[16] In David James's acute assessment,

> [they] do not document their subjects' ability to manifest an autonomous, unified self so much as narrate their anxious response to the process of being photographed. The camera is a presence in whose regard and against whose silence the sitter must construct himself. As it makes per-formance inevitable, it constitutes being as performance.[17]

Although the camera address remains constant, personal idiosyncracy stages a paradoxical return. Held in the viselike grip of frontal, evenly lit, eye-level closeups typically shot against blank backgrounds, subjects enter into sly creative exchanges with the impassive mechanism, many adopting what appear as predetermined per-formance strategies. Poet Gerard Malanga (the subject of several different tests) and dancer-choreographer Lucinda Childs turn their faces into still masks, yet every blink, twitch, or flex of facial muscles carries the weight of a microdramatic event. For in-stance, when a fly crawls across Childs's shoulder, her slight eye movements trace a host of suppressed feelings. Other sitters orchestrate minimalist comic fugues consist-ing of nods, lip movements, head twists. Some abandon any pretense to blank inertia, confecting indirect ways of calling attention to the camera's representational limits; in one roll, Nico smiles seductively and bites her fingers, then rolls a magazine into a telescope to mimic the lens in front of her. Dennis Hopper sings to himself, well aware of the stipulation of silence. Painter James Rosenquist confronts the limits of the frame, skittering around in circles on an offscreen stool. Harry Smith performs a series of complicated string figures using a cat's cradle as if to illustrate film's spatial oscillation of flat and deep. Ironically, tests with the least amount of overt movement convey the strongest impression of temporal flow, each passing moment reminding us that time is an ineluctable bearer of human change. By stringently contracting the field of dramatic action, Warhol accomplishes several contradictory tasks: he cues our sense of latent contradictions between still frame and illusion of motion, between prerogatives of film and the graphic arts; he also compels attention to normally unnoticed visual signifiers of human difference, a profoundly realist impulse.

In a number of instances, the camera, as it were, gets into the act. A three-minute take of Charles Osgood contains brief pixillation effects along with zooms that change the shot-size from medium to medium-closeup. Apparently it was not always clear who manned the camera, hence it is impossible to say why or under what conditions Warhol's premise of passivity became subverted. But the range of options is indeed striking. In one patently symbolic portrait, actress Beverly Grant seems to impersonate an anguished silent movie diva or Wagnerian harpie, pulling and mangling her thick coils of hair in operatic fashion. Curator Henry Geldzahler, another favorite subject, turns the simple knotting of a necktie into a suavely erotic spectacle.

Not surprisingly, the longer portraits often incorporate more elaborate camera set-ups and editing schemes. *Eat* (1963), a forty-minute silent study of painter Robert Indiana eating a mushroom, is remarkable in its ambiguous play of looped or repetitive footage versus singular moments of activity. Indiana bobs around in a swiveling rocking chair in slight slow motion (his enacted slowness amplified by Warhol's insistence on a slower projection speed). His face is at times shadowed by the brim of a fedora as he shifts the angle at which his chair faces the fixed camera. The effect is that of a real time cubist compilation of facial views, the absolute mutability of the artist's deadpan identity heightened by a scattered trajectory of offscreen glances. As in the bulk of Warhol's early films, the viewer's apprehension of what is happening offscreen and its relationship to the visible provokes an almost physical discomfort at odds with the conventional appeal of the scopophilic image. Here the time it takes to consume what is ostensibly a single mushroom is distended as Warhol rearranges the footage's chronology and inserts freeze-frames of images already seen. Thus the suggestion of a progressive movement toward closure—the final consumption of the mushroom—is made doubly obscure, with the subject acquiring an almost hallucinatory time-warped veneer.

Especially in the silent portraits, the format of unbroken camera takes prompts the sitter to improvise successive self-presentations around a banal, frequently oral activity. *Henry Geldzahler* (1964), a feature-length treatise on the art of cigar smoking, captures its subject reclining on the infamous Factory couch in a series of high-angle views in high-contrast lighting. As in *Eat*, the terminus of the film's unfolding action—finishing an ostentatiously huge stogie—is evident from the beginning. The subject's

Robert Indiana in Andy Warhol's *Eat*. Photograph courtesy of Anthology Film Archives.

self-appointed task was clearly to discover fresh ways of composing his face and body in relation to the central phallic prop, not simply allowing time to pass but fondling its shape through a miasma of change. The film's taxing duration allows the viewer ample time to explore different areas of the frame and attend to the material surface of the image. As if staring into a mirror, we gradually become aware of how the sitter's posture and fidgeting might parallel our own confining situation. As in other silent studies, consciousness of the weight and physiotemporal restriction of bodies produces an eerie jolt of self-recognition. Conversely, in sound portraits such as *Beauty #2* (1965) and *Outer and Inner Space*, both starring vivacious Edie Sedgwick, the interplay of direct and offscreen speech, coupled with a more densely populated mise-en-scène, redistributes reflexive energies toward the dramatic struggle between subject and various dispersed scenic "directors."[18]

Jonas Mekas was again astute in his designation of Warhol and Brakhage as "two extremes" of cinema, "the slow and the quick."[19] Not surprisingly, their antithetical approaches to film language are nowhere better illustrated than in their styles of portraiture. As Brakhage cut loose the trappings of oneiric narrative—focusing instead on detailed observations of himself, his family and friends, and isolated Colorado surroundings—portraiture emerged as a primary axis of his poetics, conjoining the celebration of intimate textures of everyday life with a constructivist, intersubjective view of identity. In this sense, he carries forward an aesthetic heritage associated with Picasso and other modernists for whom portrait depictions could no longer serve as records of an external, immutable presence but issue instead from "the artist's personal response to the subject."[20] More cogently, Brakhage's adopted practices of filmic portrayal are commensurate with the tenets of literary portraiture adopted by Picasso's notorious friend Gertrude Stein:

> I had to find out inside every one what was in them that was intrinsically exciting and I had to find out not by what they said not by what they did not by how much or how little they resembled any other one but I had to find it out by the intensity of movement that there was inside in any of them.[21]

Brakhage's signature method entails the arrangement of short repetitive bursts of imagery, the rapid alternation of adjacent views, liberal use of superimposition, and the metaphoric linkage of a subject's physical features or movements with objects in a surrounding environment.

Although he gestures in the direction of portraiture prior to the mid-sixties, this project was clarified and intensified when, following the theft of his 16mm equipment, Brakhage switched to the smaller, more intimate 8mm format and initiated what would become an ambitious cycle of thirty *Songs* (1964–70). Intended as comparatively unvarnished lyrics, several of them are explicitly described as portraits while others incorporate obvious portrait elements.[22] He plumbs the possibilities of the form most extensively in *Song 15: Fifteen Song Traits* (1965), a silent thirty-eight minute "gallery" of friends and family in which separate sections develop motifs or visual gestures that recur in other parts and then resurface in subsequent *Songs*. In the opening section, poet Robert Kelly is shown in Brakhage's home in a synecdochic flurry of hands cutting cheese, an activity intercut with shots of Kelly's face and an abstract nuclear diagram filmed off a television screen. The rhythmic cascade of hand movements suggests not only a visual affinity between subject and the filmmaker's unseen hand-held camera movements but a visual correlative for the poet's unheard rapid-fire patterns of speech. That is, what defines Kelly for Brakhage is his vocation as a creator of verbal images, the source and enunciative glue of their artistic fellowship. Further, the common sinew of domestic routine and poetic expression, their mutually invigorating energies, constitutes the dominant trope of *Song 15,* in which homey passages devoted to Jane Brakhage, or to Jane and the kids, are paired against brief appearances by poet Ed Dorn and his family, by Robert Creeley and Michael McClure, and finally by Jonas Mekas. Filmmaking, like the strain of poetry extolled by his friends, is rehearsed as an implicitly domestic enterprise.

In the fourth section of *Song 15,* daughter Crystal's dark brooding face anchors a series of animal associations, including the mordant image of caged birds. The fifth section, titled "Two: Creeley/McClure," builds consecutive miniportraits out of quite different expressive markers. As Creeley appears to rise from a chair, Brakhage repeatedly piles positive against negative images of nearly identical movements, confecting the poet as a fiercely divided personality whose self-control flickers in an imaginary internal argument. McClure's portrait bristles with an apposite tone of manic energy via harsh swish pans, pixillation, and solarized film stock. As McClure tries on an elaborate animal mask he seems to exude a preternatural shape-shifting function that Brakhage metaphorically connects with both spoken and filmic modes of performance.

Addressed in the context of Brakhage's monumental, amazingly diversified career, the portraits occupy a relatively subdued, even prosaic, niche.[23] Although underscoring his commitment to direct subjective confrontation with the particulars of daily existence, in scope and execution the portraits remain slightly peripheral to the larger imperatives of autobiography, dream and closed-eye vision, and the vicissitudes of memory. Nonetheless, their significance can be judged in several ways. They are among Brakhage's most extroverted works, countering intensely solipsistic versions of romantic isolation with a bracingly empathetic recognition of autonomous subjectivities. In an interview discussing *Scenes from under Childhood* (1967–70), created during the same period as the *Songs,* he imputes an almost therapeutic function to the intimate observation of others: "The first, simple, daily impulse to make it was to *see* my children—to see them as something much more than mine . . . Photographing them was one way (I'm most intensive and excited when I'm doing that) to begin a relationship of better seeing, or entering their world."[24] For Brakhage, the portrait offered a vehicle of social/familial connexity, an act of creative imagination establishing grounds for renewed kinship in the profilmic. A secondary aspect of the portrait impulse, especially evident in *Song 15,* links his project not only to the work of other avant-garde filmmakers but to a central task of sixties vérité documentary.[25] That is, cinema itself is proffered as both visual mediation of and instrument for the assuaging of personal alienation and social marginality. Compounding this identificatory process, the triangulation of filmmaker, subject, and viewer makes possible the continued expansion of an otherwise introverted subculture.

The spectral community sketched in *Song 15* must nonetheless be understood as a utopian wish, an act of solidarity threatened a priori by the transient and incomplete nature of filmic representation. At the same moment it declares subjective affiliation with certain like-minded individuals, it must also admit a horizon of disharmony and dispersion, the imminent release of time from the elaborate scaffolding of present-tense connexity. In Brakhage's work, as in the vast majority of avant-garde portraits of the time, a primary sign of the inability to fully render the subject's "natural" presence is the absence of direct speech. This absence can be said to stand in for the representational blind spots of the medium as a whole. To expressively render the world of any portrait subject, and to embed in that display a gestural shadow of oneself and one's aesthetic project, is in some sense to concede the gaping existential chasm at the heart of all human consciousness. It is certainly no accident that the allegorization of death is a trope linked to portraiture at least since the Renaissance. As John Welchman argues, facial images, a motif that has "shaped the very conditions of visuality," eventually came to serve as "Modernism's repressed token for the whole inheritance of pre-Modernist humanism."[26] Thus Brakhage's images of selected Others, like those of Warhol, testify to the irreducible isolation of the maker as sympathetic observer. The tension exerted between identification and detachment, presence and absence, is perhaps all the more vivid in ensemble portraits in which a sequential grouping acts to camouflage the separations subtending the triangulated gaze.

Although there are noteworthy individual sketches from the sixties—Ed Emshwiller's *George Dumpson's Place* (1965), Marie Menken's *Andy Warhol* (1965), Baillie's *Tung* (1966) and *Valentin de las Sierras* (1967), Gregory Markopoulos's *Through a Lens Brightly: Mark Turbyfill* (1967)—the portrait suite stands as the period's consummate and symptomatic achievement. The self-validation of nontraditional forms of community, an essential plank in sixties ideology, was hailed by avant-garde film in a range of styles and geographic sodalities. Warren Sonbert, following Warhol, assays ten youthful couples in *The Bad and the Beautiful* (1967), a series of in-camera "collaborative" glimpses of the underside of bohemian stardom. Hollis Frampton enlists a throng of artworld acquaintances, including some previous Warhol subjects, for *Manual of Arms* (1966), a "14 part drill for the camera" in which each section demonstrates a different visual treatment of lighting, camera movement, editing, and composition. Markopolous shot two portrait collections, *Galaxie* (1966) and *Political Portraits* (1969). In the former, thirty luminaries including Susan Sontag, Erick Hawkins, W. H. Auden, and Gian Carlo Menotti are celebrated through camera improvisations linking facial closeups with metonymic props or physical enactments related to their particular spheres of creative endeavor. Mekas's *Diaries, Notes, and Sketches (Walden)* (1968), although not strictly a work of portraiture, contains numerous brief studies of New York artists. Takahiko Iimura's *Film-makers* (1966–69) blends portrait shots of Brakhage, Mekas, Warhol, and others with slivers of spoken dialogue. In one way or another, these works embellish a common subtextual agenda: the laudatory description of an artistic coterie in which the filmmaker implicitly functions as a central mediating figure. Serving as the indigenous "face" of an anti-industrial film practice—at once recruiting poster and self-legitimating vehicle of publicity—the portrait helped secure a role for experimental cinema within a wider arena of social transformation.

Portraiture in the Age of Identity Politics

If avant-garde portraits of the 1960s were linked to the emergence of an indigenous movement of experimental cinema—a movement spurred by, but frequently diverging from, the period's countercultural ideologies—a similar trajectory in film and cultural politics can be said to inform portraiture's significance and aesthetic vitality in the following decades. By the mid-seventies, avant-garde film was undergoing a cycle of institutionalization, expanding its public viability through a network of semistable funding sources, exhibition venues, museum patronage, and university jobs. In several key respects, this process was complemented by accelerating demands for inclusion, and for autonomous bases of cultural authority, by women, gay men and lesbians, and racial minorities. Independent film and, increasingly, video were singled out for obvious reasons as prime showcases for the projection of freshly theorized subjectivities. In this climate, portraits and self-portraits functioned as a crucial idiom of personal-as-political articulation.

Although the approaches represented by Warhol and Brakhage—roughly denoted as "minimalist" and "expressionist"—continue to define important polarities in the envisioning of identity, Warhol's emphasis on the performance of contingent, de-psychologized masks of personality has been constantly ratified and endlessly reconfigured by younger artistic cadres. Neither artist was especially committed to the generational values of sixties counterculture and both were uncomfortable with calls for overtly political art. Nonetheless, an attitude toward issues of representation that might be deemed "Warholian" infuses the designs of numerous feminist and queer portraits made in the last thirty years. (Ironically, this attitude took hold despite a near-total absence of Warhol's early films from public exhibition.) Moreover, Warhol's radical version of direct observation finds its way into portraits made in otherwise disparate styles such as structural film, Super-8 punk, diary, and postmodern interview. Perhaps the most blatant gap between Warhol's seminal portraits and those of younger makers is the latter's intense engagement with the human voice, with the power of language to adumbrate, fracture, and/or renegotiate social constructions of self. Thus a predilection for sync-sound speech or voice-over narration indicates the extent to which post-sixties portraits reaffirm the collaborative stamp of one-on-one recording while questioning the primacy of image alone in capturing traces of individual character.

As is well known, Warhol's recourse to sound in 1965 was underwritten by a desire to embark on more conventional movie projects. Although portraiture would remain central to his painting, it virtually disappears from his film work after 1966. Brakhage continued to craft short, evocative portraits of family and friends: *Clancy* (1974) and *Jane* (1985) are two radiant examples. A full-length, commissioned sketch of local politician Richard Lamm, *The Governor* (1977), is a rather awkward stab at a documentary/

avant-garde hybrid. In the late eighties, Brakhage turned his attention almost exclusively to hand-painted abstract films, precluding further engagement with the genre.

Saul Levine, a prolific filmmaker whose allegiance to Brakhage's aesthetic is often tempered by considerations of social context, forged a kind of be-bop portrait whose frenetic pacing reflects both the filmmaker's nervous energy and notions of quicksilver shifts in interpersonal relationships. As is true of Brakhage, the majority of his subjects are media artists or intimate muses, depicted in the throes of creative activity. Since sound, in particular contrapuntal patterns of voice and environmental ambience, is essential to his rough-hewn method, Levine was an early proponent of the Super-8 format, which allows for heightened effects of immediacy as well as greater flexibility of in-camera procedures.[27] *Near Sight* (1978), *Raps and Chants, Part II* (1981), *Departure* (1976–84), and *Bopping the Great Wall of China Blue* (1981) demonstrate a range of subject interactions geared to musical rhythms rather than poetic metaphor.

Marjorie Keller, a noted Brakhage scholar,[28] made several portraits in the expressionist mode that offer sly responses or correctives from a feminist perspective to Brakhage's idealizations of women. *By Twos and Threes: Women* (1974) and *Daughters of Chaos* (1980) question as they celebrate, respectively, female bonding and childhood role playing. Keller's strongest portrait, *The Fallen World* (1983), exacts a heartfelt acknowledgment of the Romantic legacy in avant-garde film. Ostensibly an "elegy for a Newfoundland dog named Melville," Keller strings together montage figures linking the frolicking dog with her husband, P. Adams Sitney, whose disposition is further developed in visits to the Melville Library and to the graves of two English poets. Thus Sitney is rendered iconographically and also formally—through match cutting and musical selections—as a disciple of an art grounded in the struggle between inchoate nature and self-conscious erudition.

What I have been referring to as portraits can be—indeed have been—addressed through other generic or institutional (e.g., "video art") rubrics. Since this is a matter of critical labeling, of discovering alternative logics with which to connect and understand historical impulses within a cultural field, it is often the case that a single work can satisfy two or more categorical requirements. It is tempting, if ultimately misleading, to claim that portion of American avant-garde cinema organized around immediate representations of human subjects in nondramatic situations as fulfilling the aims of portraiture. The problems in such a stance, however, are daunting. For instance, the stipulation of "nondramatic" is essential yet fuzzy. It does not account for, say, text-driven improvisations in the work of Peggy Ahwesh, the most resourceful portraitist of her generation. In addition, it would exclude the Super-8 punk movement's provocative subcultural documentation offered in the guise of narrativized portrait galleries, of a which a cogent example is James Nares's *Rome '78* (1978).

On a related front, a common effect in Mekas's self-described "diary" films is that of an array of miniportraits interspersed with glimpses of landscape, events, and so on.[29] By the late seventies, the portrait element in his autobiographical peregrinations had assumed an expanded role. *Notes for Jerome* (1978) is the first of a group of tributes

Saul Levine. Photograph by Barbara Rosenthal; courtesy of Anthology Film Archives.

to dead friends in which scattered footage of the subject taken at different times is interlarded with quick observations on the subject's physical environment and social coterie; the fleeting images are augmented with local sounds, music, and Mekas's distinctive voice-over musings.[30] *Jerome* is followed by *Scenes from the Life of Andy Warhol* (1990), *Zefiro Torna or Scenes from the Life of George Macunius* (1992), and the video *Allen's Last Three Days on Earth as a Spirit* (1997). In general, these discrete individual sketches are less visually and aurally dense than Mekas's feature-length diary installments. They also develop undercurrents of reciprocity between subject and maker, as if the recording and arranging process was also an act of self-reflection, of recognizing personal traits in the mirror of the Other.

The Birth of a Nation (1998), Mekas's summary elaboration of portraiture, constitutes a throwback to the gallery mode of the sixties. Upbeat yet nostalgic for a lost era, the title limns Griffith's simultaneous announcement and forfeiture of cinema's visionary innocence while registering Mekas's conviction that a tribal community of *cineastes* had evolved by the early seventies into a potent cultural alternative. Nearly 150 filmmakers, administrators, scholars, and assorted fellow travelers parade across the screen in (mostly) youthful, hirsute ebullience. Framed as couples, trios, or small groups—rather than as isolated individuals—they exude a strident congeniality. Some vignettes are like comic haikus: Harry Smith sandwiched by the bookish clutter of his hotel room; gourmand Pater Kubelka caught in rapt contemplation of a slab of greasy-spoon bacon; P. Adams Sitney presiding over a barbeque grill the size of a postage stamp. The flipside to Mekas's mournful recollections of the deceased, *Birth* conjures a golden age of artistic promise and internal social cohesion.

It is to the lore of that age, particularly its outsized ambitions and aura of bohemian triumphalism, that younger filmmakers reacted by harnessing the portrait to a host of political agendas. Documentaries such as Amalie Rothschild's *Woo Who? May Wilson* (1969), Yolande du Luart's *Angela Davis: Portrait of a Revolutionary* (1971), and Geri Ashur's and Peter Barton's *Janie's Janie* (1972) had already established an arena in which portraiture could bolster struggles against racism, sexism, and homophobia. Fortified by immersion in poststructuralist theory, by feminist and psychoanalytic film and literary studies, and cognizant of a recent resurgence of portraiture in cutting-edge painting and photography,[31] avant-garde filmmakers had little stake in vérité documentary's rhetoric of exemplary role models and formal transparency. Instead, they tendered reflexive portraits in which the body is unmistakably a contested political terrain, in which "gender" is exposed as a masquerade or as the oppressive detritus of patriarchy. Primed to regard the camera historically not as a neutral instrument of recording but an ideologically complicit weapon, younger artists were determined to counter an inheritance of mainstream representations—especially those associated with Hollywood—with a blatant, personalized erotics of camera vision, in which underlying positions of dominance and submission could be foregrounded and erased.

Leslie Thornton's *Jennifer, Where Are You?* (1981), in which a girl smears lipstick over her mouth while an insistent voice attempts to "place" her, is part of a copious subset of films and videos focusing on children as ciphers for female socialization. Peggy

Ahwesh, who has used children in quasi-scripted roles more appropriate to adults and, conversely, directed adult women in riotous bouts of regressive behavior, has made portraiture a central component in her spontaneously anarchic work. In *Pittsburgh Trilogy* (1983), *Doppelganger* (1988), and *The Fragments Project* (1985–95), friends deliver monologues on past events, philosophical issues, and personal betrayals, and Ahwesh's presence behind the camera resembles a cross between master of ceremonies and ethnographer (or archeologist) of gender-role constructions. There are often palpable tensions between her and her voluble social actors. As she puts it, "It's more like me doing conceptual exercises so that I can figure out what kind of relationship I have with the person, and what kind of relationship the camera has with the person."[32] Despite pronounced allegiances to Jack Smith and Warhol, this notion of the portrait as process of mutual discovery is remarkably similar to Brakhage's prospectus for the filming of his children.

Unlike avant-gardists of the sixties, recent feminists have tended to inject their portraits with images and soundbites from mass media in order to demonstrate the difficult yet necessary task of defining a sense of self around and against prescribed, seductive stereotypes. A good example of this tendency is Mary Filippo's self-portrait, *Who Do You Think You Are* (1987), which plays off the filmmaker's painful attempts to quit smoking, with advertisements and movie clips featuring the ironic attachment of women's sexuality to the symbolic potency of cigarettes. A more oblique treatment of pressures on woman's identity is Amy Taubin's *In the Bag* (1980). As female voices announce airport departures on the soundtrack, we see close shots of hands rummaging through a purse in search of something, perhaps a lost ticket. A series of objects—mirror, address book, diaphragm, sunglasses—are displayed, then carefully cut to shreds, twisted, or otherwise obliterated. There are suggestions that this pantomime of mental breakdown is prompted by an aborted love affair. What is stowed in a purse is often adduced as a reflection of, or synecdoche for, the personality of its owner; here Taubin manages to bare the trappings of personal intimacy while withholding any scopophilic pleasure derived from exposing herself as visual image.

An equally idiosyncratic spin on feminist portraiture, Elizabeth Subrin's *Shulie* (1998) is a nearly shot-by-shot recreation of a 1967 documentary profile on art student and radical theorist Shulamith Firestone. The fake-doc gambit is executed with such precision that we assume, until the closing credits, that we are seeing the original. At one level, the film is an uncanny celebration of an influential activist and thinker by an artist of roughly the same age, living in the same city and going to the same school, as her onscreen subject. The reciprocity between filmmaker and subject in this case sets in motion a skein of subversive dialectics usually ignored in documentary portraits: fact/fiction, original/copy, spontaneous/rehearsed, art/politics. Combining profilmic performance with an emphasis on *cinematic* dexterity and visual conundrums, *In the Bag* and *Shulie* attest to a compass of approaches adopted by women in pursuit of politicized, formally reflexive renditions of personhood.

The roots of recent gay and lesbian portraits can unquestionably be traced to Warhol's early work, along with the multipersonality composites of Markopoulos and Sonbert. Not just *Blow Job* but various "Screen Tests" hitched portraiture's sub-cultural charge to the evocation of self-assured queer sexual identities. Among films with at least a loose connection to the burgeoning gay rights movement are James Broughton's *Together* (1976) and Barbara Hammer's *Women I Love* (1976). An almost accidental dip into genderbending self-depiction, George Kuchar's hilarious *I An Actress* (1977) starts as an improvised lesson in overacting but winds up encapsulating the veteran filmmaker's bedrock commitment to dramatic excess. Shooting the film during a directing class at the San Francisco Art Institute, Kuchar seizes the spotlight when a student actress is unable to summon sufficient enthusiasm for a violent roman-tic spat. Donning a stringy mop on his head and knocking around a microphone case as a stand-in for the cheating husband, Kuchar unleashes a torrent of emotions as he simultaneously narrates a chain of motivational impulses in a spasm of transvestite Method.

As the crisis surrounding the AIDS epidemic deepened in the mid-eighties, new strains of gay male portraiture emerged that bore witness to the dying as they served as beacons of resistance for survivors. Warhol's portraits raise the issue of what limits can, or must, be placed on a subject's self-representation. Since portraits in general limn an effort to establish some logic for beginning and ending, one that refuses familiar nar-rative devices of anticipation and resolution, the "arbitrary" gesture of closure instates a condition that is both formal necessity and, symbolically, universal biological fate. Portraits made in the shadow of AIDS have managed to thematize this inherent prob-lematic, with scrutiny of a subject's face and manner, in a sense, overdetermined by the prospect of imminent death.[33] Gregg Bordowitz's video, *Fast Trip, Long Drop* (1993), is a collage self-portrait of a Jewish PWA activist that mixes home movies, diary scenes, archival footage, comic skits, interviews, and fake interviews. Alongside critiques of media misrepresentations of HIV, Bordowitz documents his obsessive concern with slight changes in his facial identity. In this instance, collage functions as an emblem of fragmentation that is specific to its human subject but is also a trope shared by many queer subjects in postmodernity. Further, the juxtaposition of diffuse materials contributes to a mingling of historical periods and confusion over temporal referents, loosening time's constraints in a manner that nonetheless reminds us of the impend-ing future (a key sequence has the narrator shopping for a watch at a store called "Somewhere in Time").

Ken Kobland's *End Credits* (1994) is a straightforward look at actor Ron Vawter as he applies makeup prior to a performance of the theater piece *Roy Cohn/Jack Smith*, a double portrait of two notorious gay men who died of AIDS; Vawter himself is shown at an advanced stage of the disease. Kobland subtly evokes the textures of Rembrandt portraits, employing his hand-held camera in lyrical, caressing strokes. Aspects of character are revealed through the makeup process: patience, focus, attention to detail. At once affectionate and chilling, Kobland's film, like Marlon Riggs's *Non, Je Ne Regrette Rien (No Regret)* (1992) and Mike Hoolboom's *Positiv* (1997), recasts the framing of fa-ciality as a locus of decay and fleeting reflection, a mise-en-abime that ensnares subject and observer alike.

A different mode of lamentation is apparent in Hollis Frampton's *Gloria!* (1979), where printed texts and archival footage substitute for direct images of the filmmaker's maternal grandmother. Frampton, who began as a still photographer, continued to explore terms of an antiexpressionistic portraiture, first broached by *Manual of Arms*, in several rationalized, formally elegant sketches of artists Paul Sharits (*Yellow Springs* [1972]) and James Rosenquist (*Quarternion* [1972]). Both films present their subjects through visual tropes that evoke the signature qualities of their art. *Gloria!* can be classified as a structural film in its strict numerical and alphabetical organization of a series of verbal propositions: his grandmother's love of animals, gardening, and strong drink; her speech patterns and physical attributes. These statements are metrically juxtaposed with silent slapstick scenes of an Irish wake and a blank green passage over which an Irish folk song is played. As the film develops it becomes clear that Frampton's orderly yet passionate tribute—among other gifts, his grandmother taught him to read—highlights qualities that apply to the filmmaker's own personality and vocation.

On the surface, structural filmmaking and the aims of portraiture seem inimical, given that the human figure is typically marginalized (e.g., *Wavelength* [1967]) or expunged altogether (e.g., *Serene Velocity* [1970]) within the minimalist program. Nonetheless, a number of portraits were made in this style. Henry Hills's denatured, optically printed portrayals of George Kuchar, *George* (1980), and poet Jack Hirschman, *Kino Da!* (1981), chop their subjects into tiny, precalibrated units. In the former, Kuchar's manic energy is divided into four repetitive, alternating views. In the latter, Hirschman's reading of a poem referring to Soviet poetic/cinematic montage is turned into a machine-gun barrage of discontinuous sounds and physical tics. In *Apropos of San Francisco* (1968), Charles Levine fabricates a spirited emblem of hippie culture by transforming a brief shot of filmmaker Ben Van Meter into a five-minute looped dance with occasional variations.

Bruce Conner's *Marilyn Times Five* (1968–73), in its mobilization of looping and fragmentation to reanimate a reel of grainy found footage, has close affinities to the structural project yet it also anticipates later attempts to meld portraiture with oppositional takes on sexuality and gender. Indeed, Conner's remarkable film serves as a capstone to major concerns of this chapter. Part of a minor tradition of found-footage paeans to beloved movie actresses extending from Joseph Cornell's *Rose Hobart* (1939) to Lewis Klahr's *Her Fragrant Emulsion* (1986), *Marilyn* manipulates a set of cheesecake shots allegedly starring a young Marilyn Monroe. Just as Cornell reworks a tacky Hollywood feature to extract only those scenes in which Rose Hobart appears in sensuous dramatic predicaments, Conner breaks up the tenuous continuity of the original crude production by reordering poses and distending certain movements via looped repetition or a form of progressive looping in which a movement begins in one shot, is incrementally advanced in the next shot, and so on. Five individual sequences are built around a lush recording of "I'm Through with Love"; each successive permutation displays pieces of previously unseen footage interrupted by passages of black leader.

With its ostensibly voyeuristic address and mechanical control of the female body, *Marilyn* could be interpreted as a sadistic affirmation of the power of male desire through the coerced submissiveness of a tortured cultural icon. Such a view, however, misses the film's darker meanings and self-implicating pathos. Although the viewer swiftly realizes that the three-minute song will receive five iterations, the seemingly endless refrain "I'm Through with Love," played over increasingly dislocated nude images, makes it clear that this subject—or rather her screen image—can never really be "through with love." Her fetishistic fans will, in fact did, mine every scrap of erotic potential from her celluloid presence. Admittedly, there is a cruel exploitative edge to Conner's exercise— just as there is in the jewellike vivification of a minor star in *Rose Hobart*—but that mood is blunted and ultimately subverted by a combination of disorienting gaps in continuity and frustrating insertions of nonimage. As Conner suggests in catalogue notes, "*MX5* is an equation not intended to be completed by the film alone. The viewer completes the equation."[34] The feeling is that of being trapped inside a desiring machine gone haywire.

In the final segment, there is a quick pan over "Marilyn's" body slumped in a pose that suggests abject exhaustion or death. Her image has simply been ground into stillness. A treatise on the sexual dynamics of male spectatorship, conceived in a genre steeped in the promotion of public celebrity—and completed at least a decade before VCRs would popularize slo-mo instant replays of favorite scenes, among other libidinous rituals—*MX5* at once curdles the promise of scopophilic pleasure and reveals an ominous fold in the underbelly of avant-garde portraiture.

(2003)

3 | The Redemption of the City

> Multitude, solitude: identical terms, and interchangeable by the active and fertile poet. The man who is unable to people his solitude is equally unable to be alone in a bustling crowd.
> —*Baudelaire, "Crowds,"* Paris Spleen

EVER SINCE THE MOMENT IN 1895 when the Lumière brothers recorded the *faits divers* of workers leaving a factory, a brick wall being demolished, and a woodcutter plying his trade on a Parisian street, cinema and the modern city have been locked in an uneven yet mutually enhancing embrace.[1] To a greater degree than still photography a half-century before, cinema *required* the presence of an urban matrix at every stage of its ever-thickening economy, from the manufacture of equipment through the photographing of lively action scenes to the marketing and consumption of its product. If, as it is commonly held, cinema arose from conditions of modernity epitomized by European industrial cities, the urban function in the visuality of early cinema may be understood primarily as a reservoir of exterior scenery and recognizable social types, and only later as a source of site-specific dramatic situations, themes, and full-blown narrative idioms such as film noir. Even in cinema's first decade, however, there are occasional glimpses of symbolic modes of representation, a language for organizing urban space and time, that are fully commensurate not only with cinema's material bases of production but with a legacy of expressive figures gleaned from the previous century's literary and painterly traditions. For example, the snaking onboard camera movement in Billy Bitzer's 1905 protonewsreel, *Interior, N.Y. Subway, 14th St. to 42nd St.,* inscribes an image of underground space as labyrinth while the scenic structure of Edwin S. Porter's *The Kleptomaniac* (1905) reifies a notion of urban social divisions—wealth coexisting with stark poverty—common at the turn of the century. A host of other films evidence iconographic or syntactical tropes for speed, hierarchal social relations, human density and heterogeneity.

Marshall Berman joins a long line of commentators in asserting an isomorphic relationship between urban dynamics and the celebration in modernist art and literature
of the fragmentary, the aleatory, the transient, the artificial, and the synchronic.[2] In a
reciprocal flurry of innovation, capitals of twentieth-century culture—Paris, Berlin,
Moscow, New York—inflected the development of film language in distinctive ways,
from the temporal dislocations of Rene Clair's *Paris qui dort* (1924) to the haunted facades of German "street films." In return, commercial cinema supplied mass audiences
with easily comprehended stories and stylistic devices that aided in the cognitive mapping of otherwise chaotic phenomenological impressions. That is, cinema helped make
the complex experience of modern cities more legible. Following the venerable literary
opposition of City of Vice and a City of Virtue, movies of the 1920s had developed a
repertoire of images by which urban space was characterized as a Machine or, alternatively, as Organism or displaced pastoral; Fritz Lang's nihilistic *Metropolis* (1927) and,
in a more celebratory vein, Dziga Vertov's *Man with a Movie Camera* (1929) are examples of the former while pastoral tropes dominate the second half of F. W. Murnau's
Sunrise (1927).[3] To be sure, the roots of these ostensibly cinematic patterns are firmly
embedded in the soil of Western culture, from the Bible to Baudelaire. Rhetorical strategies that cast urban society in vivid, largely negative terms were refracted through
particularities of disparate historical periods or social backdrops, yet roughly the same
tropes have circulated with slight variations across a range of filmic genres and modes
of production. From the outset, then, the filmed city found itself immersed in a dialectical play of original insight and received wisdom, futuristic visions and shopworn
metaphors.

The observation that American avant-garde cinema has promoted, and in turn been
sustained by, an unmistakably nostalgic urbanism placed at the service of a radically
revisionist program of urban representation is at once obvious and insufficient. In the
history of the movement, the urban regime is not simply a prominent topos in a larger
field of subjective visual investigation. Rather, an overarching stake in an "urban-
ist" methodology can be said to underwrite the entire experimental film enterprise,
constituting one axis in a shadow grid for which the Hollywood industry serves as a
mirroring coordinate. Even at its most ardently pastoral—in work by Stan Brakhage,
Bruce Baillie, or Larry Gottheim—the avant-garde retains an urban imprint, tem-
pering Romantic contemplation of nature with the pressures exerted by a decidedly
nonpastoral apparatus, a "machine in the garden" tied inexorably to the demands of
an industrial society.[4]

Filmic constructions of urban space and social relations, including the static views
of documentary newsreels, are rarely grounded in techniques of transparent reflection.
If, as writers such as Thomas Pynchon, Don DeLillo, and Paul Auster have intimated,
the city is a "text," it can be deciphered or translated through quite different optics.
Implicit in any rendering of the city, however, is the necessity of fragmentary or synecdochic modes of address. In this sense, the privileging of editing as a means of instating urban rhythms, and reliance on spontaneous subjective recording as a measure of
human-scaled spatial negotiation, feed into core practices in avant-garde cinema. For

Ken Jacobs and the New York skyline. Photograph by Mike Chikiris; courtesy of Anthology Film Archives.

instance, if there is a paradigmatic procedure or physical circumstance for this broad body of work, it is a single cameraperson scrutinizing the hidden visual properties of a public domain. For any location-based filmic practice, the indexical weight of photography militates against the fantasy of a universal or indeterminate cityscape—although Kuleshov's montage theory of "creative geography" authorized instances of urban fusion or interdependency in Soviet cinema of the twenties. Hence the avant-garde has tended to frame a handful of cities that have proven most receptive to marginalized cultural initiatives. In noncommercial American city symphonies, the focus of attention is inevitably precise and often hailed in titles: *Manhatta* (1921), *A Bronx Morning* (1931), *Notes on the Port of St. Francis* (1952), *Under the Brooklyn Bridge* (1953), *On the Bowery* (1956), *NY NY* (1957).[5] Moreover, while Peter Emanuel Goldman's *Pestilent City* (1965) and Robert Frank's *Life Dances On* (1981) are among a group of films promoting dystopic visions of a City of Dreadful Night—to invoke poet James Thomson's late-nineteenth-century lament—the prevailing attitude is surprisingly affirmative, if not outright exultant. Despite an enveloping cultural context of virulent antiurbanism, dating at least from Thomas Jefferson's well-known characterization of cities as a "cancer," experimental filmmaking in America has consistently represented the inner workings of urban society as a source of personal redemption and collective nourishment.[6]

In films of the fifties and sixties, especially, a familiar urban site is mined through its formal convergence with aspects of recording and/or editing. Proceeding from a request from Joseph Cornell, Brakhage's *Wonder Ring* (1955) transforms a ride on the Third Avenue El in New York into an elegant, if silent, fugue of jiggling hand-held camera movements against layered planes of buildings, ghostly subway passengers, and the onrush of parallel trains—all of which are superimposed through natural reflections on glass surfaces. The film has a pellucid development, with a gradual acceleration in speed and visual complexity encapsulating expressive gestures widely associated with city life. Emphasis on the outlined shape of train windows and imperfections in the glass create a metonymic link with the camera lens. A recurrent figure in disparate films, the window-as-aperture indicates a crucial boundary separating self from society, interior from exterior, private from public space. An automobile windshield serves as aperture in Hilary Harris's *Highway* (1958), a musical tour of Manhattan's circumambient roads—backed by David Hollister's jazz track—that utilizes the curves of exit ramps and guard rails shot from the side to rhyme banal architectural elements with notes on a musical staff. Harris enlists zoom shots, exposure changes, sections of crisp cutting, and undercranking to engage shifting moods and to underscore the "symphonic" conceit.

Shirley Clarke's *Bridges-Go-Round* (1958), with a bop score by Teo Macero, animates the cables, struts, and steel towers of a Manhattan span through kinetic editing, superimpositions, and color gels that lend the motif a choreographed, lilting propulsion suitable to sharp changes in tempo. Clarke's award-winning *Skyscraper* (1959) applies a similar style to the monuments of what architect Louis Sullivan called "vertical modernism."[7] Critics have contended that Clarke's films, along with Francis Thompson's *NY NY* and other urban studies of the period in which human figures are absent or nearly absent, illustrate a dominant impulse toward abstraction, turning cities into deracinated expanses of purified line and color, motion picture equivalents of Mondrian or Franz Kline paintings. While it is a potentially useful analogy in relation to, say, the funhouse distortions of *NY NY,* the motifs in Clarke's films, and those of her avant-garde cohort, are rarely severed from their denotative identities or their instrumentality. Moreover, unlike *NY NY,* Clarke's urban idioms create personalized, hand-wrought textures permitting access to the shaping consciousness behind them; they are hardly the mechanized products of an unfeeling camera eye. A stronger correlation, perhaps, lies in the still-photographic practices of Walker Evans and Andreas Feininger, among others, that exploit tensions between abstract urban shape and realist social inscription.[8]

Closer to an ideal of cinematic abstraction, Marie Menken's *Go Go Go* (1962–64) relies on single framing and short bursts of imagery to turn pedestrians on crowded streets and parks into fleeting dabs of color posed against static backgrounds (one of her earliest films actually records a Mondrian painting in bursts of isolated detail). A time-crunching walk across the Brooklyn Bridge conveys a humorous impatience that nonetheless pinpoints the structure's indelible beauty. In *Notebook* (1962), sidewalks and lit windows at night offer pretexts for similar environmental reanimations. The style in both films is casual, diaristic, wry—a collection of hasty sketches made in transit, or about transit, in the course of a quotidian schedule. Jim Jennings, a younger filmmaker whose gorgeous black-and-white studies revise urban vocabularies pioneered by Brakhage, Menken, Clarke, and others, fashions a luminous ode to the New York subway at night in *Silvercup* (1998); in *Painting the Town* (1999), he captures the brightly lit visual circus of Times Square in the manner of Thompson's *NY NY* by filming the distorted reflections of building facades on automobile hoods, windows, and sidewalk puddles.

Empire by Andy Warhol. Photograph courtesy of
Anthology Film Archives.

Despite obvious affinities such as the jazz-related orchestration of commonplace urban sites, the films of Clarke and Menken represent distinct visual idioms. Clarke selects icons that stand for New York in the same sense that a picture of the Eiffel Tower evokes Paris or the Golden Gate Bridge acts as a synecdoche for San Francisco. Immediately recognizable locations are transformed into *emblems* that, depending on the manner in which they are shot and edited, engender specific elements of a city's public identity. Hence Manhattan itself, adduced as "imposing" or "steely" or "edgy" in countless portrayals, is signified visually through Clarke's angular juxtapositions of the hard reflective skins of skyscrapers—a metaphoric use of camera positioning already apparent in Paul Strand's and Charles Sheeler's *Manhatta*. By the same token, *Wonder Ring* appropriates the subway route in order to realize ideas of speed, repetition, and architectural variation.

The *emblem* is one of roughly a half-dozen separate, loosely defined, and not mutually exclusive configurations apparent in avant-garde city films. Additional ways of organizing urban space and society include the *tour, catalogue, microcosm, diary,* and *essay.* Most of these approaches have analogues in documentary cinema, and they often bridge specific periods, styles, or social ideologies. There are as well several types of avant-garde urban narrative, from the Beat picaresque of Robert Frank and Alfred Leslie's *Pull My Daisy* (1959) to George Kuchar's melodramatic sendups in *Mosholu Holiday* and *Hold Me While I'm Naked* (both 1966), Warhol's subcultural epic *Chelsea Girls* (1966), and back alley punk excursions such as Vivienne Dick's *She Had Her Gun Already* (1978) and Becky Johnstone's *Sleepless Nights* (1980). The emphasis here, however, will be on formal constructions of urban space.

Not only can the same neighborhood or site be recruited for disparate purposes, the same idiom is amenable to various stylistic options. For instance, Warhol's infamous eight-hour fixed-frame *Empire* (1964), undoubtedly the longest "establishing shot" in the history of the medium, suggests an extreme limit point for the *emblem.* The Empire State Building is a favorite postcard image of Manhattan, and Warhol's seemingly static film hinges on the reflexive paradox of still frame and moving image; but at the same time it solicits a more active attention to tiny shifts in light and tonality (augmented by roll flares and printing errors) as it magnifies pseudodramatic incidents such as the movement of a flock of birds at dawn. In a canny play on art history, *Empire* recalls the method of Monet's cathedral paintings or Cézanne's mountains while simultaneously mocking the clichéd opening shots of dozens of Hollywood thrillers. Transcending its phallic joke on erection, the film becomes another testament to New York as the scene of remarkable endurance, a space in which the potential for "eight million stories" exists just offscreen. Instead of Weegee's Naked City, *Empire* shows the City stripped bare—formally bare—by her profligate bachelor.

Menken's work, instead of depicting famous monuments, guides the viewer along fast-paced topographic *tours.* The visual premise here is familiar to conventional travelogues: present a series of diverse urban views implying a cross-section for which expressive forms accentuate a given city's uniqueness or current importance. *Wonder Ring,* blending prerogatives of both emblem and tour, covers a swath of New York

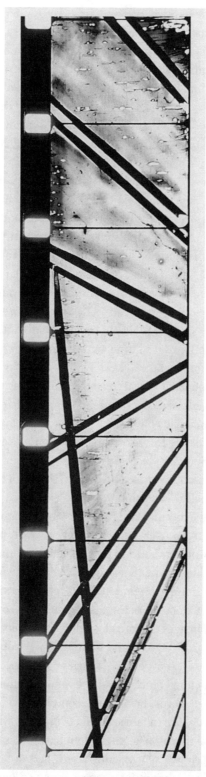

Notebook by Marie Menken. Photograph
courtesy of Anthology Film Archives.

real estate—a parade of neighborhoods and architectural facades—yet its path is clearly fixed and impersonal, unlike the idiosyncratic *flaneury* in Menken's films. Rudy Burckhardt's *The Climate of New York* (1948) is an early example of fractured travelogue, with individual segments devoted to separate districts or kinds of activity. Hollis Frampton conducts a minimalist tour in the central section of *Surface Tension* (1968), clicking off single frames at regular intervals as he travels Manhattan island from top to bottom. *Eureka* (1974), Ernie Gehr's found footage journey down San Francisco's Market Street circa 1901, is predetermined by a trolley route. By printing each original frame multiple times, Gehr distends the hectic movement of a traveling shot in order to savor a rich medley of horse-drawn and pedestrian traffic.

Notebook, along with *The Climate of New York* and other Burckhardt films, incorporates aspects of yet another discursive type, the *catalogue*. Once again, these labels are not intended as rigid obligations; they sketch a range of signifying practices by which cities are made legible to the viewer. The primary symbolic thrust of the catalogue form is that of infinite variation. Although accumulation of similar objects or architectural features is a common strategy—for example, Burckhardt groups together images of water towers, residential entranceways, and sidewalk vendors—in a number of films the collection of transient snapshots almost automatically imbues a sense of extreme heterogeneity. In Standish Lawder's humorously eerie *Necrology* (1970), the camera appears to glide in a continuous take over an endless line of dispirited faces that, as the title implies, meld into a phalanx of waking dead (in fact, the shot was made with a stationary camera aimed at a descending office-building escalator at 5 p.m., then printed to run backwards). At the conclusion of the traveling shot, Lawder attaches a long list of fake credits identifying participants according to various vocational or personal criteria. More recently, Scott Stark's *Acceleration* (1994) weaves an apocalyptic aura around a procession of San Francisco street faces, frozen in a flash of bleak light as if caught at the instant following a nuclear explosion.[9]

A seminal example of structural film, and possibly the greatest city symphony produced by the American avant-garde, Frampton's *Zorns Lemma* (1970) is governed by an extensive inventory of Manhattan's public signage, of the cacophony of printed language that surrounds our urban experience. Without delving too deeply into the intricate numerical axioms used to generate the film's structure, Frampton takes the twenty-four-letter Roman alphabet as linguistic/cinematic constant. He edited twenty-four frame (one-second) images of words found in the streets, presenting a word that starts with "A" followed by a "B" word and so on. Every twenty-five seconds—allowing for one second of darkness—a new cycle of images commences. Eventually, nonverbal depictions—many of which reference urban sites and activities—are inserted as substitutes for the emblazoned words. Prior to the completion of this process, however, the viewer is treated to a *textual* urban fabric the sheer scope of which mirrors the material resources of a commercial metropolis, its random harmonies and striking dissonances. The New York of *Zorns Lemma*, a stringently controlled riot of color and shape and semantic meaning, enfolds a cheerfully modern Tower of Babel that we understand, at least initially, as an impossible onslaught of rapid-fire signs but gradually come to

Zorns Lemma by Hollis Frampton. Photographs courtesy of Millennium Film Workshop.

master conceptually, just as the inhabitants of actual cities learn to master their physical perambulations.

A subgenre manifesting some of the same social-ecological tenets as the tour and the catalogue—namely, diversity and density—is the *microcosm*. Here, instead of navigating urban pathways in random or predetermined arrangements, films explore a single precinct by assembling contiguous views or by adopting a fixed frame of reference capable of revealing covert visual patterns. Jay Leyda's *A Bronx Morning* offers an early version of the former method by piling up short musical segments of neighborhood kids at play, of storefronts and rhymed vertical movements. Leyda pays poetic tribute to Vertov and Eisenstein, but his film also limns a historically telling vignette of immigrant conditions during the Depression. The trope of neighborhood as self-contained universe resurfaces in Helen Levitt's, Janice Loeb's, and James Agee's *In the Street* (1952). In an awkwardly sententious prologue, the "street" is addressed as a theatrical stage and battlefield. In the ensuing action, lower-class children act out rituals of aggression, submission, and compassion. Shot on an East Harlem block rife with ethnic and racial differences, *In the Street* is marked by a cool, unobtrusive visual style. There is, however, little evidence that poverty stifles the energy or imaginations of these kids; they seem to invent tribal customs through pantomimic language, donning masks and costumes that subvert adult pretenses to stable identity. A point worth underscoring is that, unlike similar procedures found in works of fiction or documentary, urban categories discussed thus far do not focus on individual diegetic protagonists or role hierarchies. Thus along with other aspects of urbanism, they inscribe decentered, or democratic, modes of address.

Microcosmic idioms flourished during the seventies, spurred by structural film's minimalist formal prescriptions. A fashionable tactic situated the camera at an open window as quasi-mechanical witness to street-level spectacles. Thus in David Rimmer's *Real Italian Pizza* (1971), a "slice of life" long shot charts the compressed interactions of several generations, ethnic groups, and social strata as subjects stroll in and out of a field anchored by the eponymous eatery. Tensions between systemic recording and an unpredictable exterior flux enlivens the final portion of Michael Snow's *Wavelength* (1967) once the film's forty-minute zoom shot approaches a bank of windows overlooking a busy commercial avenue. Barry Gerson's *Generations* (1969) unsettles the stability of framed residential vistas by making small adjustments in focus, camera position, and exposure. The space in front of and behind an open doorway is magically reconfigured in Ken Jacobs's *Airshaft* (1967) through oscillations in focus and exposure.

Without question the master of the fixed-frame microcosm is Ernie Gehr, an urban ethnographer in the guise of avant-garde filmmaker, who since the early seventies has harnessed ingeniously revealing camera protocols to urban expanses that are perceptually turned inside out and upside down. *Still* (1971) assays a scene divided into planes by a multilane street bounded by sidewalks. Activity in the opening passages unfolds at a straightforward, leisurely pace, after which superimposed layers of the same view begin to complicate perception through a play of transparency and opacity, presence and absence. Ghost images of cars seem to overtake more solid shapes; store windows darken or burst with reflected light; the shadow of a tree bends and recedes. Passersby strengthen the illusion of depth; when they exit the foreground, the view flattens out. Like all successful exercises in (filmic) urban renewal, *Still* prods us to experience quotidian motifs simultaneously as ciphers of cinematic ontology and sociological knowledge.[10] In *Untitled 1981* (1981), brief intimate close-ups of a Brooklyn street corner, shot from an extremely high angle, are stitched into a crazy quilt of garish colors, textile patterns, and odd personal body languages culled from a crowd of what appear to be mostly elderly inhabitants of an immigrant Brooklyn neighborhood. Fragmented glimpses of worn shoes, crutches, handbags communicate information that is both visually concrete and suggestive. The editing has a strong musical cadence but does not feel metrical or formulaic, and the velocity of filmic exchange runs counter to the labored movements of the film's aging denizens.

Untitled 1981, as is true of many Gehr films, points to an underlying process in avant-garde city symphonies by which workplace, home, and social milieu are collapsed into a single visual domain—a convergence that reverses modernity's ever-increasing social-ecological disjunctions. To put it bluntly, filmmakers who are taking up residence in former industrial areas, such as New York's Soho, or in economically depressed neighborhoods have managed to carve out aesthetic programs from intensive observation of their immediate surroundings. The urban anomie and alienation conventionally registered by Hollywood narratives, and certainly by the modernist literary canon, is largely absent from avant-garde film; leaving aside their economic marginality, filmmakers have discovered relatively unalienated, artisanal forms of work within a medium that quickly adopted assembly-line models of production and within a social setting that is the very epitome of depersonalized interaction. Indeed, it is precisely during the fiscal crises plaguing New York and other cities in the early seventies that the movement gained notable footholds in some of the very neighborhoods most in need of economic help, re-envisioning those spaces as vital, nourishing fields of investigation. In a sense, then, the avant-garde inadvertently tried to reestablish the kind of workplaces—and their attendant social relations—characteristic of premodern urban societies. Instead of aimless, deracinated subjects, the avant-garde imagines, and in certain ways enacts, the power of blatantly subjective agents to transform the decaying core of postindustrial cities and revive moribund elements of community.

The hyperbolic instance of a studio merging social, artistic, and domestic functions was, of course, Warhol's Factory, for which a precedent might be found in the bohemian quarters of *Pull My Daisy.* His obsessive documentation of a disreputable subculture can be read as introverted exercises in social bonding. Gehr's oeuvre in particular deposits successive traces of domestic dwellings, like deflected renderings of the traditional artist's studio, as it mediates reconciliation between a hermetic version of self and a disenfranchised social setting. The act of filming, along with its reverberations at the distribution and screening stages, becomes a means by which to integrate an otherwise alienated creative sector with disparate collective histories. As Ken Jacobs explains, in a production note to *The Winter Footage* (1964/84):

We lived alongside the Manhattan side of the Brooklyn Bridge, a ghost town night and weekends. A big walker and looker, I became familiar with many objects comprising our neighborhood and invited them to the cine-dance I threw. Framing drew them together and splitting them in ways they could never understand but together we achieved some animation.[11]

What Jacobs playfully describes encompasses a broader paradigm, the "home movie of the street." Of course the quintessential form of this activity is the *diary* and its ultimate practitioner, Jonas Mekas, has confirmed: "If one has a camera and wants to master it, then one begins to film in the street or in the apartment."[12] Since discussions of Mekas's work appear elsewhere in this volume, I will forgo the opportunity to consider it here. Suffice it to say that in his greatest achievement, *Lost, Lost, Lost* (1976), the early melancholia of a postwar displaced personhood is gradually assuaged as Mekas constructs a new home for himself in New York's working-class and bohemian enclaves. As is true in other urban diaries, place serves as a harbinger and quicksilver repository of personal identity. Although overt trappings of dire personal circumstance, of exile and culture shock, do not inform the work of other urban diarists, some of Mekas's integrative energies are evident in Howard Guttenplan's *N.Y.C. Diary '74* (1974), Peter Hutton's *New York Portrait: Chapter One* (1978–79) and *New York Portrait: Chapter Two* (1980–81), and Mark Lapore's *100 Views of New York* (1996). From one angle, it matters little whether the avant-garde/urban encounter is staged as an open-ended audition for movie stardom, a predesigned set of instructions with which to navigate a public realm, or a diaristic regime of spontaneous observations. Nonetheless, the threshold separating Warhol's approach from that of Mekas—as well as those of Gehr, Menken, Clarke, Frampton, and others—is the latter's intuitive stake in what Michel de Certeau refers to as "perambulatory optics," the formal embodiment of pedestrian liberties as counterweight to the vertical thrust of administered power.[13] Although it is hardly as concrete as a geographic neighborhood, avant-garde cinema binds its human and man-made themes in a rear-guard struggle against the encroachment of "faceless" corporate controls, empowering localized *gemeinschaft* values amid the ruins of a late capitalist landscape.

As Mekas concludes, "After a while the streets begin to talk back to you."[14] What might start as a protocol for shaping immediate visual impressions eventually involves the filmmaker in a reciprocal, socially charged contract. The idea of talking streets is a piquant image, but it is ultimately misleading. Streets rarely speak, directly or otherwise, in avant-garde city films, in large measure because of the prohibitive costs of sync-sound recording and printing. Instead, the evocation of place tends to rely on visual rhythms or, at times, the contrapuntal use of music. *Lost, Lost, Lost* is a glorious exception insofar as it features Mekas's voice-over commentary and sporadic bits of conversation, yet nothing is synchronized with the image. Thus, in general, the sensory fullness of urban experience is somewhat curtailed, with the eye claiming precedence over the ear.[15] Ironically, the avulsion of sight and sound returns to the artist a semblance of autonomy forfeited by the ranks of commercial realist directors.

Before turning to two exceptional, nearly unclassifiable city symphonies, it is instructive to pay a brief visit to the *essay* subgenre. A slippery category at best (see chapter 4), the essay would seem a natural vehicle with which to anatomize or reconstruct the layered history of urban ecologies. Nonetheless, surprisingly few avant-garde essays derive their overall meaning from cities. Yvonne Rainer's *Journeys from Berlin/1971* (1980) is a seminal essay yet only peripherally treats the role of urban society in the development of women's political resistance. Jack Chamber's collage epic *Hart of London* (1969–70) reveals submerged psychological and political patterns governing a small Canadian city, but it lacks the weave of personal and social histories that characterizes the essay project in general. The same can be said of Pat O'Neill's lustrous *Water and Power* (1989). Chantal Akerman's *News from Home* (1977) seems at first glance a version of the minimalist tour, concentrating on long-take fixed-frame studies of offbeat lower Manhattan sites. However, the addition of a series of letters from the filmmaker's mother in Brussels, read by Akerman in a thick accent, creates a rich essayistic counterpoint of presence and absence, American and European urban cultures. A less equivocal version of the urban essay is Jem Cohen's *Lost Book Found* (1996), a brooding meditation on chance encounters, talismanic objects, and the fathomless enigma of New York street life. Blending the discourses of diary, autobiography, fable, catalogue, and abstract architectural study—and trailing obvious debts to Poe, Paul Auster, Frampton, and cartoonist Ben Katchtor—Cohen unfolds a story about working as a pushcart vendor and momentarily acquiring a notebook crammed with arcane markings. This symbolic "text" serves as the hub of ideas about the mutability of urban space and the volatility of urban social relations.

Since the vast majority of avant-garde city symphonies are informed by a "hometown" sensibility, instances of touristic excursions are rare (Guttenplan and Hutton have both filmed extensively in foreign cities). An interesting exception is Gehr's microcosmic treatment of a Berlin intersection, *Signal—Germany on the Air* (1985), which also brings to bear a highly original application of music and voice. On the surface, *Signal—Germany* looks like another exercise in technically choreographed human and vehicular movement. To a greater extent than in earlier works, however, Gehr eschews defamiliarizing photographic maneuvers in favor of an ostensibly pared-down recording method: a series of adjacent or overlapping views of a bustling central location, adorned with all manner of signs and symbolic demarcations, from a freestanding clock above an advertising logo of an eyeball to a profusion of painted lines directing the movement of auto and foot traffic. The dense, almost oppressive semiosis apparent in this scene is, at first, divided into individual motifs and kinetic patterns, then gradually reconfigured conceptually in terms of national character. As in city symphonies of the 1920s—including Vertov's *Man with a Movie Camera* and Walter Ruttman's *Berlin: Symphony of a Great City* (1928), in relation to which Gehr's film stands as ominous response—new elements are added that complicate established patterns of physical freedom and constraint. A deserted lot frames a deteriorating building labeled in several languages as the former site of a Gestapo torture chamber. A shot of nearby railroad tracks forges a heuristic connection to the Nazi era.

Signal: Germany on the Air by Ernie Gehr. Photograph courtesy of Millennium Film Workshop.

When the crowded square reappears, it is accompanied by sound fragments recorded directly from contemporary radio broadcasts: orchestral music, a cabaret song, a woman's voice speaking in German. The date of a Glen Miller tune is announced as 1942. As Gehr builds an overlay of past and present, the weight of formalist investigation begins to recede in favor of an anxious reckoning of personal history and the vicissitudes of memory. Played off against shots of a siding with dilapidated boxcars, the intersection begins to acquire a facade of historical complicity—what events took place here?; who walked across this patch of banal asphalt?—as a bilingual radio program issues dialogues around accusation and guilt: "You got us into this mess"; "Don't blame me"; "You people are all the same." The sound is at once immediate and removed, a faint echo of the camera's orientation to the populous street. What is invisible, and irretrievable, breaks through a veneer of aesthetic, and social, order. *Signal—Germany* announces its visual and dramatic climax in a cascade of nearly a dozen panning shots executed at different speeds and angles across the still-active square. They resemble mechanical arcs of a surveillance device yet at the same time impose an almost expressive, subjective burden of entrapped desperation. Historical memory and immediate observation are intermingled. Analytic shaping of urban locales cannot remain uncoupled from individual, or collective, signifiers of consciousness. As it happens, Gehr's visit to Berlin was not a casual vacation. But for an accident of history, it would have been his childhood home. Thus his Berlin microcosm emerges as not just another urban field ripe for perceptual conundrums. It is the field that haunts Gehr's dossier of urban renovations, albeit in profound, if not quite impossible, absence.

Ken Jacobs's urban exertions are decidedly more improvisatory and anarchic—especially in his early collaborations with Jack Smith—than the dialectics of control inherent to Gehr's work. Yet *Signal—Germany* and Jacobs's "Nervous System" live performance of *New York Ghetto Fishmarket 1903* (1993), for dual single-frame advance projectors, constitute intriguing bookends to a self-questioning problematic of urban dislocation and memory. Indeed, both are underwritten by subtle discourses of immigrant survival. In *Fishmarket,* a dizzying assortment of eye-popping effects is extracted from a turn-of-the-century Edison-produced newsreel. The original high-angle traveling shot moves along a row of open-air wagons and market stalls frequented by working-class customers and vendors. Jacobs retards the progression of found footage in order to concentrate on details otherwise buried in the grainy swirl of densely packed figures. For instance, he pauses to investigate the activities of a heavyset woman arranging and weighing her goods, repeating tiny increments of her motion in a strobic, stuttering rhythm; later, he singles out a young boy darting around umbrella-covered stands for similar treatment. Some figures are passed over altogether while others receive elaborate scrutiny; since Jacobs improvises his projector riffs from a loose score, each rendition of the piece is slightly different.

As in other "Nervous System" performances geared to archival footage, sociological details of clothing, gesture, hairstyle, and so on are granted a vivid cultural specificity far exceeding their impact in "real time" projection. In this case the filmic subjects are symbolically, if not literally, the ancestors of Jacobs's childhood friends and neighbors in Brooklyn and, not incidentally, they are conceivably among the first patrons of motion pictures. In other words, what we are exposed to is the face, or faces, of an ethnic as well as technological heritage, a double primal scene. Approximately halfway through the piece, Jacobs lowers a red filter over the lens. Encouraged by singer-composer Catherine Jaunieux's mournful variations on Yiddish folk melodies, and abetted by the intermittent blurring of focus, a vision of the catastrophic historical trajectory of Eastern European Jewry is wedged into the proceedings. Skin seems to melt from bone, tortured postures are frozen in a Goya-esque tableau of mass murder. Presumably the Jewish fishmongers and customers captured in the Edison vignette were spared the fate of their Old World kin, but Jacobs invites the viewer to imagine the historical abyss hovering over their spectral presences.

In *Fishmarket*'s final moments, Jacobs lifts the shroud of Holocaust implications to stage a return to everyday routines of urban life: buying and selling, rounding up stray kids, casting a vigilant eye on roaming detectives. Immigrant culture feels revived, but not without the intrusion of an uncanny warning. As the last frames of the Edison reel expire on screen, Jacobs finds a darkly handsome young man who separates himself from the crowd to stare head-on at the camera. His demeanor mixes shock with outrage. Looking into the lens, it is as if this marketplace Elijah has peered into the future, a panorama compounded of human suffering and cinematic representation.

Examined from our critical vantage, avant-garde city films may occasionally speak to pessimistic concerns, even as they promote vestiges of an old-fashioned, affirmative modernism. The urban spaces they confect are alien to the exhausted ruins of postmodern discourse. There is little pastiche and even less evidence of accepted assertions of a "crisis in language" or the loss of "signifying potencies that [cities] once seemed to possess."[16] In their place, the postwar city symphony makes common cause with homegrown urban theorists William H. White and Richard Sennett, for whom the "primacy of the streets" or the "humane value of complexity" retain an urgent legitimacy.[17] Finally, it is possible to align a spectrum of avant-garde work with Fredric Jameson's call for an antidote to the "unmappable" domain of postmodern culture: "practical reconquest of a sense of place, and the construction or reconstruction of an articulated ensemble which can be retained in memory and which the individual subject can map and remap along the moments of mobile, alternative trajectories."[18] At least provisionally, the nonnarrative city film merits inclusion among alternative, if not quite utopian, cultural trajectories.

(1991)

4 | The Resurgence of History and the Avant-Garde Essay Film

Chance cannot be studied separately from necessity.
—*Emmanuel Le Roy Ladurie*

OR NEARLY THIRTY YEARS AN UNSPOKEN DESIRE in American avant-garde film was to exist outside history, to operate in a realm of aesthetic expression that elided any recognition of a socially shared past. This aspiration was of course impossible, a supreme fiction, but the interlocking set of refusals and affirmations it authorized served as the motor for a powerful revaluation of cinema under the sign of personal imagination. Ironically, the circumvention of history eventually assumed its own historical trajectory, approaching an apex in the late sixties in which the full flowering of a poetic-lyrical tradition collided with an initial wave of structural filmmaking. In other words, Brakhage met Snow at the crossroads of the autonomous image, where phenomenological celebration of filmic presentness eclipsed the functional vestiges of verbal language—hence linear narrative—in the attempt to visualize more directly the dynamics of change. Revoking by one means or another the conditions through which narrative establishes itself in cinema as the bearer of motivation, causality, and closure, each camp laid claim to an image domain freed from not only the encrustations of Hollywood storytelling but the chains of social determination.

From our perspective, the gaps left unsealed by tautologies of self or formal system—for instance, the sexual politics of *Dog Star Man* (1961–64) or the description of an urban microcosm in *Wavelength* (1967)—now appear as potent as the aesthetic programs these films so stridently transmit. That is, like other artistic factions, no matter how reflexively focused, avant-garde filmmaking harbors contours of a political unconscious. Since the early seventies, however, the movement has been increasingly infused with unprecedented, or perhaps merely renewed, historical energies. There are in truth two interrelated initiatives at stake here: a desire to collate private depictions of everyday life with broader, collective experiences and events; and the desire to discover formal or thematic connections between contemporary and silent-era , or "primitive," cinematic practices. Whether nestled in a rubric of New Narrative, first-person essay, or postmodern collage, a disparate group of films are examining key aspects of historical representation and the filmic discourse of social memory. This movement, if it is that, may be understood as a refusal of a prior refusal, signaling a rupture in the movement's internal preoccupations but also a revision of longstanding concerns associated with the avant-garde's core mission: the uses of autobiography; the dissection of photographic illusion; the contradictions of subjectivity in cinema. Nonetheless, it is clear that if the repressed is making its inevitable return, the idioms in which it is conveyed are still light years from historiographic conventions of most documentaries, to say nothing of fictional treatments of history in recent European or American "art" cinema—Bertolucci's *1900* (1975) and *Reds* (1981) are two honorable examples.

Before addressing recent tendencies in the treatment of historical themes, it is necessary to give a more detailed account of the status of history—more accurately, antihistory—in the continuum of avant-garde practices. Symptoms of the avant-garde's mistrust of language, and of the "language" of linear narrative, were quite varied, especially in the antiauthoritarian climate of sixties culture. At one extreme, making films without sound was held to ensure the "purity" of image apprehension against intrusions of socially constrained meaning. Music or concrete noise could help articulate rhythmic or affective elements but the human voice was either proscribed or served up in abstracted (nonsemantic) forms. Even written film titles were jettisoned or tacked unobtrusively onto the end of works. Because language was a culturally shared entity, because words came equipped with supposedly banal or regimented associations, they were inferior vehicles for expressive—or in the case of structural film, nonexpressive— motifs, ranging from children at play to shifting light patterns in an urban loft.

An inchoate poststructuralist recognition of the regime of language and its reinforcement of status quo knowledge is discernible, in which curtailment of verbal speech is merely the flip side of later deconstructionist or New Narrative suspicions of language-as-power. Nevertheless, over several decades the combination of radical subjectivity, heightened present-tense temporality, the leveling of relations between the human figure and landscape, and the suppression of storytelling turned avant-garde aesthetics into a kind of poor stepchild of American abstract painting. The idea of standards or symbolic markers for cinematic objectivity, typically "guaranteed" in documentary and fictional discourses, were deemed irrelevant to avant-garde perspectives, rendering moot the representation of a shared past. Since the profilmic order, whether scripted or spontaneously recorded, could never "speak for itself," it was impotent to speak *to* an invisible network of causes and explanations governing collective experience. The sole enunciative authorities vested in photographic images were individual perception and the mechanical limits/possibilities of the apparatus. History, as we usually think of it, had become that which turned cinema away from itself.

The avant-garde's epistemological resistance to representations of history has an interesting by-product that could be called the "First Film/Last Film" syndrome. An offshoot of the "myth of the Absolute film,"[1] it is evident in otherwise disparate stylistic approaches and is underwritten by a desire to supplant all previous versions of a given theme or formal practice. By taking a facet of cinema to its furthest point of logical development, works such as Brakhage's *The Art of Vision* (1961–65) or Snow's *Rameau's Nephew by Diderot (Thanx to Dennis Young) by Wilma Schoen* (1974) situate themselves as beyond the reach of historical incorporation. Apocalyptic undertones vibrate through these films, as if the scale of ambition practically dooms them to artistic exhaustion; indeed, several would not be completed (anecdotally, Brakhage, Jordan Belson, Kenneth Anger, and Hollis Frampton have each suggested that an especially arduous project would be coterminus with their actual death).

The First Film branch of this phenomenon seeks to envision cinema's prehistory, a visual moment prior to either the invention of movies or their institutionalization through narrative codes. Thus Michael Snow could say of Ernie Gehr's *History* (1970), "At last, the first film," an apt description given its "primordial" swirling patterns of white grains on a dark ground. The same impression is elicited by Tony Conrad's *The Flicker* (1966), Brakhage's *The Text of Light* (1974), and Ken Jacobs's double-projector "Nervous System" performances. At the opposite end of historical time, as it were, Christopher MacLaine, in *The End* (1953), amplifies the dramatic enactment of a nuclear holocaust through a breakdown in narrative structure itself. Frampton tries to create the last word on cinematic relations between still and moving in the unfinished *Magellan* (1972–85), Snow assays the possibilities of fixed-base camera movements in *La Region Centrale* (1970–71), while Harry Smith signals the finale of split-screen imagery in the semifinished *Mahagonny* (1980). Films in the latter group often take an encyclopedic or anatomical angle on a particular item of cinematic ontology. Others have a narrower purview: Owen Land's *On the Marriage Broker Joke as Cited by Sigmund Freud in* Wit and its Relation to the Unconscious, *or Can the Avant-Garde Artist be Wholed?* (1980) didactically, and hilariously, posits itself as the "last" structural film, after which any additional explorations are made redundant.

In whichever direction the suprahistorical axis in these films is pointed, the result is an implied immunity from erosions and revisions of time figured as social-cultural history. The absolute or First/Last prerogative was itself a historically specific impulse, emerging emphatically at a time when the American movement was benefiting from institutional expansion spurred by the promise of increased funding and access to sophisticated equipment. Significantly, the artists adopting ultimate strategies were largely veterans of earlier, more impoverished phases of avant-garde activity. Consequently, the optimistic tone in their work inevitably masks an ongoing anxiety over future production. That is, given the avant-garde's obvious and persistent economic and cultural marginality, wildly ambitious aesthetic agendas may be seen as harboring deep uncertainty over the real possibility that a particular line of development could be abruptly canceled from lack of resources or suddenly obsolete technologies. The desire

The Art of Vision by Stan Brakhage.
Photograph courtesy of Anthology
Film Archives.

to circumvent history, then, serves at once as an index of utopian schemes and a talisman against the collapse of a fragile system.[2]

Ironically, some of the same factors that encouraged an escape from history in the early seventies also fueled the movement's reengagement with issues of historical consciousness. The expanding profile of film history in the study of popular culture and the rapid growth of academic film theory and historiography helped create a tiny opening for New American Cinema in university curricula, museum exhibition, and publishing. If mainstream film history largely ignored the contributions of the avant-garde, a generalized interest in conserving, restoring, and rediscovering film artifacts made a range of intriguing footage available for recontextualization by nonnarrative filmmakers. The 1974 publication of Sitney's *Visionary Film* gave the avant-garde its first rigorous historical overview.

Like other aesthetic topoi, the return to history was inflected by a combination of internal dynamics and extracinematic forces. Especially important are a set of influential Anglo-European discourses that gave impetus to new forms of envisioning the past. The ascent of Foucault's notion of "archeology," along with the French *Annales* school's exacting focus on everyday life, presaged a shift in the nature of historical evidence—the actual documents from which accounts of events are drawn—that favored social groups traditionally downplayed or ignored altogether as historical subjects. In the United States, so-called revisionist historians in the wake of William Appleman Williams boldly reinterpreted the explanations for and direction of Cold War American foreign policy, a review that was sparked by the growing debacle in Vietnam and by domestic protest. Other figures such as Howard Zinn, Noam Chomsky, and Hayden White offered powerful critiques of the tools of conventional history writing, especially in regard to the ideological underpinnings of objective or positivist enunciation. If cinema was clearly tangential to this wider enterprise, there was nonetheless extensive debate about the functions of film as source of historical evidence and as potential agent of change.

By the end of the decade, the contraction of cultural as well as social expectations in the face of a wilting economy and domestic political retrenchment helped to spell the end of one stage in the avant-garde's modernist self-interrogation. As it happens, that outcome was given a hefty shove, first by feminist political demands and theory and then by queer initiatives. For both factions, countering longstanding traditions of male heterosexual privilege required fresh confrontations with mechanisms for representing the past.[3] At the same time, feminist and queer artists managed not only to redirect avant-garde film's distinguishing constellation of styles and themes but—insisting on the need to grapple head-on with perceived biases in *conventional* modes of film narration—embraced long-abandoned hybrid or nonartisanal methods of production. It is from this swirl of (mostly) complementary departures that the movement's historical imperative takes shape. Of three discernible, though not mutually exclusive, strands, by far the most significant is the rise of the avant-garde essay film.[4]

A notorious maverick even among loosely cohesive nonfiction genres, the foundations of the essay film derive from three landmark documentaries: Alain Resnais's *Night and Fog* (1955), Jean Rouch's *Les Maîtres fous* (1955), and Chris Marker's *Letter from Siberia* (1958). What the American avant-garde assimilated from European precedents was, in part, a basic framework for reconfiguring past events and social dynamics in nonlinear, interrogatory segments often pitting language against image and vice versa. Because the essay is a form without pretense to completeness or finality, claiming an aesthetic (and political) virtue in the fragmentary and the heterogeneous, this emerging paradigm offered a possible solution to—equally univocal, hence equally tainted—ideologies of mastery pervading avant-garde as well as fictional practices. Just as the idea of history answered certain supposedly apolitical deficiencies in prior avant-garde approaches, essayistic strategies were appealing because they could retain seemingly indelible avant-garde concerns—childhood trauma; sexual identity; the rhythms of urban space—while eschewing the trappings of a unified creative self intrinsic to the validation of poetic and, in a different register, structural idioms. Subjectivity as central problematic is not jettisoned but rather uncoiled to accommodate a conceptual machinery of dispersion, contradiction, and multiplicity. Found footage is nearly axiomatic for essay projects—ranging from archival shots to Hollywood product, home movies, science and promotional documentaries—as it is for other historicizing strands. Significantly, in essay films such materials are neither fetishized nor passed along as neutral carriers of information; instead, they are prone to oppositional readings produced by visual juxtaposition, voice-over commentary, and other tactics.

The historical dimension addressed in New Narratives is, first and foremost, the shaping of personal identity and experience—particularly in the arenas of gender difference, sexuality, and conformist social behavior—by classical Hollywood genres and by ancillary commercial sources. Autobiography or first-person enunciative presence is more oblique here than in other historical tendencies. Due to a combination of budget limitations and fascination with coded, symptomatic meaning, film noir and domestic melodramas of the forties and fifties have been favorite dramatic sources and intertexts. In particular, a standard figure like the private eye is turned into a cipher through which, say, tropes of male dysfunction and female anger are reenacted for what they reveal about current dilemmas in gender roles. To put it another way, it is precisely those genres which recall the charged atmosphere of postwar America that are adopted by the avant-garde for purposes of "liberating" Hollywood fantasies from their reactionary contexts, while also chastising the imprint of screen memories on contemporary attitudes. Already a well-known acid test for feminist film theories and ideological critiques, film noir is at once honored and demystified in Manuel de Landa's *Raw Nerves* (1978), Bette Gordon's *Variety* (1984), Leandro Katz's *The Visit* (1986), Yvonne Rainer's *The Man Who Envied Women* (1986), and Abigail Child's *Mayhem* (1987). Although autobiographical connections are usually submerged, it is telling that frequently the commercial films recast by New Narratives were popular during the filmmaker's childhood, indicating a personal sense of primal cinematic past.

Eschatological themes, the search for individual and/or collective origins *in* cinema, are an important undercurrent in a second group of films. Reverting to artifacts from the first decades of film history or to the nonindustrialized precincts of home movie or fringe documentary, Gehr's *Eureka* (1979), Marjorie Keller's *Daughters of Chaos* (1980),

Child's *Covert Action,* and Alan Berliner's *The Family Album* (1986), among others, advance two ideas simultaneously: that old footage is capable of exposing through its visual qualities something of the social matrix in which it was produced; and that extant images either predating the onset of industrial codes or eliding them through private production participate in historical and aesthetic trajectories that culminate in the achievements of the American avant-garde. That is, where New Narrative implicitly traces its lineage to postwar Hollywood, these films claim a productive, not merely cele- bratory, exchange with less public manifestations of cinema. Frampton's *Gloria!* (1979), positioned near the end of his huge calendrical cycle, *Magellan,* clarifies a crucial aspect of this tendency. Made as a tribute to the filmmaker's maternal grandmother, it quotes from several early slapstick comedies about Irish wakes. We learn that Gloria herself was born in 1894, nearly coincident with the birth of cinema, and Frampton parlays that fact into a subtle elegy for the looming endpoint of living, biological contact with witnesses to the medium's early development. Thus the metaphysical question of "Where do I come from?" is spun to encompass family, ethnic, and formal roots.

A linchpin among different historicizing tendencies, Rainer's *Journeys from Berlin/ 1971* (1980) is genuinely mercurial and proved highly influential, especially to women artists. Utilizing found footage, direct camera observation, and enacted scenes, Rainer segues diary entries from her adolescence with ruminations on women's work and conditions of radicalization, excursuses on homegrown anarchism, and the outrageous state suppression of the Baader-Meinhof gang. It maintains a deeply personal tone

Journeys from Berlin/1971 by Yvonne Rainer. Photograph courtesy of Anthology Film Archives.

while sifting in a variety of spoken historical texts and archival materials. Essays refuse the impression that shots and sequences are governed by a single rationalized or, for that matter, unconsciously motivated system; they are rather the product of a twisting, a priori unmappable mental journey. They unfold through skeins of accumulation, one thing after another, allowing for sudden excursuses, unexpected epiphanies, and reflective pauses.

Essays, then, tend to inscribe a central mediating consciousness that is itself engaged in active questioning of materials and the processes of their ordering, able finally to secure only provisional truths. The representation of history becomes, in Howard Zinn's fine phrase, "private enterprise," with the strong implication that it cannot be otherwise. Lacking the guarantees of a stable, self-assured narrator, the notion of a shared past is rendered fluid, plurivocal, riddled with the incursions of popular culture, high theory, the vestiges of earlier avant-garde styles. Among recent films taking this hybrid approach are Leslie Thornton's *Adynata* (1983), James Benning's *American Dreams* (1983), Dan Eisenberg's *Displaced Person* (1981), Morgan Fisher's *Standard Gauge* (1984), Ken Kobland's *The Communists Are Comfortable* (1985), Craig Baldwin's *RocketKitKongoKit* (1986), and Jean-Pierre Gorin's *Routine Pleasures* (1986). In each case a core of distant events—accessed through found objects, personal narratives, and/or direct camera observation—are subjected to a sinuous interaction of semiautonomous parts made up of different tenses, rhetorical voices, and visual styles. At their best, they can create collage effects that thicken and enliven our understanding of historical time.

The Nightmare from Which We Are Trying to Awake

A structural description of *American Dreams* is deceptively simple. Along a narrow border at the bottom of the screen a handwritten transcription of passages from Arthur Bremer's 1972 diary, leading up to his assassination attempt on George Wallace—his original target was President Nixon—crawls from right to left over the entire length of the film, like a hastily scrawled TV bulletin. Above this text a chronological series of baseball cards and promotional or commercial memorabilia from the career of Hank Aaron is shown in a steady cadence, first the front (usually a photo or cartoonish drawing often accompanied by an advertising logo), then the reverse side (providing batting statistics, anecdotes, trivia questions, mini-interviews, and so on). Numbers that we gradually realize are the year-by-year totals of Aaron's home-run stats punctuate the images. Finally, overtitles indicate by year, identity of speaker, and at times by social context the sources of fragmentary speeches and songs on the soundtrack.

In a rhythm not precisely matched to the display of visual documents, portions of popular music alternate with political speeches, ads, and radio news broadcasts that are presented chronologically from the beginning of Aaron's career in 1954 to its conclusion in 1976. A double time scheme is thus embedded: Bremer's diary starts off chronologically in advance of the boyish baseball materials but the latter gradually catch up and then pass Bremer's wacko narration, only to jump back at the last min-

American Dreams by James Benning. Photograph courtesy of Millennium Film Workshop.

ute for an oral replay of Aaron's record-breaking home run. As in Benning's earlier films, in which simple temporal and spatial rules—such as fixed-camera single takes of determinate length—govern the structure, *American Dreams* pairs off the functions of sound and image in a welter of reciprocal relations. There are two kinds of writing (not counting the denotative titles): diary entries and baseball chatter. They can be distilled into seemingly polar categories: script/printed text; continuous/discontinuous appearance; private/public; subjective/objective; deviant/socially honored; and, less obvious at first, white male/black male.

In another register, the musical hit parade replete with lachrymose lyrics contrasts sharply with the high seriousness of spoken political rhetoric. Tropes of romantic longing and rejection infuse the music with private emotions—although, during the late sixties segment, a few mild political sentiments are expressed musically—while violence, social unrest, and international conflict occupy the bulk of "official" speeches. Significantly, neither Aaron nor Bremer—two exceptional instances, "A" and "B," of American masculinity—is given a literal voice in the proceedings. What we learn about these men is a product of reading, in one case from a text so hermetic that much of its meaning is opaque, in the other from a collection of depersonalized images and factoids that tell us little about the man himself. Neither the deranged outcast nor the sports celebrity is capable of fully realized representation. They are figments of popular imagination, apprehended only through traces, set like filigree into a fabric of familiar historical moments.

Like the two oblique narratives cast in different registers at the center and bottom of the frame, Bremer and Aaron's paths cross symbolically then diverge. Bremer visits a baseball game, rants about problems of racial inequality, longs for a public visibility attainable only through an explosive gesture which, like the home run, can be read as a sign of displaced sexual prowess. Metaphorically as well as visually, Bremer's thoughts form an undercurrent to Aaron's exploitation by organs of mass media. Aaron, a rather shy Southerner (born in Wallace's Alabama!), obsessively chases a white man's supreme standard of athletic potency in a period that spans the Civil Rights and Black Power movements. Meanwhile, Bremer, an abject failure, acquires an abiding resentment toward outward signs of power as he stalks first Nixon then the racist governor.

Despite sparks of correspondence, the two stories cannot truly be followed in unison. It is impossible to simultaneously read the cards and attend to the constantly moving diary entries. The viewer must fixate on one trajectory or, more likely, alternate haphazardly between them. Navigating through the overlapping grids of information—two visual plus two aural diachronies—becomes a task subject to all manner of chance encounters. And the viewer's desire to locate cohesive patterns, alignments, and causes is inflected at every turn by sequencing, the order of apprehension for any given moment of intersection, and of course by personal experience and memory. For instance, a song familiar to one viewer will prime adjacent materials to resonate along lines not available to another viewer. The temptation is to regard the disjunct historical vectors as not only pieces of a narrative whole but as indicative of a larger social predicament whose salient tropes are those of counterpoint, repetition, irony, and accelerating pressure. In this sense the film encourages us to view its dual protagonists as (unlikely) historical catalysts.

There are, predictably, some weird connections: Elvis is interviewed about a rumor he once shot his mother, as Bremer notes the ease with which guns can be hidden in an automobile. Nixon is heard excoriating JFK for pessimism over race relations and poverty, then Frank Sinatra breaks in singing "High Hopes." A reporter announces the White House line on the Bay of Pigs invasion just before Brenda Lee chimes in with "I'm Sorry." The song "Red Roses for a Blue Lady" invokes the grief of Jackie Kennedy while Bremer's inane self-pity unfolds below. Aaron nears the homer record as Bremer writes, "There's going to be an explosion soon." The cheesy ballad "Tin Soldier" draws a loop around Bremer, Aaron, and news about the war. Irony springs from coincidence and there is the potential to assign every juxtaposition an integral role in a discursive network of meaning. Yet to do so would be to risk the kind of paranoid thinking that was displayed by Bremer and, as we now know, haunted Aaron as his pursuit bred increasing death threats and racist taunting. It is, however, hard to resist the inference that pop music took its cues from headline news and government policy mimicked dominant themes in popular culture. Aaron is heroic but also, according to Benning, a corporate marketing tool; Bremer tells us, "I liked to think I lived with a television family with no shouting and no hitting me." We are propelled by the need to locate causal relations, primary and secondary effects. We imagine that the music and radio broadcasts we hear were shared cultural terrain for Bremer and Aaron, and for baseball-worshipping Benning as well, but the film never says so explicitly. Evidence, then, is what we make of it.

American Dreams is, to be sure, relatively constrained in its social-historical horizons. A sense of an ending, as befitting a film employing the rigid design of the structural "school," is made obvious early on: Bremer *will* shoot Wallace; Aaron *will* break Babe Ruth's mark. And through this conjunction the film will end. The expectation of closure, a logical and dramatic resolution to the braided series of events, folds back upon the question of authorship. Although his work is energized by an autobiographical impulse, Benning nonetheless hides himself in the shadows of time. With the Rossellini of the historical films he can proclaim: "It's all in the documents. Nothing is invented."[5] We need not know that Benning's earlier (and later) films swirl around themes of murder, rage, restless travel, alienation. It isn't necessary to know that Bremer was Benning's neighbor in Milwaukee or that the filmmaker counts among his greatest achievements pitching batting practice to the Milwaukee Braves in 1962. As externally shaped and motivated as it appears, *American Dreams* embodies a dark and self-conscious meeting of personal and public desires.

Spectators unacquainted with Bremer's published diary—which also served as the premise of Paul Schrader's script for Martin Scorsese's *Taxi Driver* (1976), as well as for several avant-garde theater pieces—might reasonably think, until the mention of stalking Nixon and then Wallace, that the diary is Benning's. The recognition of similar handwriting on various baseball membership cards and the diary crawl furthers this inference. But the parallels do not end there. Bremer's obsession with a particular type of fame accords not only with Aaron's obsession with Ruth's achievement but with Benning's hoarding of baseball souvenirs—and again with their relentless display as "art" objects. Searching for causes, Benning's diffuse historical materials lead us to see Bremer's story and Aaron's story as a double allegory (the light and dark sides, as it were) cloaking an absent, or merely effaced, personal narrative of youthful ambition and alienation staged at a crucial juncture. There but for accidents of birth—physical ability, creative talent, family upbringing, genetic disease—goes the veiled subject of *American Dreams*, Benning himself.

The journeys of *three* itinerant men through cities and small towns form a palimpsest of failure and success, each figure marginalized in separate and telling ways, each a product of attitudes, fantasies, and ideologies heard murmuring across the soundtrack. Yet they are as well agents in the public enunciation and propagation of interlocking systems of masculine ambition, cognate versions of a central cultural myth encompassing race, sexuality, and celebrity. Benning's innovation here, in the context of his film career and given the avant-garde's recent turn toward historical discourse, is the positing of a ground on which the distanced articulations of the structural style and the private voice of the diary can be productively folded into a vision of a common past. It is as if the constraints of systemic, nonnarrative organization could paradoxically enable fresh alternatives to what Hayden White has dubbed the "emplotting" of historical evidence.[6] White's critique of history writing, its borrowing of codes from narrative fiction, could be taken as implicit endorsement for avant-garde film's scattered, self-implicating, and contingent modes of inscribing actual events. Indeed, his discussion of the shape of medieval annals and chronicles suggests certain parallels with the avant-garde essay.[7]

As I have argued, *American Dreams* and other essayistic treatments undermine the sort of totalizing perspectives found in previous avant-garde styles and, of course, in orthodox histories as well. Recent films have in consequence paraded subjectivity as a marker of partial knowledge while, reciprocally, foregrounding the representation of collective experience as a hedge against the unbridled, solipsistic imagination. Apart from selecting quite different historical *issues* as bases for filmic articulation, a recurrent set of features binds the work: heterogeneous visual and sound materials; voice-over narration as separate authority to that of image; the fixity of printed texts contesting descriptive or affective functions of photographic imagery; found footage and other forms of textual appropriation; the interweaving of two or more "plotlines"; the intermixing of documentary, avant-garde, and fictional techniques.

This conspectus begs a comparison between American avant-garde and European versions of the essay, especially since both factions gathered steam during the same period of late-sixties political turmoil. At the risk of oversimplifying, works such as Dusan Makavejev's *WR: Mysteries of Organism* (1970), Jean-Marie Straub's and Danielle Huillet's *Introduction to Arnold Schoenberg's Accompaniment to a Cinematographic Scene* (1972), and Marker's sublime *Sans Soleil* (1982) harbor a kindred faith in heterogeneous materials as a formal tool in the splintering or decentering of univocal frameworks of knowledge. To be sure, the European examples tend to be more explicit in their politics and cognizant of their status as counterhistory. On the other hand, as might be expected, the autobiographical impulse, the idea of cinema as a vehicle for expressing personal memories and ideas, is less prominent among European makers. Operating in commercial industry settings, with divergent budgets and economic expectations, European essayists in general prove less hostile to fictional codes while for Americans the recourse to trappings of scripted narrative is often overshadowed by reflexive scrutiny of space and time. By the same token, European films are more intent on constructing adequate signs of closure, if not outright resolution. Finally, there is empirical as well as anecdotal confirmation that European New Wave initiatives, those of Godard in particular, have inflected the work of Rainer and Benning but little evidence of influence flowing in the opposite direction.

A final question remains that cannot, at least for now, yield a definitive answer. Are there current or previous historical methodologies to which the discursive patterns of *American Dreams* and its cohort can be aligned—in roughly the same manner as, say, Hollywood biopics of the 1930s can be said to adopt the tenets of "Great Man" theories, or that Rossellini's made-for-TV epics install a materialist depiction of historical change? Dispensing with objective criteria, by which divergent historical interpretations can be weighed and adjudicated, avant-gardists insist on an antipositivist rehearsal of conflicting claims and explanations. Personalizing the presentation of history, and placing it within culturally specific limits, Benning and company adopt a direct and empathetic—"Verstehen," in the German historical tradition—identification with the flux of social development. They do not stand outside processes of transformation, and, with Foucault, they invest significance in the "capillary" action of institutional power, peeling back a wide swath of popular sources and ritualized activities to expose hidden orders of manipulation.[8]

Such speculation, though, is hardly conclusive. The effect of these films is not, if truth be told, primarily historiographic but aesthetic. History appears as by-product of longstanding concerns in avant-garde practice, reanimated by pressures of a shared past and by recent currents in intellectual thought. Yet the attempts by avant-garde film to imbricate history with flights of subjective consciousness may have a less palpable, heuristic value. Traditional historians of various schools would likely agree that change must be amenable to consistent, far-reaching explanation. If history does not constitute, as Augustine put it, "the great melody of some ineffable composer,"[9] it must at least have a discernible meter and recognizable motifs. Tolstoy, in the epilogue to *War and Peace,* offers a more modern analysis: "If the will of every man were free, that is, if every man could act as he chose, the whole of history would be a tissue of disconnected accidents."[10] As *American Dreams* might suggest, in lieu of a central melody, historical developments can be rendered through the application of "accidental" harmonies, along with a steady, and not unhelpful, syncopated beat.

(1989)

5 | The Last of the Last Machine?

FROM A CURRENT PERSPECTIVE [1985], nearly all that is vital in American avant-garde film—along with much that isn't—aspires to the condition of television. This unanticipated, if not outright shocking, development is the by-product of a gradual assumption by film of formal imperatives that, taken together, limn the terms of TV's address to its viewers, anchor its centrality in postmodern aesthetics, and contribute to its immensely powerful social scaffolding. Needless to say, avant-garde film's reworking of television's formal ontology has been conducted without a trace of the latter's all-embracing commercialism and is thus devoid of TV's controlling ideological mix of status quo motives and nervous prohibitions. In this sense only, films made under the sign of the televisual retain an experimental impulse. For at least a portion of avant-garde film, morganatic engagement with mass culture has had the effect of reclaiming some of the anarchic cultural energies—if not the utopian social aspirations—of American cinema in the sixties. Ironically, it is the pervasive codes associated with TV, already an impossible "subject" and even less promising model of production, that have provided a tentative solution to the avant-garde's impasse between subjectivist reflexivity and antisubjectivist reflexivity—roughly, between so-called poetic modes like the Brakhagian lyric, and vestiges of structural film's rationalist ethos. This outlet has surfaced, however, at a time when formal innovation is being questioned as the paramount criterion of value and institutional vagaries of fund-raising, distribution, and exhibition often trump critical arguments about "cutting edge" assaults on older styles.

Disparate points of contact link recent experimental films with TV: highly segmented, plurivocal, and materially mixed arrangements of image and sound; written language texts as overlay or replacement for the photographic image; de-emphasis on internal markers of cohesion such as whole/part symmetry and dramatic closure in favor of something resembling nonhierarchical "flow;"[1] iconographic accumulations encompassing multiple strata of image production and historical provenance (i.e., found footage in its broadest definition). None of these qualities is unique to the television medium, and most of the work I have in mind—disparate in approach, content, and tone—is not focused on TV per se, neither its cultural reality nor its symptomatic terms of spectatorship.[2] Yet what is shared by films made in the last ten years by Owen Land (George Landow), James Benning, Yvonne Rainer, Hollis Frampton, Leslie Thornton, and others is an attitude concerning the availability of popular entertainment, or rather its languages, as vehicle for overturning certain modernist shibboleths and recasting venerable themes in the avant-garde film canon (e.g., the dreamstate, autobiography, myths of childhood).

The acknowledgment through form of the collapse of high-art prerogatives into mass media is characteristic of what is called the postmodern. Nonetheless, this acknowledgment must necessarily operate differently in the margins of experimental cinema than it does in, say, painting or performance art. Film is clearly not the only enterprise involved in a critical recontextualization of TV, and the American avant-garde is not the only mode of filmmaking so engaged.[3] Issues engendered within the limited discourses of avant-garde film might resemble those in other art forms (e.g., appropriation versus originality) but diverge substantially in both articulation and cultural status. Apart from the total absence of a viable commodity, or even the lineaments of an artistic vocation, what separates this brand of cinema from adjacent practices such as video art or photography is a history organized around deeply ambivalent negotiations with cinema's popular face; that is, Hollywood remains the animating skeleton in the avant-garde film closet.

Oddly enough, today the branches of the movement that still aspire to the medium-specific condition of *film* appear the least progressive and innovative. At one extreme are residues of the structural onslaught, no longer seditious but constituting a mode of obdurate, institutional authority. At the other end of the experimental spectrum is the politicized, "deconstructed" narrative feature. In apposite ways both are burdened with an essentially modernist conviction that the materiality and processes of signification in film are culturally detachable, that they are self-governing texts amenable to endless elucidation and revision. One problem is that even when the structural legacy results in fresh perceptual experiences, or when New Narrative successfully retools the reactionary baggage of fictional codes, they wind up reinforcing patterns of heightened polarization and polemical friction in the avant-garde community. In this sense aesthetic contrasts represented by these antithetical stances are rather different from previous avant-garde skirmishes.

At first glance the reflexive program of structural film's adherents and the social thrust of New Narrative situate these camps as not only separated by production methods, means of circulation, and funding requirements but antagonistic in their address to audiences. Another reading, however, positions them as reverse sides of a dependent artworld coin regulated and loosely validated by a nexus of elite public institutions. If in the past, partial compensation for the lack of visibility was stylistic transience, the freedom to switch visual approaches from project to project, a sizable chunk of current avant-garde production has neither. To be sure, current narrative and structural modes are connected through Warhol's great early films; and both acquired their separate agendas during the late sixties surge of minimalist spatial "dramas." Where the justly celebrated examples of *Wavelength* (1967), *Institutional Quality* (1969), *Zorns Lemma* (1970), *Serene Velocity* (1970), and *Tom, Tom the Piper's Son* (1970) held in suspension contrasting dynamics of subjectivity and enunciative detachment, material process and meaning, the expressive and the antiexpressive, recent practice has shown a tendency to follow a less complicated path through these terms. If there is currently a salient opposition in avant-garde film, it is between work molded by the exploration of cinema and work molded by TV. Of course some films—arguably the best—carve out territory that acknowledges both vectors; a flagrant example is Land's *On the Marriage Broker Joke as Cited by Sigmund Freud in* Wit and Its Relation to the Unconscious, *or Can the Avant-Garde Artist Be Wholed?* (1980).

TV's function in relation to current avant-garde aesthetics is finally less that of a culturally potent, unattainable Other than a handy, as it were "readymade," cipher for arranging what happens between internal parts and configuring the ever-present gap between personal and social experience. In this way the notion of TV recalls critical categories such as "mythopoesis," which, as explained by P. Adams Sitney, acted as an organizational mandate for an earlier generation of makers.[4] Unlike the specter of Hollywood, TV was never really an object of disavowal for the avant-garde; it was simply off the map of potential aesthetic identifications.[5] In the current climate, having failed to secure workable alliances with related avant-garde movements of the seventies (modern dance, experimental theater, contemporary music), experimental film may regard television as an, admittedly unlikely, economic partner on several possible levels: for instance, music television as a conduit for production, or PBS and cable TV as possible venues for exhibition.[6]

According to various scholars, the pivotal period in New American Cinema was roughly between 1970 and 1973, and it was precisely during this period that TV surfaced as an alternative source of mediation distinct from either Hollywood or the precincts of traditional art. It was nonetheless a moment of remarkable onscreen achievement, of tenuous social consolidations, the influx of academic theory, and the reemergence of comedy and parody (Robert Nelson and William T. Wiley's 1970 jape, *Bleu Shut*, is a key work here). Any thoroughgoing assessment of the present must return to this period, in particular to the broad project of structural film, from which ensued a decisive chain of responses, openings, and refusals. Further, a host of external factors inflected the movement's transformed horizons: feminist and gay perspectives in politics and art making; the apogee of fighting in Vietnam, the "TV War"; the growth of video art; the expansion of film in university curricula. What follows offers a rather more constricted account, one that takes structural film as a sort of critical plumb line in order to redraft a few ostensibly fixed boundaries and cultural significations.

The limitations of such a purview are all too evident. It turns a twenty-year cycle into a contest between two rather obscure aesthetic programs, eliding what was in fact a messy forum of ideas, regional contrasts, and quirky individual careers. It is, inevitably, oversensitive to academic arguments and privileges 16mm films by established figures shown in prominent, mostly East Coast, venues. Stressing *North* American film practices, I occasionally make reference to work produced here by Europeans but steer clear of rich developments in other global avant-garde centers. I also give short shrift to the vigorous efforts of Super-8 and 8mm filmmakers and the (sometimes) interesting products of video artists. Regrettably, discussion of the state of political documentaries, a sector of independent production that over the past several decades has manifest intriguing parallels with the avant-garde, falls outside my basic objectives. Finally, to avoid arguing for the hundredth time the efficacy of the terms "avant-garde," "experimental," and "independent," I have chosen to be blithely inclusive.

Critical positions routinely announce themselves and their objects in rhetorical gestures of crisis and renovation. Only at a distance do contours of resemblance surface across the bulwarks of cultural combat. When claiming affinities between, say, structural films and New Narratives, it does not follow that they could ever be mistaken for one another experientially.

Further, the purposes of this inquiry will be facilitated by dividing New American Cinema into three inexact phases or generations: artists who began exhibiting work prior to the advent of the Cooperative movement in 1962–63;[7] those who emerged before the period commonly associated with institutionalization, 1970–73;[8] and filmmakers who have become known over the past decade or so. The idea of generations prevents a given artist from being stapled to one corresponding style or communal doctrine; indeed, an important virtue of the movement until recently was its capacity to sustain contradictory impulses in the careers of its most innovative practitioners—Brakhage is, once again, the preeminent example.

Especially in the last half dozen years, two widely endorsed critical-historical injunctions have informed a swath of writing on avant-garde films, pulled along by or operating in tandem with renewed practical engagement with narrative conventions and bracketed by a desired convergence of feminism, academic film theory, and avant-garde resistance to dominant cinema's ideologies.[9] The first project is the dissolution of artificially maintained discursive barriers separating experimental from commercial cinemas. What is required here is the rewriting of avant-garde history to demonstrate the avant-garde's imbrication in the metathemes, if not the techniques, of the Hollywood industry. This proposal is often accompanied by attacks on "academic," "idealist," "romanticist" film writing, as epitomized by P. Adams Sitney.[10] A related admonition proceeds from the belief that formalist film analysis is burdened with disabling flaws. The proposed remedy is some type of sociological or materialist hermeneutic that would take criticism beyond the text to show, on the one hand, relations between the avant-garde and pressing social concerns and, on the other, the historical place of experimental film within larger networks of cultural dissemination. The role of meaning would be dispersed from a single axis onto a field composing relevant features of production, distribution, publicity, and so on. This proposal is often accompanied by attacks on "academic," "phenomenological," "complicit" film writing, epitomized by P. Adams Sitney, or alternatively, a chimerical "Sitney-Michelson power base."[11]

These two critical initiatives are imagined as hooking up with narrativizing currents to augur greater accessibility for avant-garde work along with an unprecedented political responsiveness. In this optimistic prognosis, the ghettoization (or outright exclusion) of avant-garde film from the construction of film history and theory would be redressed by the same hybrid energies attempting to rewrite mainstream movie expectations. The vision summoned by these injunctions is nearly irresistible, despite being laden with internecine grudges and unwarranted accusations. Unfortunately, there have as yet been no large-scale attempts at laying a new groundwork for avant-garde historiography.[12]

The Avant-Garde and Its Others

In the early seventies, the avant-garde edged at least to the outskirts of the academy and found its way into such previously unsympathetic channels of prestige as *Artforum* magazine, the New York Film Festival, the Leo Castelli Gallery, the Whitney Museum of American Art, and the *New York Times*. The outpouring of "minimalist" films generated a different order of attention and support because of the presumed overlap in formal practices with movements in adjacent arts. Avant-garde filmmakers and celebrated artists and musicians shared the same urban environments, the same organs of journalistic publicity, often the same exhibition spaces. However, as the decade proceeded disjunctions between art world and film world became increasingly apparent; indeed, the expectation that the byways of elite American culture could accommodate yet another passenger of the minimalist persuasion proved elusive. For starters, avant-garde film's expensive and unpredictable projection equipment inhibited the spread of installations in galleries and museums. The occasional forays into film by established artists such as Richard Serra, Robert Morris, and Dan Graham, despite obvious correspondences with structural work, never resulted in reciprocal opportunities or additional interest from art journals or gallery owners; nor was the avant-garde ultimately able to command regular coverage in the mainstream press.

Unlike, say, modern dance's ability to recruit new audiences and convert audiences faithful to classical ballet, avant-garde film had no backlog of audience exposure to "difficult" films on which to draw. Part-time college teaching jobs, museum showings, and the odd review in tiny film journals could not translate into ongoing economic viability. To make matters worse, rising production costs—especially in film stock and processing—and the proliferation of video threatened to eclipse even the crude technological options secured during the sixties. In retrospect, the no-budget Super-8 punk insurgency and the industrialized New Narrative were twin responses to an ongoing, yet rarely discussed, economic predicament. From our current vantage, it is clear that not only did structural film change the organizing principles that characterized earlier stages of the avant-garde, it inadvertently mandated a shift in the level of production by relying on sophisticated, costly items such as electric cameras, optical printers, and intervolometers. To put it another way, it will always be cheaper to edit footage than to shoot long takes. This altered sense of technological dependency, an expansive base nourishing a reductivist aesthetics, is an unacknowledged facet in the investigation of pure filmic properties of camera movement or photographic illusion.

It is well known that filmmakers in the first several decades of cinema freely borrowed and mixed elements from a range of middle-class entertainments: popular and classic novels; newspaper and magazine articles; still photography; theater. Among various reasons why the established arts became an explicit (e.g., France's Film d'Art theatrical reproductions) or implicit (Griffith's glosses of Dickens) source of authority in early films was the desire to cloak the movies' "disreputable" social origins and lower-class stories in a mantle of bourgeois respectability.[13] Similar gestures of self-validation are scattered across the histories of both fiction and nonfiction film genres. At least since the late 1940s, the American avant-garde has declared itself committed to investigating what constitute the unique qualities of the medium while simultaneously buttressing the movement's cultural profile through comparisons with—primarily—painting, music, and poetry. That is, for filmmakers and critics alike, specific films or styles contain aesthetic assumptions, procedures, and/or epistemological issues redolent of other art forms. To be sure, the assimilation by film of prerogatives associated with traditional practices has been a two-way street: for every self-proclaimed "cine-poem" or instance of "eye music" there are pseudocinematic paintings or theatrical designs.

In the past ten years or so, the avant-garde's (philosophical) scission from mass culture finally transformed itself into a thematized ambivalence. In this light previous denials of contact may be seen as not just therapeutic but as inoculations against an assortment of threats defining cinema as a *popular* medium: collective authorship, formulaic content, third-person enunciation, and, of course, wide circulation. While it is probable that the current ranks of commercial directors were largely university-trained in the craft of cinema, the majority of avant-gardists are still refugees from the study of, or fledgling careers in, adjacent arts. The adoption of, say, poetry as aesthetic model and original artistic practice differs, however, in one telling respect from current allegiances to TV and Hollywood: the latter are predicated on personal *spectatorship* rather than direct participation. In other words, if poetic models for filmic inscription implied parallels or continuities in method and experience, for the most part identification with television is marked by a practical *discontinuity*, a distanced and fragmented relation to an enabling Other.

This might sound like a commonplace generational complaint usually accompanying a lament for the waning of humanist values. Yet the existence of a cache of cultural knowledge shared with a broad generational cohort—versus earlier bohemian creative investments in elite culture—has putatively strengthened the avant-garde's potential appeal while weakening the kinds of subcultural bonds that invigorated and sustained the aesthetic aspirations of Maya Deren, James Broughton, Bruce Baillie, and Brakhage, among many other makers who abandoned or converted their training in traditional mediums. Hence the avant-garde's delayed arrival in the Age of Television has had the unanticipated consequence of negating older communitarian values built upon the concurrence of nonpopulist production and nonpopulist aesthetic paradigms.

The "Mystique" of Structural Film

In its heyday from 1967 to 1972, or roughly from *Wavelength* to Frampton's *Hapax Legomena*, structural film acted as a powerful lever for avant-garde activity, prying loose then hoisting previously submerged but latent features of composition as it demoted signature techniques such as hand-held camera movement or montage.[14] A principal site of revaluation was the notion of metaphor, the use of editing (or occasionally superimposition) to create figurative meaning from the meeting of two or more images. Contrary to hard-line modernist views, structural film did not so much expunge metaphor as shift its status and position within the perceptual process. The question raised as subtext is whether metaphor is inevitably at the service of an idealized imagination, and whether what I want to call "material metaphor"—image content at the service of the apparatus—actually breaks the vise-grip of allusion. For instance, is the isomorphism of the long corridor in Gehr's *Serene Velocity* (1970) and the zoom lens with which it has been shot not an alternative inscription of metaphor?

At this late date there is little merit in debating which films should or shouldn't be counted in the structural group, or to what extent the structural program coincides with that of minimalist painting and sculpture.[15] If *Dog Star Man* stands as the exemplar of an approach favoring dense visual correspondences and expressive techniques in framing, exposure, angle, and so on that trample on standard cinematographic practice, structural work *discourages* moment-to-moment reading in deference to an equally active but less associative or "constructive" mode of viewing. Hence it asserts a more democratic version of nonnarrative film experience in which dream material, traces of myth, references to literary texts, and other extracinematic frameworks gave way to the rigors, and pleasures, of discovering the logical systems created for ordering shots and entire filmic durations.

Several ramifications for subsequent, post-1972 developments can be distilled from this account. First, the felt presence of creative labor becomes displaced from stages of shooting and editing to an a priori moment of design. Second, although it might seem counterintuitive, many structural films exhibit a hyperbolic strain of Bazinian realism in their insistence on seamless, objectified recording of actual settings. Of course the purposes to which the straightforward images are applied can hardly comport with Bazin's belief in transparency. Nonetheless, following the lead of Warhol, structural film deploys variants of a long-take aesthetic to instill appreciation of the temporal unfolding of spatial paradox. Places and objects photographed in a minimalist style are strongly legible or, alternatively, their illegibility is rendered as a carefully calibrated process subtended by a recognizable image source—the case in Land's *Thank You Jesus for the Eternal Present* (1973).

The passage from structural idioms—supposedly, the last modernist bastion against twin pressures of narrative and social content—to the rejuvenation of fiction in avant-garde practice is circumstantial yet provocative. In effect, the former reintroduced the script, albeit in the form of blueprints, mathematical formulas, and logical propositions. In earlier styles, evidence of exacting instructions for a film's completion would have been construed as lack of spontaneity or imagination, a failure to make sensual contact with the outside world. By the early seventies such documents had become a sign of salutary removal from the vagaries of subjective vision and the all-too-slippery realm of nonliteral expression. The distance between theoretical blueprint and full-fledged screenplay has proven closer than it appeared. Like narrative scripts, structural documents were useful in practical contexts: as fodder for grant proposals, as ancillary exhibition materials, and as "crib notes" for critical appraisals. Paul Sharits, Peter Kubelka, and Michael Snow have displayed design notes in gallery or theater settings; Rainer and James Benning have published scripts for narratively oriented projects in important journals. For the sake of clarity, I am not suggesting that anyone fabricated designs in order to impress a funding committee. Structural film and its offshoots, unlike New Narrative, retain the imprint of artisanal production yet they are also undergirded by various theoretical disciplines, and it is no accident that Frampton, Sharits, and Kubelka have made important contributions to contemporary film aesthetics.

On a formal or iconographic level, a number of recent avant-garde narratives—Sara Driver's *You Are Not I* (1981), Curt McDowell's *Sparkle's Tavern* (1981), Tom Palazzolo's *Caligari's Cure* (1983), Lizzie Borden's *Born in Flames* (1983), Bette Gordon's *Variety* (1984), and Sheila McLaughlin's and Lynn Tillman's *Committed* (1984)—continue to mine strategies associated with structural film, including fixed-camera takes and repetitive camera movements. Moreover, structural film's lofts, street corners, and deserted commercial spaces are in essence repopulated by New Narrative, turned into "bit players" instead of given starring roles, as they are in the structural ethos.[16] To the extent that New Narrative invokes the framework of subjective perception, it does so almost exclusively through character perspective and not as the film's controlling consciousness. One way of thinking about New Narrative, then, is as the invidious meshing of Hollywood genre conventions and structural protocols.

In a spasm of fraternal age, filmmaker Gary Doberman published a diatribe against structural film titled "New York Cut the Crap."[17] Doberman's stance in this article was immediately perceived as reflecting, if it did not simply echo, objections voiced primarily by Stan Brakhage. Structural film and its attendant debates had been around for more than ten years when Doberman entered the fray, and although nowhere is the trend toward narrative addressed directly, the timing of his piece plus the terms he employs in vilifying minimalism beg the question of interrelationship. His main argument is familiar and sententious: structural filmmaking "replaced more complex negotiations with the Muse" (24); it strenuously stifled emotions and strangled

Variety by Bette Gordon. Photograph by Nan Goldin; courtesy of Millennium Film Workshop.

cinema's natural expansiveness through deadening predictability and a "tautological narcissism" (24). It is the "zenith of academic cinema" (26) and he attributes its enduring power to an Eastern intellectual cabal centered around the control of institutional resources (a canard repeated in recent years with distressing frequency and conviction).[18] Doberman is nonetheless correct in thinking both that structural film was and is decidedly East Coast in origin and that there exists a wellspring of undervalued regional, "personal" filmmaking. By contributing to the myth of "reductivist" aesthetic absolutism, Doberman inadvertently joins forces with his staunchest adversaries, the English "materialists" Malcolm LeGrice and Peter Gidal for whom metaphor and expressivity were not just problematic but anathema.[19] Looking again at celebrated work by Snow, Frampton, Gehr, Land, and Barry Gerson, it is hard not to reach a very different conclusion: far from weeding out all concerns extraneous to the filmic apparatus and the perceptual transactions generated by it, these films sustain rich covert dialogues with some eminent cinematic constructions of social reality.

If a portion of avant-garde activity since the early sixties has operated tangentially to the realm of documentary, structural film could be said to gloss nonfiction codes in direct ratio to its expulsion of tropes for inner consciousness. That is, *Zorns Lemma* or Gehr's *Still* (1971) lose none of their reflexive power by also tendering metaversions of the City Symphony. Joyce Wieland's scintillating *La Raison avant la passion* (1968–69) reconfigures elements of both newsreel and travelogue through a grid of starkly material functions. Owen Land's *Diploteratology* (1967) lampoons the pretense of scientific research footage while his *Institutional Quality* (1969) gives new meaning to industrial training exercises. Traditional documentary themes that infiltrate the structural style include depictions of the artist's studio (*Wavelength*; Gehr's *Wait* [1968]), anthropological field research (David Rimmer's *Real Italian Pizza* [1969]; Standish Lawder's *Necrology* [1969–70]), and portraiture (Frampton's *Manual of Arms* [1966]).[20]

Perhaps this is simply to suggest that the best films operate beyond categorical limits and that part of their impact is to make us rethink the interests served by definitions stressing the sovereignty of mediumistic interrogation. Regardless, it is evident that the single-minded pursuit of filmic demystification, or Gidal's "empty signifier," is itself an illusion. The point is that socially resonant iconographic motifs add to rather than subtract from the confrontation with cinema's mechanical substrate.

The Featurization of the Avant-Garde

The historical trajectory that begins with *Wavelength*'s loft break-in and culminates in *Variety*'s motel room break-in can hardly be read as a continuous arc of development. Critic Manny Farber famously found in Snow's film "a straightforward document of a room in which a dozen businesses have lived and gone bankrupt."[21] Annette Michelson, citing Farber, declared that Snow had managed to spatialize the cognitive dynamics of Hollywood suspense narratives.[22] What neither could have predicted was that fifteen years later, *Wavelength*'s bristling physical milieu and its fragmentary human events would be amplified into a semblance of linear diegesis and placed under a rubric of ideological resistance.[23] In the course of Snow's stuttered zoom shot, a bookcase is moved into a loft, a radio blares the Beatles' "Strawberry Fields," an offscreen crash heralds the entrance of an unkempt man who then collapses, and a woman telephones for help, saying that she thinks the man is dead. These events belong to a dramatic register that has come to occupy the foreground of an increasingly significant branch of avant-garde production and, not incidentally, theory.

The aesthetic underpinnings of this tendency issue from a conflation of traditional New American Cinema thematics (e.g., the journey of sexual discovery), revised plot conventions, iconography, and psychological frissons from Hollywood genres (especially film noir's existential crises of identity), and a coolly distanced presentational format adapted from structural film. Certain elements of minimalist self-inquiry, such as the play of flatness and depth in the image, reappear yet seldom do they cancel the forward progression of story in a given scene; unlike the early trance films that New Narratives often evoke, they proffer vague critiques of narrative illusionism enacted on the terrain of narrative cohesion.

Where European models of narrative infraction—Godard, Fassbinder, the Straubs— take as their starting points a fully articulated narrative system that is then subjected to a series of ruptures and distortions, recent avant-garde narratives seem to start from an assumption of material process, or the autonomy of spatial depiction, onto which is grafted a battery of storytelling devices. Because dialogue, dramatic structure, and the burden of causation are here the *alien* mechanisms, there is a feeling that if the characters were suddenly withdrawn, there would still be enough to constitute a plausible (experimental) film: the blank camera stare, a concrete parcel of space, a concern with ambiguities of still and moving. One cannot, I think, say the same of New Wave European cinema. This discrepancy limns a heightened spatial presence in the avant-garde narrative but also a notable awkwardness of execution caused by incommensurate levels of technical address; in short, a lack of writerly or directorial chops in relation to dialogue and acting.

The problem has very little to do with narrativity itself, with the desire to fashion stories or rework the social attitudes embedded in film-narrative codes. The idea that storytelling impulses were ever completely abolished in avant-garde practice is tenuous at best. Pockets of narrative invention have persisted even in periods of the most adamant formalism or anti-industry rhetoric. For individual careers, such as that of Kenneth Anger, it is sometimes hard to separate imagistic from narrative motives, and in the crucial case of Brakhage a narrative bias has occasionally served as a term of resistance plied against the usual demands of an inwardly fixated subjectivity; it is in this regard interesting that the oddly linear *Wedlock House: An Intercourse* (1959) follows close upon *Anticipation of the Night* (1958) and that the quirky comedy *Blue Moses* (1962) appeared directly after *Thigh Line Lyre Triangular* (1961).

It is not simply that there have been narrative exceptions like George Kuchar and Jack Smith who have kept this issue alive until its current revival; there are enough progenitors to constitute an avant-garde counterhistory.[24] Moreover, New Narrative itself is considerably less homogenous than its advocates would admit. Its ranks include not only theory-laden novices and refugees from the structural style but also filmmakers better known for poetic approaches, for whom narrative seems to represent a slightly different container for longstanding themes—Gunvor Nelson, George Manupelli, and Tom Pallazzolo fall into this category.

It could be countered that New Narrative refers only to a particular type of avant-garde project—that is, not all avant-garde narratives are New Narratives—yet it is unclear how to distinguish a "cutting edge" narrative from, say, a "reactionary" spoof. In this light, the notion that it is less the presence of story elements than a return to socially charged imagery that defines the current movement may again derive from a disturbingly parochial vision of avant-garde history. To believe that there has been a sustained period in which the social was evacuated from image making would refute basic implications of the avant-garde/mass culture interchange.

This is not to deny important changes in the configuration of American avant-garde film, of which the most telling isn't the renewal of narrative but what I want to call "featurization," the mobilization of resources attending feature-length, preplanned and budgeted (i.e., nonartisanal) production underwritten by assigned roles and divisions in paid or semipaid labor. A number of corollaries are attached to this shift in relations of production: increased dependence on state and parastate subsidies (although not restricted to feature-length narratives, such funding is obviously more essential to their completion); the revision of historical expectations for avant-garde distribution and exhibition stemming from the mandate to break with "elitist" patterns of avant-garde circulation.[25] Typically, a more sophisticated coordination of social and technical resources is required for narrative features, hence an increase in formal contracts, business arrangements, and the like.

In addition, featurization almost inevitably means a decrease in prospects for individual productivity; according to reports, recent New Narratives have taken on average three to four years to complete. There is nothing terribly ominous in the gap between successive projects—especially since if one measures output by total minutes rather than number of films, productivity may not actually drop—but it does remove a traditional margin for failure, revision, and discovery through trial and error, factors informing the dynamic growth of numerous individual careers. In the mutually validating logic of granting agencies and feature-length projects, the "short" may again acquire the dismissive status of apprentice work for longer, more serious efforts. Yet even if smaller-scale work does not wind up devalued in avant-garde film culture, there has been a demonstrable, if subtle, pull on nonnarrative as well as New Narrative filmmakers to think in terms of larger undertakings.[26]

Some of the pressure is economic, the realization that features command a different quantity of attention at all levels and that, as in the commercial industry, it is often easier to obtain financing for high-profile projects than for those intrinsically modest in scope. Imagine, for instance, a granting agency (or, at a later stage, a distributor, an exhibitor, or a programmer) faced with two competing projects: in the first, a young woman is forced from her reclusive bohemian existence to play detective in a gangland regime of spooky locations, violent threats, and million-dollar exchanges of cash; in the second, a filmmaker pledges to explore the shapes and color patterns in an office suite holding a glass ashtray over his camera lens. Regardless of the manifest aesthetic quality of these, as it were, hypothetical films, it seems undeniable that the avant-garde is entering an age in which the "concept"—as opposed to previous values such as spontaneity or experimentation—wields an unprecedented and unpredictable balance of power.

A secondary pressure to make work of a certain scale and public ambition comes not from above but from peripheral, academic precincts of film theory—feminism in particular—which have championed not just narratives but full-length antispectacles. Buried in prescriptions for expanded audiences, along with ideological imperatives of unmasking narrative film discourse and construction, is a repudiation of not only previous avant-garde styles but their handmade organs of circulation. What has recently come under attack is the system of personal appearances by filmmakers in specialized venues, aka self-distribution, and at least implicitly, the practice of anthologizing groups of films on programs classified by region, theme, technique (e.g., optical printing), and so on—a tactic that has almost defined public access to the movement. Some believe that the stipulation of artists appearing with their work enhances the cult of individualist authorship and that it fuels the validation of mastery as a culturally ingrained prerogative of the male ego.[27] In a similar vein, omnibus programming is held as conservative and preservationist, a means by which critic-curators propagate their own aesthetic choices while ensuring that the avant-garde remains in a culturally marginal position.

On balance, there are a few useful correctives uncovered by the critical allies of New Narrative. What is not evident is how the desired hybrid model of sponsored/independent feature production and limited commercial distribution, while primed to displace a controlling "boys club" ethos, might possibly achieve its political and cultural agendas. More puzzling still is how feminist—or for that matter, nonfeminist—applications of the narrative apparatus create new possibilities for women in the avant-garde. There is as well an unresolved contradiction between principled refusal of mastery and the advocacy of a system that *requires* hierarchies of labor and decision making, to say nothing of the active patronage of a coercive, instrumental network of consumerist marketing.

Admittedly, the position of women in the American avant-garde, at least since the time of Maya Deren, Marie Menken, and Shirley Clarke, has been ill-defined and perhaps provisional.[28] Yet it is difficult to understand how featurization will foster greater levels of female participation or organizational impact. It could be said that structural films are in fact domestic movies devoid of the domestic. They gaze past human facades of home, workplace, neighborhood, local landscape to foreground the interaction of photographed objects and medium-specific properties. In their refusal of admittedly discordant mechanisms of identification imposed by narrative and certain antinarrative styles (e.g., the voyeuristic look), they question film's subjective register. Unfortunately, for all of structural film's "democratic" rhetoric of the image, it has proven to be—with the exception of Joyce Wieland, Yoko Ono, and Vickie Z. Peterson—perhaps a more segregated male preserve than any previous style. Empirically, there is likely a higher percentage of women involved in narrative forms than there was in earlier avant-garde styles, but what that means for women working in other, nonnarrative idioms is not at all apparent.

Two suppositions of the New Narrative program could use a further bit of critical scrutiny. First is the actual potential to create a crossover model for avant-garde reception via independent, nonstudio distribution and art-house exhibition. The second concerns Hollywood genres, the manner in which conventions and their ideological subtexts can be simultaneously invoked and reformulated or unmasked.

There has been relatively little written on independent film distribution and exhibition and what there is suggests a dim prospectus for the avant-garde feature—that is, short of duplicating the singular success of avant-garde fellow traveler Jim Jarmusch's *Stranger Than Paradise* (1984).[29] In a helpful overview not primarily directed toward avant-garde features, Mitchell Block states that all nonstudio (foreign plus independent) distribution accounts for less than 5 percent of the total American market.[30] Of approximately 16,000 theatrical venues, less than 400 cater to independent films; of these, perhaps one-third mix independent work with classical studio repertory. According to Block, an independent feature is generally unable to gross more than $250,000 in a single year, based on roughly 100 bookings and 60,000 viewers. Subtracting the exhibitor's share of box-office receipts, typically 50 percent, and the costs of printing, advertising, and the distributor's cut, the balance left for a film's producer is only slightly more than $10,000, not nearly enough to finance a subsequent feature or, presumably, attract the interest of significant new investors.

New Narrative's desire to leap over the established system of avant-garde distribution and exhibition—artist-run cooperatives; museums and regional showcases—is predicated on the idea that semicommercial circulation affords access to a demonstrably different audience and a more substantial return on a filmmaker's labor. Neither axiom is plausible, or at least not in the glowing terms in which they are frequently discussed. In a hypothetical case of self distribution, a new film—of any length, subject, or style—by a well-known avant-gardist might be booked into twenty-five or thirty single showings around the country in twelve months, with or without the artist being present. If each date averages only forty viewers—an estimate based on conversations with administrators and on personal experience—then over a thousand people will have seen the work within a year. And at the current scale of honoraria in avant-garde circles, the filmmaker would realize roughly $5,000, or half the amount earned from a narrative feature, with only a fraction of the latter's audience. Thus if the primary motive behind theatrical distribution is increased profit, the New Narrative does not seem vastly superior to previous paradigms—even granting possible sales to cable TV, the acquisition of foreign rights, and some overlap with the regular avant-garde circuit. Moreover, *only* narrative features can be accommodated through a semicommercial system.[31]

If the primary task of featurization is gaining a popular audience, the evidence is just as murky. Sixty thousand viewers is more impressive than one thousand, but it is still the proverbial drop in the bucket compared with studio product, even the most abjectly unsuccessful studio product. The notion that by landing a distribution deal with an adventurous company like New Yorker Films a practitioner of New Narrative will reach a more socially diverse viewership is questionable at best. As with self-distribution, the number of potential markets is largely limited to urban cultural centers and college towns. For each market, one or two venues will be available and in all probability they will be patronized by a similar, if not identical, profile of single, lower-middle-class, college-educated types found in avant-garde screenings across the country.

I am not arguing that the dream of commercial distribution was doomed from the start. Nor would I claim that lugging one's work around like a pro bowler on tour is the best of all possible situations. The narrative feature seizes an evening, a show date, with a force that makes it difficult for either daily journalism or mass-circulation magazines like *American Film* and *Film Comment* to conduct themselves as if the avant-garde did not exist. And as Yvonne Rainer has shown, the feature format can be recruited for visually and intellectually exhilarating dissections of the urge to narrative.

In defense of the anthology program format, it should be said that it has served and can continue to serve salutary social as well as economic functions. For example, it gives the avant-garde maker a reliable opportunity to display new work almost regardless of length or style or film gauge. Perhaps more importantly, it fosters a system in which the work of younger artists comes into contact with, and can be evaluated against, that of more established figures. Film programs, as well as the individual films, can be addressed as texts, and although such a reading is beyond the scope of the present essay, there is much to learn about the history of the avant-garde from studying the art of programming. To abandon the makeshift "accidents" of avant-garde exhibition for a slightly wider social ambit may have tactical rewards, but to do so in the name of resisting Hollywood's hegemonic rule makes little sense.

In lieu of a more statistically responsible, and theoretically nuanced, account of the avant-garde's push for commercial viability, and as a way of concluding my case against featurization, it pays to briefly consider two related aspects of New Narrative's appropriation of genre conventions and the dynamics of Hollywood narration. The first issue remains under the sign of economic-technical dilemmas. Stated simply, avant-garde filmmakers are not trained to adequately duplicate or revise the protocols of visual articulation and dramatic development associated with classic Hollywood films. (Indeed, many current industry directors, laden with obscene budgets, have a hard time executing competent match cuts, much less expressive mismatches.) When individual scenes or entire stories require the simulation of realist or even allegorical—as in *Born in Flames*—versions of social interaction, basic criteria of mise-en-scène, line readings, continuity, and general production values come into play. In a Kuchar extravaganza, no amount of kowtowing to Hollywood realism could conceivably make one line reading better than another; moreover, a barrage of technical inadequacies complement one another perfectly, instating a poignant and convincing fantasy of un-power vis-à-vis the dominant system. The chief deficiencies in the avant-garde feature are centered less on "bad acting" or "bad scriptwriting" than on the pretense of technical facility, the—albeit ambivalent—guarantee of narrative continuity and dramatic cohesion. In short, in order to structure suspense codes, even if the objective is to reveal their underlying misogynist effects, it is necessary to have available at least a semblance of an old-fashioned studio apparatus.

Supposing the avant-garde could summon the skills with which to execute facsimiles of generic idioms, there would still be a theoretical stumbling block. Actually there would be a double, mutually reinforcing blockage. In what I take to be a misconception

Born in Flames by Lizzie Borden. Photograph courtesy of Millennium Film Workshop.

of narrative film theory, current practitioners appear to believe that mechanisms of "subject construction," such as identification with the look of the camera, are absurdly easy to accomplish. Have two people walk into a room and, bingo, there is diegesis; have them look at one another and there is strong projection of fictional lives and selective spectatorial sympathy.[32] The underlying assumption is that codes of narrative centering and transparency are simultaneously extremely subtle and devious, but they are arrived at with only the barest effort and understood on the basis of skimpy cues. Indeed, it takes something like informed vigilance to keep these functions from erupting and a powerful exercise of distanciation to undermine them when they appear.

This is not the place to frame a discussion of how narrative structures perform their tasks and how these tasks might be productively challenged by avant-garde film. But it does seem worthwhile to issue a caveat that relates to my initial premise of what the movement has acquired from its engagement with television. Forms and conventions, like technologies and iconographic motifs, are not ahistorical. They can be extracted from a sediment of specific meanings engendered in and through their period location, the economic and sociopolitical conditions surrounding a given production, but doing so without the mediation of some legible process of transformation—for instance, parody or nostalgic homage—threatens to dilute the force of any critical autopsy. The dramatic tics of film noir minus the ideological confusions of Cold War society, the domestic melodrama without the glaze of fifties corporate liberalism or the myth of upward mobility, exist in avant-garde features but as reservoirs of more or less empty signs, vaguely in tune with contemporary aesthetic or cultural theories acting as replacements for a nexus of historical contradiction.

A crippling problem, then, for avant-garde narratives that burrow into a fictional past for thematic and stylistic templates is their twin inability to reproduce the salient aspects of their sources at face value and/or to render a framework for interrogation in which recognition and comparative understanding proceeds from—and gets reinvested in—material contexts. In a pervasive climate of crumbling cultural distinctions, death-match struggles between narrative and nonnarrative, abstract and iconographic, reflexive and socially engaged are decidedly archaic. It is simply no use arguing for the "purity" of a cinema of structure, or poetic rhythm, or personal confession, or . . .

For the avant-garde, adopting TV as an emblem of composition paradoxically holds out the option of low-tech or quasi-artisanal filmmaking, keeping alive some of the hard-won aesthetic interventions of the sixties yet devoid of nostalgia or high-art pretense. It accomplishes this through a revaluing of montage, in its broadest sense, as the avant-garde practice least economically dependent and complicit yet most responsive to visual dialectics. Unlike the codes of classical Hollywood narration, what TV delivers to the avant-garde is precisely the reverse of its assumed amalgamation of disjunct material sources. It proposes a (usable) model for placing in juxtaposition, not just suspending, separate planes of historically resonant social representations. The dossier-like assembly of "televisual" films internalizes in a positive manner decentered, serially skewed social markers of traditional avant-garde consumption: heterogeneity stripped of anomic isolation. TV's ghost in the avant-garde machine can succeed in forcing a

discernible bracket around the languages of commercial cinema, making them appear already partially undone, ripe with potential antagonism and dysfunction. Thus
far, the inflated products of featurization have managed only to re-present imperfectly
imagined targets as perfect wholes, unencumbered by self-conscious discord and, in
bowdlerized translations, incapable of wit or irony. The avant-garde feature, then, is
nostalgic in an impossible fashion, creating a graveyard of spare parts to a Hollywood
system that never really was without the power to expropriate that system as it never
could be.

(1986–87)

6 | The Western Edge: Oil of LA and the Machined Image

I had to admit to myself that I lived for nights like these, moving across the city's great broken body, making connections among its millions of cells. I had a cray wish that some day before I died, if I made all the right neural connections, the city would come all the way alive, like the Bride of Frankenstein.
—*Ross Macdonald,* The Instant Enemy

In the Belly of the Basin

Dreiser called it "the city of the folded hands." H. L. Mencken said it was "the true and original arse-hole of creation." Malcolm Lowry called it a "barren deathscape," exactly the sort of hell to which a suicidal spirit would gravitate. Faulkner concluded that "they don't worship money [here], they worship death." Brecht had a slightly different eschatological vision:

> In these parts
> They have come to the conclusion that God
> Requiring a heaven and a hell, didn't need to
> Plan two establishments but
> Just the one: heaven. It
> Serves the unprosperous, unsuccessful
> As hell.[1]

The object of such warm sentiment is, of course, Los Angeles, or at least that piece of the city inseparable from its stand-in in popular imagination, Hollywood. Long after a sour cohort of literary lions moved on to other habitats, the denigration of LA remains a favorite sport of artists housed in this nexus of urban postmodernity. A closely related activity offers invidious comparisons between the perceived styles and underlying philosophies of creative work produced here and in New York City, as if these two locations were the sole arbiters of national taste.[2] Indeed, when the topic of discussion is cinema, the bicoastal cliché—like many other Angelenocentric truisms—contains more than a smidgeon of truth.

The notion that LA is a cultural wasteland would seem to mute the announcement of an alter-ego relationship with NY. Yet frequently subtending jeremiads of self-proclaimed inferiority are nods to the inarguable power wielded by popular culture industries, especially TV and music recording, based in and around the city, cheek-by-jowl with manifestations of elite culture. As cliché has it, nowhere in America are the demands of High and Low as blurred or as reciprocal. Hence a visual artist in LA whose work is defined as peripheral to codes or social attitudes associated with mass media consumption must contend with a kind of double-edged estrangement: perceived by opposing camps as either "in denial" or suspiciously nostalgic for an ethos of bohemian detachment. It is hardly surprising, then, that beneath the veneer of much "LA Cool" painting and sculpture of the past two decades is a choked anxiety symptomatic of a cultural setting only ostensibly immune to residual dogmas of modernism but a setting that registers simultaneously as omnipresent and amnesiac.

If only because institutional networks of publicity and financial reward are so meager, the situation for avant-garde filmmakers—as opposed to painters or even photographers—is rather different. Further, the discrepancies mirror but also diverge significantly from the plight of avant-garde filmmaking elsewhere. For instance, LA's experimental film scene has tended to be excluded from discussions by, predominantly, Eastern critics and scholars and when it *has* gained recognition there is a tendency to identify it with the terms of a specific "look" or technical facility borrowed from art-critical discourse on LA. As is the case with other avant-garde centers, a number of filmmakers began their careers making gallery art, and local painters and sculptors have occasionally ventured into alternative cinema; nonetheless, genuine collabora-tions between these creative arenas are erratic at best. On the other hand, instead of pragmatic or stylistic affinities, an attribute arguably shared by both groups is an iconographic fascination with Southern California's unique mixture of natural and manmade environments. Although the same claim might be made for the output of various cities, alternative filmmaking here seems unusually galvanized by indigenous, physical conditions of possibility. Which raises the issue of regionalism, a nexus of idio-syncratic responses to reigning aesthetic ideas—say, the ongoing impact of structural film's reductionism and reflexivity—couched in a cluster of local idioms. The outlines of such a position are already evident in David Curtis's early designation of a "West Coast optical/kinetic movement."[3]

Although this offers a tempting line of inquiry, several caveats are in order. Among the factors inhibiting a cohesive definition of regionalism is a tenuous relationship to the idea of a "national" or dominant avant-garde paradigm; in this sense, it could be held that all alternative filmmaking has a regional cast. Additionally, local participation has not only been relatively limited in scope but bears the consistent imprint of several makers who have worked and taught in the area since the sixties; for instance, Pat O'Neill's name appears as informal or technical advisor in the end credits of a sizable number of films. If there is a case to be made for regionalism, it must take into account two unavoidable, and interrelated, predicaments: the proximity of the commercial film industry; and the role played by high technology in the region's postwar economic development and its contemporary social mythology. That is, my admittedly provisional use of regionalism as critical framework focuses on tensions between industry, or technology, and environment. Before surveying some recent versions of this tension as inscribed in representative films, a brief historical detour is instructive.

These days it is easy to overlook the fact that the origins of experimental film in America and in LA coincide exactly. What we know of the making of Slavko Vorkapich's, Robert Florey's, and Gregg Toland's *The Life and Death of 9413—A Hollywood Extra* (1928) indicates the terms of a recurrent ambivalence. All three directors—and one could also include the less blatant experimentalists Paul Fejos and Charles Vidor—adapted production methods, iconography, and syntax from nonmainstream European sources. They subsequently applied visual approaches discovered in the relative freedom of independent production to their industry careers. Vorkapich's condensatory montage sequences of the thirties and some of Toland's scale-obliterating work in *Citizen Kane* constitute well-known instances of this conjunction.[4] To be sure, individual and collective debts to German Expressionism and Surrealism were increasingly diluted by homogenizing pressures of the studio regime. It is clear, however, that the presence of a loosely knit film community and heightened access to professional equipment facilitated, and in turn deflected, the noncommercial impulses of aesthetically adventurous movie novices.

A second strand of the Hollywood interaction appears in the 1930s in abstract films by Oscar Fischinger and James and John Whitney,[5] a starting point for the later propensity to harness color and movement studies to the capabilities of animation and optical printing. This fusion of formalist invention and artistic application of sophisticated and costly imaging systems—engineered and controlled by large corporate interests—is shadowed by an often frustrating cycle of courtship and rejection, technical alliance and outright theft, that remains a singular feature of the West Coast avant-garde. While the Whitneys kept their distance from the lures of Hollywood production—except for ill-paid excursions like the credit sequence for *Vertigo* (1958)—John's projects required close cooperation with emerging technologies of data processing and data communications, realized through association with Bell Laboratories and IBM. Sponsorship in the form of direct and indirect grants, technology time-shares, or more nebulous exchanges of access and publicity continues to affect a wide swath of local art, for which precedents in avant-garde film served as partial models, if not cautionary tales. Although hardly confined to LA, the desire of a generation of visual artists to enlist resources of advanced industry blossomed in the late sixties with the acclaimed "Art and Technology" exhibit at the LA County Museum. Fittingly, one characteristic of this show was a profusion of cinema-aided and protocinematic installations. A less sanguine, yet telling feature was an implicit disavowal of the political meaning of high-tech borrowings.[6]

LA also played an underacknowledged role in the evolution of avant-garde psychodramas in the forties. Maya Deren's *Meshes of the Afternoon* was shot in the kind of lush hillside neighborhood that figures prominently in the stories of Raymond Chandler and proved a staple of forties film noir iconography. Even discounting Deren's interest in Wellesian flashbacks, the LA-based trance films of the period have a distinct kinship with the existential themes and strident lighting patterns of Hollywood noir. Several years after Deren moved east, Kenneth Anger, Gregory Markopoulos, and Curtis Harrington all completed their first important films in and through the sites and mythic subtexts of LA/Hollywood. They were close acquaintances, exchanged equipment and advice, and nurtured disparate attitudes toward the movie industry; perhaps most telling is Harrington's transition to feature film directing in the early sixties. The subsequent trajectories of these filmmakers are typical of the early avant-garde: a short-lived burst of activity followed by migration or a change in creative commitments. Without stretching the point, transience has often served as a multivalent trope in the description of both indigenous social arrangements and the exigencies of avant-garde production in LA.

A resurgence in the mid-sixties of nonlinear animation, and looped or optically printed treatments of found footage, revived an experimental niche in the promotion of technically polished image surfaces, a trait known in the artworld as "finish fetish." In retrospect, it was a halcyon moment for American experimental cinema in general, in which the vision of a broader, receptive youth audience jolted avant-garde enthusiasts into fresh alliances with adjacent art forms. In this heady climate, alternative films acquired immediate leverage from their imbrication with the counterculture: rock concert light shows (in LA, the collective Single Wing Turquoise Bird included filmmakers Pat O'Neill, Peter Mays, and Peter LeBrun); hallucinogenic street festivals; electronic music; and, to a lesser extent, local antiwar activism. Films that epitomize the youthful energies of the time—such as Burton Gershfield's stroboscopic lament for the genocide of Native Americans, *Now That the Buffalo's Gone* (1967)—hang together via an inflamed thematics of "dehumanization" and, paradoxically, a passion for rhythmic repetition.

By the mid-seventies, rapidly evolving institutional ties and fledgling artist-run organizations resulted in enhanced opportunities for screening and distribution,[7] increases in funding, and the gradual incursion of filmmakers into academia. Although the prime resources of the area's two giant film programs, USC and UCLA, continued to be staunchly dedicated to narrative and documentary discourses, nodes of experimental activity coalesced around strong personalities: O'Neill, Ed Emshwiller, Chick Strand, and Jules Engel at CalArts; Shirley Clarke at UCLA. On the other hand, local geography, the vagaries of educational employment and film exhibition, and the growing popularity of video tempered prospects for the type of bohemian urban community that helped sustain avant-garde momentum in New York or San Francisco. As production costs mounted and funding leveled off in the early eighties, artists such as Gary Beydler abandoned film altogether. The LA Independent Film Oasis, a loose screening and discussion collective that attracted some of the area's best-known makers, went dormant, leaving just two isolated venues in which to present new work.

Infrastructural cycles of boom and bust are of course the lingua franca of marginalized film production. In LA, however, such issues are inflected by broader creative and economic trends in Hollywood and its attendant or tangential industries. For instance, just as the utilization of fiberglass and polymer resins in airplane manufacture—also in surfboards and custom cars—has had an impact on LA sculptors such as Larry Bell and John McCracken,[8] Hollywood's accelerating reliance on intensive special effects is reflected in stylistic shifts in avant-garde visuals. It is, of course, significant that a host of local artists support themselves financially through commercial film production. Moreover, their labor, for the most part, is not limited to semiskilled laboratory or projection jobs but involves specialized editing, optical printing, titling, and sound recording. Hence it is curious to discover in the waning technical credits of, say, *The Empire Strikes Back* (1980) a full roster of avant-garde talent. But the significance of commercial involvement is discernible only alongside a near-total dismissal of influence of, or even fascination with, popular genres. Rather than trying to lump together a bunch of recent avant-garde films under the rubric of "nativist" allegory, it pays to look more closely at particular relationships between physical environment and techno-culture as they surface in a few exemplary films, including the summary achievements of Pat O'Neill.

Manifest Destiny

Tom Leeser's *Gratuitous Facts* (1981) and Betzy Bromberg's and Laura Ewig's *Marasmus* (1982) evoke, in rather different ways, confrontations with an enveloping social milieu based on pervasive media images and an aura of mechanized human contact. They share a basic strategy of unleashing skeins of referentiality inside formal structures whose purpose is to short-circuit or upend coded significations of popular culture. All three have made films elsewhere, but Leeser's work has a clear, if ultimately superficial, resemblance to the West Coast avant-garde stereotype: beautifully crafted; awash in dazzling color and varied textures; conceived around optically denatured bits of TV or movie found footage. *Facts*, along with Leeser's previous LA films, *Renee Walking/TV Talking* and *Opposing Views* (both 1980), negotiates between iconographic context (or how it structures meaning) and descriptive or denotative elements contained by a given image; as Leeser puts it, "how we perceive an image as object, and as cultural and political information."[9] In *Renee*, the mediating climate is the multichannel flow of daytime TV, shown as a concatenation of seamless yet alien languages of identification, from detective dramas to advertising, soap opera to news reportage. The core of this seductive assault is its inevitable seepage into the dynamics of intimate, personal relationships, a transference that imbues the banal events with a hyped, disfiguring dramatic logic. Conversely, we see how TV solicits, perhaps requires, individualized readings of its mass-produced contents.[10]

The pretext in *Opposing Views* is the polarized design of Cold War rhetoric and the formal pun on ideological conflict drawn through the narrative convention of shot-countershot. This initial insight is amplified by a variety of tacky spectator and sports-action shots arranged in the same editing figure, creating a syntactical as well as an iconographic framework for competition. This is close to the analytical territory honed by English structural filmmakers Peter Gidal and Malcolm Le Grice, but in contrast to their didactic rigor, Leeser's focus on history and cinematic language is constantly buoyed by playful, associative linkages predicated on shape or movement.

In the same way that a well-known clip of the 1959 Nixon-Krushchev "kitchen debate" functions as generating source for *Opposing Views,* fragments of a poorly made industrial advertisement for a Styrofoam decanter spawn the structural shape of *Gratuitous Facts.* The film begins with titles in stenciled lettering, as if on a crate or commercial package, superimposed over a field of video dots. Color-saturated, diagonal video patterns, mimicking the common malfunction by which color images dissolve into black-and-white, recur as visual static. These abstractive patterns are compared to walls and cyclone fences enclosing industrial sites; both are spatial interruptions that also carry their own intrinsic meanings separate from the objects they surround. The flow of the film suggests a sharply condensed daily TV schedule with the camera position alternating between commercial transparency and pointed subjectivity. A salient perspective is that of reporter, or perhaps archeologist, digging through and recontextualizing a group of strange artifacts in the form of kitsch footage: a tooth held by pliers, a desert-bleached skull, a fossilized rock—all held up to the camera for close scrutiny by unseen sleuths.

Similarly, found footage from a variety of sources is sewn together and tested for co-herence through criteria of shape, color, or narrative activity. A dominant, all-purpose shape or gestalt is given at the outset: a light bulb glows lurid red then gets even bright-er. This image is roughly continuous in graphic outline and symbolic association with a parade of objects: the Styrofoam decanter, an underwater diving suit, an astronaut's space suit, John Glenn's domelike head at an American Legion banquet, a dolphin leaping for fish, smokestacks at a refining plant, and, last, the cartooned word "idea." Leeser's method here is to cue visual symmetries or odd displacements by rapidly jux-taposing materials already altered by filters, optical matting, and related procedures. In one chain of reference, a petroleum plant—involved perhaps in the manufacture of the decanter—appears next to shots from a B-movie space epic; it's a plausible sequence of "airtime" that ties Hollywood product to the depredations of oil conglomerates.

Marshall McLuhan's outmoded thesis of "warm" and "cool" mediums is recalled in alternating images of heat or water, expressed at times by red or blue overlays. An ingenious trope finds television itself vouchsafed as an ocean, with the iron-suited diver as immersed spectator, or alternatively, a surrogate for the struggling artist. Voices on the soundtrack create an additional layer in the decoding of media artifacts, especially an officious documentary narrator who extols the virtues of Pompeii "be-fore the long silence fell." Other spoken conduits of information—announcements of time, weather, topical headlines—are filtered by a haze of white noise. Leeser creates an implicit contrast between Pompeii artists "representing the ordinary life of the people" and the social alienation felt by contemporary avant-gardists. When did the rupture occur? Attempting to evoke the late stages of a "great silence," *Facts* sketches a society that has learned to love the (media) Bomb, spending its days stockpiling images of its own slow-motion destruction. The last shot at first seems like an anomaly, a young girl posed self-consciously in a crude home-movie remembrance. The isolation and reflective authority of the image derive from its raw, unadorned recording of "ordinary life." Appearing as something left over, a remnant, it calls into doubt the mercurial completeness of what has gone before; as if a piece from an avant-garde autobiography had wandered into the visually scrambled array. The ending benefits from a strange poignancy, which acts to seal Leeser's distance from prerogatives of both poetic and structural styles (the latter is given a playful nudge through a dialogue of "conceptual" intertitles).

Leeser has insisted that in his work the "tyranny of the surface" is not the issue. Yet what remains problematic for the viewer is the delicate balance between exposing origins and cultural meanings of distinct shards of image and welding them into a dense, kinetically pleasing container. Although the syntactical flow of Leeser's films could never be mistaken for that of TV, looming disparities and contradictions are at times subsumed by fascination with a composite image's technical brilliance. Rather than a capitulation to forces of mass manipulation, however, ambivalence toward the machined image reveals something useful about the reciprocity of fabrication and packaging, an insight that extends from heavy industry to the more illusionistic realm of movies. In its condensatory power, *Facts* approaches, as it simultaneously refuses, the condition of smoothly rendered commodity (the decanter, which, as the ad shows us, is appropriate for both "hot" and "cold" substances). Like its plastic analogue, *Facts* situates itself as a newfangled object retrieved from the detritus of a "multistaged energy conversion," whose facile surfaces are neither tyrannical nor totally divorced from their original productive contexts.

It should be stressed that *Gratuitous Facts* does not satirize or deconstruct specific film or television genres; nor do its techniques obviously mirror those employed by Hollywood in the creation of fictional worlds. Nonetheless, there are tantalizing connections between the LA avant-garde's interest in denaturing processes and commercial genres that rely on integrating partial images from discrete sources (say, live action and animated models) into compelling dramatic scenes. Science-fiction and horror films are not only Hollywood's special-effects sentinels, they are currently the two most financially successful genres in international as well as domestic markets. In science fiction, displays of futuristic technology inherently celebrate the "alien" sovereignty of immense capital outlays directed at ever-more dehumanized film processes; in horror films, the technological imprint is usually masked by themes of human resistance to supernatural forces. Avant-garde work manifests a version of the sci-fi ethos in no-budget hi-tech quests aimed at transcending parameters of space and time, and also through the iconic fusion of natural-mechanical beings (think R2D2) or landscapes. Needless to say, since experimental cinema disregards conventions of linear narrative, the effect of reordering—i.e., mechanizing—photographic recordings is validated in rather different terms. Recent films specializing in optical printing techniques evidence a submerged stake in issues raised in standard sci-fi fare: for example, Diana Krumins's *Babobilicons* (1981), Diana Wilson's *Rose for Red* (1980) and *Eclipse Predictions* (1981), and Lyn Gerry's and Estelle Kirsh's *Abacus* (1979) deal in slippages between things we usually identify as organic versus those we designate as mechanical. Not all contain conspicuous sci-fi imagery, like *Gratuitous Facts* and a group of late-sixties West Coast films,[11] yet their tentative acceptance of technological transformation as both inevitable and capable of triggering redemptive knowledge limns a major conceit in commercial sci-fi.

Although frequently grounded in present-tense, recognizable settings, horror films address consequences of technological domination, also common in sci-fi, but they do so in less thematized, more ambivalent idioms. As films such as *Alien* (1979) and *Altered States* (1980) attest, generic boundaries between horror and sci-fi are highly permeable. At the risk of overstating the distinction, technology in horror is brought to bear not on landscape or objects but on "unnatural" bodies, either by destroying them in ever more gruesome ways or by reconfiguring their exterior or internal structures—a familiar motif is that of scientifically altering some subhuman/superhuman species.[12] Instead of the natural world as machined, horror replaces body parts with complex filmic effects. The manifest project in horror is, however, clearly the inverse of "bionic" corporeality: upholding an unfathomable uniqueness of human form *as* consciousness. In contrast to humanoid figures in sci-fi, monstrous creatures are almost always outcasts from society and their trajectories of dehumanization serve as displaced reactions to universal feelings of powerlessness and isolation. Hence sci-fi and horror films pose complementary versions of our relationship to emerging technologies, with the instrumentality of E.T. and Yoda—ushering in a desired fulfillment of human consciousness—answered by the return of atavistic impulses in the technobeasts of *The Howling* (1980) or *An American Werewolf in London* (1981).

From this angle, Bromberg's and Ewig's *Marasmus* can be seen as a kind of feminist avant-garde horror film, the Bride of Frankenstein set loose in a postindustrial wasteland, the choking maw of monster LA. Bromberg's earlier films, *Ciao Bella* (1979) and *Soothing the Bruise* (1981), segue tiny bursts of narrative action with seemingly random bits of domestic life. Neither personal documentaries nor poetic diaries, they shift gears with razor-edged velocity, tossing together disparate materials—color and monochrome, positive and negative stock, straight photography and optically distorted images—in aggressive combinations of emotional tonality. Visualizing what *Bruise* refers to as "speaking in tongues," they hover on the edge of control, caught in a circuit of female victimization and female resistance.

All three films offer scenes of women in agitated movement against some unseen male violence: go-go dancing, tumbling down a barren hillside, lurching in circles around a mountain parapet. The central, deracinated figure in *Marasmus* moves through a series of brightly hallucinatory spaces, alternating between offices in a sterile skyscraper, bleak industrial sites, and even bleaker canyon terrain. There are multiple references to and metaphors for birth, death, and abortion. The protagonist's body, covered by a clear plastic shroud, lies near an oil pipeline, the stillborn product of this environmental blight, or perhaps its deceased victim. The relation between industry, female reproduction, and disease is signaled by the film's title, a childhood ailment found in the urban slums and rural poverty areas of underdeveloped countries, caused by gross malnutrition. It is a disease where infants acquire the blank inanition, painful motion, and wrinkled skin of the elderly, with bloated bellies that grotesquely recall pregnancy. The plastic shroud, a dry bush held in front of the woman's face, and skin seen through water all suggest an attempt to empathize with the condition of starvation through psychophysical metaphors of self-abnegation.

A chorus of Third World women is conjured from a succession of ethnic costumes, topographic allusions such as desert landscapes, dancelike performances, and phrases of non-Western music. It is an intentionally vague evocation—part Middle Eastern, part Asian, part African—a vision culled from dreams or, differently, cognizant of the dangers of privileged identification with depressed cultures. The dire plight of women, the film seems to imply, is a transnational reality. *Marasmus*'s heroine is often gaudily dressed and made up; she delivers eye-rolling expressionistic grimaces and exaggerated hand gestures indicative of madness or bodily "possession." She is a minatory incarnation of the voice heard at the beginning of the film: "What am I supposed to do? Feed the starving children, starve my own country?" But she is also the angry voice of former congresswoman Bella Abzug: "We have nothing to apologize for. We don't make policy," a line heard over a shot of the protagonist raging in front of the walking-beam of an oil pump. It's a crucial moment: the female outcast, disenfranchised and metaphorically starved, confronts a mechanical and, we sense, patriarchal edifice that has sired her condition.

Technology, or rather the social ecology it has engendered, is inscribed as Other— and as unavoidable. Suspended between glittering corporate spaces and barren (but somehow feminized) wilderness, the outcast finds solace in neither. Through iconography and enacted events, a venerable avant-garde theme of dehumanized corporate technology is subjected to feminist rereading. For an older generation, romanticized visions of battles with technology helped validate tenets of independence, personal freedom, and creativity.[13] Here the problematic of technology as creative antipode is less idealized. The formal language of Bromberg's previous films is exceedingly rough, providing much of their vital energy. An immediate shift in *Marasmus* is the degree of formal control, including the removal of fictive events from contact with a spontaneous, documentary milieu. Editing rhythms are more regular and there is greater reliance on filters and optical printing. One could account for this change by citing the important collaboration with Ewig or simply remarking that it is a *later* work. Another possibility involves rooting the tensions between surface execution and anarchic structure in a specific cultural context. That is, contemporary LA art can be said to prioritize responsiveness to the look and functions of technology as a means of "cultivation" or control of natural elements. In *Marasmus*, the symbolic compass of control, including technical mastery, is understood as inherently gendered, and is actively challenged by tactics of (female?) disruption.

Bromberg's and Ewig's film also needs to be recognized as contributing to recent revisions in the avant-garde psychodrama, a form originated by Deren and Anger among others. Like Deren's early productions, *Marasmus* is anchored by a changeling figure making her way through a threatening environment. Other revisionist psychodramas include Michael Guccione's *Legions* (1981), Vivienne Dick's *Beauty Becomes the Beast* (1978), and Ericka Beckman's *Out of Hand* (1980). What is significant is that the form is being appropriated largely by women filmmakers and repositioned within broader cultural discourses, in which the dilemma of image production (a marker of cultural power and sexual difference) is no longer peripheral. If the new versions are less subjectively tortured, they are just as angry and erotically charged.

The Shadow and Its Shadow

It is possible to reformulate the technocentric "alien agenda" operating beneath both Hollywood's megalith and the fringe cadre of the LA avant-garde film. During the last decade or so, the dominant industry has strayed from a visual paradigm of straight photography of recognizable backdrops—a cinematic benchmark of realism, tweaked by appropriation of cinéma vérité techniques—toward a ruling ethos of artificial, phantasmic worlds with a concomitant disengagement from overt social themes. Put another way, the prime locus of industry creativity has begun to shift from mise-en-scène, the stage of photography and acting, to a moment of production which privileges *rephotography,* opticals, and postproduction generally.[14] In cruder terms, this development represents a return to the studio environment and its aura of Taylorized oversight, but it also underlines an increasing creative practice of subcontracting in which directors (George Lucas, for one) assume roles closer to those of engineer or project manager than auteur.

On the other hand, an implication of special-effects practices is that commercial directors have, in certain respects, moved closer to the creative stances of local avant-gardists. In fact, several ballyhooed technical achievements were pioneered by experimental makers for the depiction of otherworldly states. To take one example, *The Demon Seed* (1976), an otherwise dismal sci-fi/horror concoction, contains abstract sequences crafted by Jordan Belson, who has done effects for other films and from whom, it is rumored, the penultimate slit-scan sequence in *2001* (1968)—the progenitor of recent space epics—was purloined. Belson's contributions are deployed in the visualization of an omniscient supercomputer bent on ruling the world. Stripping away the film's admittedly silly narrative trappings, it features the sort of fusion of "higher consciousness," advanced technology, and graphic abstraction that corresponds to one popular profile of avant-garde cinema.

Studios have as well employed experimental filmmakers as consultants. Among other notable projects, Scott Bartlett managed to leave his stylistic stamp on the Warner Brothers flop *Altered States*. A lexicon of devices familiar to avant-garde enthusiasts—flicker, solarization, multiple superimpositions—are discernible in, for instance, *The Black Hole* (1980), *Wolfen* (1981), and *One from the Heart* (1982). In a similar vein, effects gurus John Dykstra and Douglas Trumbull have parlayed rudimentary knowledge of the avant-garde canon for kinetic light shows etched into *Star Wars* and *Close Encounters of the Third Kind* (both 1977).[15] The point here is although Hollywood has a long history of inserting visually hyped passages into otherwise straitlaced narratives—starting with dance numbers in thirties musicals—today's interludes are not only semiautonomous in their stylistic ruptures but feature a level of abstraction unusual for Hollywood in any era.[16]

It might be tempting to conclude from these observations that a portion of the most successful commercial genres is now devoted to aesthetic principles consonant with those of the LA avant-garde. Such a position is grossly misleading. A more grounded explanation for the seeming convergence would address the myth of (Hollywood) technology in an era of broad economic instability and the challenges to longstanding bastions of American industry—such as automobiles and aerospace—from countries such as Japan. That is, there are ideological ramifications to effects-driven genres that exceed any speculative alliance with experimental methods or objectives. For starters, the visual elegance and fantastic themes of recent sci-fi and horror films serve a typical goal of deflecting attention from pressing social ills. On another, perhaps more salient, level, displays of technical mastery—regardless of the apocalyptic stories they illuminate—help to embed a set of beleaguered national values as *formal* cinematic properties: Innovation, Efficiency, Expansiveness, Power.[17] No comparable jingoistic markers can be dredged from the sleek surfaces of Lesser, Bromberg, and their colleagues.

Nonetheless, in granting essential and unalterable polarities between the two uses of the medium, it still serves no critical purpose to deny common areas of discourse, or to segregate avant-garde from industrial epistemologies in the name of aesthetic purity. One intriguing filament of connection is that images produced, separately and in collaboration, contain implicit defenses of the authority of those tools by which movies are defined in the public imagination. There are, to be sure, various reasons why the local avant-garde has resisted competing claims of personal-poetic filmmaking and the analytical, reflexive practices of the structural style. LA might be said to constitute a "third stream" of development, were it not for the existence of additional regional streams and tributaries. At the risk of oversimplifying a local spectrum of formal approaches, a notable preoccupation involves coupling densely packed referents with coolly distanced—i.e., nonsubjectivized—frameworks of enunciation. The tendency to maintain a neutral organizing presence is, in many instances, accompanied by the absence of didactic gestures of demystification. Image construction is couched as neither spontaneous recording nor the execution of a blueprint. And image succession is rarely a matter of exclusively logical, or psychological, coordinates. Finally, there is a certain—or rather, *uncertain*—optimism regarding the place of the machine in an artificial fabric that indulges as well as transforms the immediate physical environment.

Surface Tensions

Last year, an evening hosted by David James to honor Pat O'Neill was held in an ornate theater at USC, a venue more accustomed to the intricacies of Alfred Hitchcock or Herbert Ross than those of a scion of the avant-garde. In this case, the location enabled

O'Neill to screen two recent 35mm projects, *Let's Make a Sandwich* (1982) and sketches from an as yet untitled film [*Water and Power*, 1989]. The former takes a piece of commercial kitsch—a domestic primer in how to prepare a weird sandwich, produced to plug the virtues of natural-gas cooking—as a jumping-off point for layering a deck of diverse images (animals, a seascape, an animated digestion diagram). The untitled film has extensive time-lapse photography of light phases and human movements set against urban, coastal, and desert backdrops. If aspects of both films signal a departure for O'Neill, they also extend the condensatory, defamiliarizing tactics that galvanize his previous work. His decision to switch gauges was predicated on a desire for greater scale and more exacting control of the image surface, qualities clearly enhanced by the size, brightness, density, and clarity of 35mm images. Exploring O'Neill's films, it is important to consider the notion of "surface" as a site of intense transactions, a realm where themes of regulation and disruption, the everyday and the fantastic, are intertwined in comic and menacing articulations.[18]

After studying industrial and graphic design at UCLA, O'Neill started making films in the early sixties, having abandoned an interest in sculpture. Within a few years he had become a hub of local energies by dint of his films and teaching, but also through his exceptionally generous technical counsel and production assistance. At the core of his reputation is the recruitment of the optical printer as primary tool in the hermeneutics of image construction and reception. The shadow of the printer hovers over O'Neill's work in a manner similar to the way camera movement invigorates

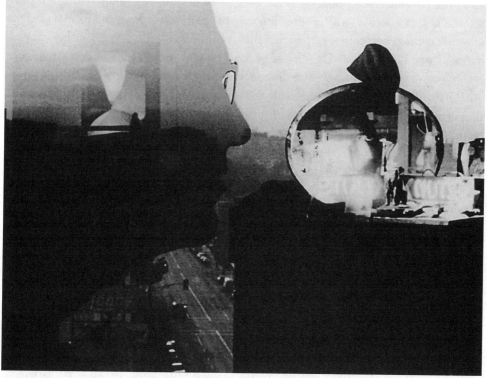

Water and Power by Pat O'Neill. Photograph courtesy of the filmmaker.

Michael Snow's oeuvre or the splice acquires sweeping metaphoric significance in Stan Brakhage's filmography. The point is not that these films are *about* their instruments of production, but that a specific technique, fixing and privileging one stage of production over other stages or operations, authorizes a powerful union of imagination, creative exigency, and formal execution.

A few (untutored) observations are necessary on the nature of optical printing—which I am using to cover an assortment of procedures including stationary and traveling mattes, image enlargement and reduction, even subtitling. As practiced by O'Neill, composing with a printer fundamentally means making images of images, working at a minimum of one remove from the photographic recording of reality. It adopts the individual frame as principal unit of filmic utterance. But unlike, say, Peter Kubelka, for whom the frame is an absolute unit of syntax, O'Neill's fascination with optical printing posits the single frame as divisible, as a field capable of sustaining internal juxtapositions among noticeably discrete parts. Changes within a given sector and changes in relations between areas develop in the course of what are perceived as single takes, deflecting the usual place of editing in the generation of meaning. Though it is often thought of as a somehow streamlined or automated process, O'Neill's version of optical printing is as painstakingly "hands-on" as almost any technique known to film; indeed, its closest relatives are cell animation and hand-painting.

A typical O'Neill image consists of three or four iconic components occupying separate planes—sometimes just a corner, sometimes the majority of the frame. These fragments frequently diverge in scale, in material (animated shape, found footage, straight recording), coloration, iconographic category (indoor/outdoor, organic/cultural), and so on. There has been a loose progression over the years in the look and formal range of O'Neill's planar compositions. In earlier films such as *Runs Good* (1970), either a foundational image is "decorated" with one or more rectangular, screenlike cutouts, or several levels are melded through superimposition. In a more recent film like *Foregrounds* (1978), the device of miniframes inside the larger frame gives way to a closer integration of planes in which designations of "primary" and "secondary" are rendered moot. Despite this compositional shift there has been a persistent theme of "projection," in which human or mechanical shapes, whether moving or stationary, take on the function of screens on which new image permutations appear. Sometimes the master trope of objects as reflective screens is literalized in footage displaying the mechanics of film projection. In *Sidewinder's Delta* (1976), regular pieces of paper placed on barren desert ground begin to glow with eerie, metallic color transformations and are then gently rolled and turned as if by the wind. The image suggests both a mini–movie screen filled by desert light and an organic formation, some rare geometric desert flower that breathes new colors at the touch of scorched air.

Projection screens, a shape that *is* but also *contains* something else, can be read as an allusion to the mechanical relationship between projection and recording, or re-recording, of parallel filmstrips inside the printer. In successive print generations the composite image gets farther away from conventional camera illusion, more constructed and hermetic. The irony is that O'Neill's films are also strongly evocative, even cannily descriptive of a real Southern California environment itself often discussed as an illusionistic amalgam of disparate features.[19] As if in imitation of the method of their fabrication, compositions often begin slowly then build to moments of visual intensification, then begin to fade. Entire sequences in the later films pile up in a similar fashion: a fluid configuration is added to another without discernible narrative or formal trajectory. Rhythms may accelerate or slow down, referential fragments may become more abstract; there is often a brief wry coda. The critical difficulty in describing O'Neill's work stems in part from the complexity of individual images, but it is also a consequence of their laconic, transient organization, re-presenting familiar objects as prone to mysterious incursions.

It is possible to regard the optical printer as a kind of alchemical device acting on original photographic materials to bend, recolor, dissolve, replace, even reverse their coordinates. Indeed, a prevalent image category is the turning of apparent solids into liquids or gaslike transparencies, giving visual shape to otherwise ephemeral phenomena. The title *Sidewinder's Delta* is instructive: it suggests a riverbed of snakes, but delta is also the symbol for change, and the sidewinder is a rattler that thrusts its body forward in a series of loops. Hence it poetically invokes the movement of film through printer or projector (the filmstrip as snake is parsed most spectacularly in a late sequence of *Foregrounds*). Sometimes the agency of change is explicitly cued as the banuasic Artist: hands encased in editing gloves snap their fingers at the start of *Easyout* (1972); a godlike fist assumes the shape and scale of a mountain in *Sidewinder*; the toe of a work boot meddles with the bottom of an image in *Saugus Series* (1976), where boots later serve as an abstract expressionist canvas for sprays of intense color.

More often, however, the mediator of change is associated with something mechanical. Electronic music or machine noises on O'Neill's soundtracks frequently provide an initial linkage. A sputtering generator in *Sidewinder* seems to fuel an extraordinary exchange of colors between an electric lamp and a cactus; when the generator shuts down, so do the tonal variations. Machine sounds are also used to mock their ostensible synchrony with an image, as when an annoying saw in *Saugus* eventually defies its own rhythmic command. Natural elements such as clouds move with the cadences of wind-up toys; a stream is redone in the tones of an industrial paint job; a potted cactus soars like an airplane. The theme of nature and/as/versus machine can be split into a cluster of antinomies: animal instinct versus learned behavior; the prerogatives of animal versus human; conformity and its opposite as benchmarks of contemporary society; the cycle of growth and decay.

An early indication of how O'Neill treats these tensions is evident in *7362* (1967), named after a high-contrast print stock and featuring split-screen laterally symmetrical images of, primarily, an oil pump and a nude dancer. At one point the movements of these two figures, flattened and abstracted, seem to merge, but eventually the human form asserts its distinctive prerogatives of nongeometric shape. The film is a redaction of Férnand Leger's *Ballet Mecanique* (1924) fitted to the specifications of LA's nightclubs and oil facilities. If the body-as-machine conceit is open to social critique, the affect of *7362* is nonetheless staunchly abstractive.

Runs Good (1970) is O'Neill's most concerted effort at picturing a malignant mass society. It relies heavily on found footage and recalls the films of Bruce Conner in its sour millenarian mood. It opens with a drive through a tunnel into a blinding light (perhaps that of LBJ's gift to the lexicon of the Vietnam War), and what follows is a "newsreel" from a postholocaust future. People and animals have been reprogrammed in their behaviors: women act like dogs in a piece of soft-core pornography and, for good measure, their stunts are looped to blunt the erotic effect; animals at a pet show pretend to be human; a lonely bison humps the ground as a voice on the soundtrack singles him out as a nonconformist. A gigantic snail clicks across the screen, dwarfing an airplane and a crowd of sun-worshipers. Entertainment is reduced to strict utilitarian limits, with a football game compared to military formations and the lockstep of a digital clock repeating a countdown from ten. Even an orange grove is depicted as part of a horrifying manmade order. A counterweight to the film's overabundance of control is signaled by intermittent breakdowns in the image. In fact, a recurrent tactic has an image or sequence reaching a level of mechanical refinement—subtended by the domination of natural elements—that precipitates a disruption by nonrepresentational blobs or lines gone haywire.

Sequences that resist, as they simultaneously affirm, a mechanical or rational order occur in *Runs Good, Easyout, Saugus Series,* and *Sidewinder's Delta.* Over the course of O'Neill's career, the unraveling of old footage thematically redolent of domestication or institutional constraint—in *Runs Good,* this includes shots of a lion-tamer, cops, and a wedding ceremony—seems less agreeable than doctoring culturally unhinged images such as cartoon characters. In later films, O'Neill adopts objects or elements that would appear to be completely immune from visual reconstruction: twigs, rocks, plants, clouds, streaming liquids—things whose irregular or transient shapes, random arrangements, or immeasurable durations make mechanical intervention all the more surprising. In *Saugus,* for example, a three-pronged stream of viscous fluid is at first mistaken for a waterfall in front of foggy rocks. The original photographic source for this deluge is perceived as nonmanufactured, while the sinuous shapes described by the separate prongs are inferred as neither animated nor looped. Yet as the colors inside the stream start to change in harmonious patterns, like a color organ, the unavoidable conclusion is that rational agents have caused the permutations. Further, the artificially saturated colors suggest an industrialized homogeneity. The composite image is a typical O'Neill "oasis," a refreshing hybrid composed of natural elements altered to resemble mechanical objects, or ostensibly artificial parts that acquire amorphous properties of a natural regime. The ultimate fiction of loss of control, the purposive confusion between manmade—meaning regimented, at the service of culture—and natural is amplified by the filmmaker's amazing technical mastery. *Techne* is elevated to the status of a theme because it is clearly in excess of the quotidian image-contents and because it emblematizes a friction attributed to the geographic context to which those images refer.

Finally, it is worth noting that ambivalent transactions with technology have been a potent idea in LA artmaking at least since the sixties. Two characteristics are especially

Water and Power by Pat O'Neill. Photograph courtesy of the filmmaker.

relevant to O'Neill's films. The first is the adoption of materials and processes expressing contradictory relationships to the natural world. Among prominent examples from
the sixties are Kenneth Price's ceramic eggs, Craig Kaufman's swelling plastic reliefs
(which recall animal carapace or rock formations), and Ron Davis's "marbleized" paintings. Of more recent vintage are Eric Orr's environmental sculptures that employ water,
fire, and precious metals.

A second characteristic relates to avant-garde film's vaunted project of perceptual
retraining. Specifically, vacuum-formed or other advanced industrial materials are
wielded to emphasize the role of light in fluctuations of shape and color. Though they
differ vastly in aesthetic goals and applications, James Turrell, Doug Wheeler, Ron
Cooper, Jerrold Ballaine, and Robert Irwin have all constructed work highlighted by
conflicts between real and implied projection, translucency, and reflection, and underwritten by the shifting apprehension of form as alternatively intrinsic to the object or
produced by a viewer's contact with a contingent environment. Thus a parallel exists
between the aspiration to "paint with light" and the avant-garde's rigorous interrogation of the depth illusion.

Larry Bell is perhaps the artist whose aesthetic vocabulary, commitment to perceptual process, and complex handling of technology most closely resemble O'Neill's accomplishments in film. And although he has never been concerned with explicit social
imagery—unlike, say, Ed Ruscha, who shares with O'Neill an affinity for surrealist

visual condensations drawn from local scenery—Bell's sculpture poses a convoluted relationship to his increasing sophistication of means. His private annexation of the production machinery of commercial plating, his well-documented establishment of a factorylike studio, and the increasingly *organic* connotations exuded by that technology have interesting correspondences in O'Neill's career; for starters, a self-described turning point was his purchase of an optical printer.

Bell's large glass constructions made since the early seventies—including *Homage to Griffin, Dilemma of Griffin's Cat* (both 1980), and the *Cat Variations* (1981–82)—actively engage the spectator in a play of perceptual contradictions whereby reflected and directly transmitted shapes appear to materialize and dematerialize as our gaze shifts or we move around a given piece. Spontaneous, chance occurrences in the experience of this work stand in blatant contrast to the precise control exerted (and felt by the viewer) during the design and building stages. To be sure, if the tone of Bell's sculpture is antithetical to that of several of O'Neill's films—highly theatrical, metaphysical, utterly devoid of wit or self-mockery—his suspension between natural and manufactured formal properties is strikingly similar. The poet Robert Creeley, in an introduction to a recent catalogue, compares the experience of Bell's art to a "changing sky or river." The plying of metaphors from the natural world is indeed a common critical response to his art. Bell himself, in the same introduction, says that a series of vapor drawings "represent very strong personal feelings. Not anguish, pain or joy but daily mundane drama . . . most of all they contain my efforts to overcome strict technical discipline, to become spontaneous, intuitive, improvisational in my approach."[20]

A central problem, then, for both Bell and O'Neill is the balancing of advanced technological processes with overtones of a natural disorder or anomaly. If the look of Bell's sculptures suggests a liquid recontextualization of the smooth architectural skins of skyscrapers, O'Neill carves a similar niche between city and country in his transformative welding of machine life and elemental vitality, although unlike Bell's, his iconography of the manmade is funky, unpredictable, antiutilitarian. Moreover, their shared concerns echo a traditional ambivalence in American culture toward the position of nature in historical trajectories of progress, simultaneously threat and providence, that is famously, and convulsively, manifest in the nineteenth-century writings of Thoreau, Emerson, and Melville.[21] O'Neill clearly recognizes the personal as well as the collective status of his opposing forces; they are not idealized or made redemptive by his approach but situated on a continuum that reflects, as it constantly reinvents, its origins in an indigenous milieu.

Postscript: O'Neill's City Symphony

Water and Power begins with a high-wire act, a defiance of natural law by human—or rather, technology-aided—resolve. Then immediately there is a fall. A time-lapse low-angle shot shows a soaring bridge at dusk beneath which scuttle tiny beachgoers; a lone figure walks across the trestle, pauses, climbs the railing, then leaps into the evening sky like a shooting star. How the shot was made, its degree of verisimilitude or artifice, remain opaque. We realize only later that this sumptuous opening is practically the least complicated image in O'Neill's remarkable 35mm short feature, a lambent rush of quasi-narrative, documentary, and formalist prerogatives. The first image is a bridge, as it were, initiating cyclical rounds of accretion and dissolution, ebb and flow in its widest sense, permeating every quadrant of the LA basin, the extended body of a city rife with anxious illusion.

A city symphony in the great 1920s tradition of Dziga Vertov, Joris Ivens, and Walter Ruttman, O'Neill's film is a flagrant hybrid: a "big-budget" (approximately $60,000) avant-garde epic produced over nearly a decade and sporting optical effects every bit as polished, as innovative, as those of Hollywood blockbusters—in particular, a personally designed computer-driven time-lapse camera program capable of minute increments of motion between frames. Moreover, there are specific references as well as identifiable moods that connect O'Neill's portrait of LA to commercial movie genres of the past. Hollywood—in the form of quotations from film noir, De Mille, two early von Sternberg dramas, allusions to westerns and to irradiated sci-fi monsters from the fifties—floats over the proceedings like a ghost in a dream factory, creating a zone that encompasses not only streets and city skyline but adjacent desert landscapes and ocean tidepools. They are all part of an omni-production line. Once again there is the trope of an oasis, inhabited this time by human wanderers whose impossibly sped-up movements are answered by glacial topographic shifts in seashore and desert floor. Ultimately, the film both is, and is about, the clockwork mechanisms of human/natural interdependence.

O'Neill accumulated footage slowly, often through trial and error, by taking long solitary treks into remote areas. In some sequences, durations of up to six hours are compressed into minutes. With the basic photographic materials in hand, he then subjected them to varied processes of matting, superimposition, and so on. The painterly studies that emerged from this arduous gestation were then stitched together into a loose narrative fabric secured by informational titles, a vague historical progression, and an ominous mélange of movie voices and obscure verbal anecdotes.[22] In a manner analogous to his construction of images, the history of LA is sedimented in overlapping layers, from references to Native American and pioneer outposts to the laying of the infamous 1910 pipeline from Owens Lake that spurred the growth of a modern urban matrix. Allusions to different eras drift through scenes of contemporary ethnic diversity in LA's bedraggled downtown district and the cookie-cutter sprawl of middle-class suburbs.

Predictably, O'Neill's film has been compared with Godfrey Reggio's ecological attack on urban blight, *Koyaanisqatsi* (1982), yet the disparities between the two are more illuminating than any superficial congruences. While Reggio's film flaunts, even fetishizes its time-lapse vision of technological society run amok—in essence, denying any complicity between his fancy camera apparatus and corporate domination of society—O'Neill is typically sensitive to, and skeptical of, his own inscribed mastery. Indeed, at times *Water and Power* seems to comically taunt the puny resources of cinema as wan metaphors for the heat and light and ceaseless animation of natural elements. A *bricoleur* almost without peer, O'Neill is ever mindful of the material limits of his art.

Unlike the distanced, if also enraged, narrational presence in Reggio's work, *Water and Power* is imbued with a tantalizing nimbus of subjectivity. On one level, it is possible that the film's framework of knowledge derives from one or more of its dramatic "characters," intermittent figures that perform small tasks within scenes of extreme temporal compression or that narrate individual sections. Another reading is that the source of enunciation is O'Neill himself. A bunch of signature images (a running dog; a porkpie hat) recall earlier films, the filmmaker takes a fleeting turn before the camera, and several characters share a rough physical resemblance to O'Neill. Behind the trappings of a city symphony, then, may lurk the shadows of avant-garde psychodrama. To be sure, *Water and Power* is a synoptic project that touches upon and reformulates a number of persistent themes, including O'Neill's participation in commercial fiction films and TV ad campaigns.

There is even an enigmatic central location, a locus from which the film's hallucinatory journeys might radiate: a loft in downtown LA with a view of surrounding streets and looming mountains. Depending on how it is filmed, or the type of images that infiltrate its drab interior spaces, it looks like an abandoned industrial building, an artist's studio (in one sequence, a nude model poses in blurry fast motion), a large camera obscura, and a barebones movie studio in which memory, projection, and photographic observation are conjoined in a labor-intensive drama of image production. To put it another way, *Water and Power* operates in a no-mans-land, a cinematic ground zero. In its scale and ambition, its flirtation with narrative, and its profound reckoning of technology, O'Neill's tour de force is at once a boldly original initiative and a film that raises unsettled questions for the future of the avant-garde movement in general.

(1982–83)

7 | Springing Tired Chains: African American Experimental Film and Video

Facing down, the ground springs tired chains. Voices spring from the eye there, at corners-sleep. Hoarseness becomes rhetoric seasoned / as first distinct words lacerate grim oppression reality, a behind vision tomb widowed enfeoffment jettisoned
—*Cecil Taylor*

Extending the Boundaries

On the face of it, the assertion of a distinct African American avant-garde cinema seems dubious, perhaps faintly dismissive. Indeed, there is little in the extensive history of post–World War II filmic experimentation that appears conducive to a black presence. It is not that the movement's aesthetic foundations, institutional paradigms, or political agendas barred inclusion; it is simply that until recently the domain of avant-garde concerns and practices appeared culturally irrelevant—and often economically prohibitive—to black artists. Further, while there were many examples of black involvement in cutting-edge American literature, painting, and especially music, no comparable models existed for nonmainstream filmmakers during the germinal period of heightened avant-garde production and public visibility.[1] Despite the utopian rhetorics and intermittent social activism associated with alternative film groups of the 1960s, the avant-garde's egalitarian aspirations, directed simultaneously at organization building and image making, were rarely extended to people of color. By the end of that decade, as a less overtly politicized countercultural ethos gained prominence, the prospect of a truly interracial avant-garde all but disappeared. Thus the recent surge of nonmainstream work by black film/videomakers, at once imbricated in yet separate from cultural ideologies and practices common to white avant-gardists, could easily be taken as a wholly autonomous development. Nonetheless, for reasons that I hope to make clear, understanding the motives and strategies of black experimentalism requires a mapping of substantial exchanges and aesthetic intersections with, as well as divergences from, the wider historical field of avant-garde activity.

Among the most telling obstacles to earlier black participation was a historically contentious relationship between black aesthetics and tenets of European modernism, in particular the imperative of medium-specific formal exploration adopted by successive generations of experimental filmmakers. Alain Locke, a canny and tireless promoter of the Harlem Renaissance, called for a fusion of modernist literary techniques with black vernacular idioms, a fusion manifest in the visual arts by, among others, Romare Bearden. By the late 1960s, this stance had been repeatedly discredited as counterproductive, if not insulting, to black cultural self-determination, with the most strident repudiation expressed by advocates of the Black Arts Movement.[2] Conversely, independent film had by that time abandoned previous critical engagement with issues of racism, conformism, and militarism—admittedly couched in narrative hybrids such as John Cassavetes's *Shadows* (1959) and Jonas Mekas's *Guns of the Trees* (1961)—in favor of more subjectivized, reflexive modes of resistance to dominant values. Thus the handful of black actors, writers, and directors who were fellow travelers during the underground, Beat phase of the movement drifted into other cultural spheres.[3] For the next twenty years, with the singular exception of the LA Rebellion of the 1970s,[4] the prospect of an indigenous black cinema was entirely bracketed on the one hand by the positivist goals of traditional documentary and, on the other, by the popular allure of Hollywood.

It is only in the last decade or so that grassroots pressures for greater inclusion of nonwhite cultural perspectives have furnished conditions for a black presence in the landscape of avant-garde cinema. Heightened sensitivity to perceptions of racial exclusion has prompted a long-delayed process of outreach by funding agencies, museums, exhibitions venues, academic media departments, and public television. At the same time, avant-garde cinema's ongoing revision of formal approaches in tandem with renewed interest in the treatment of social issues has created a unique opening for artists of color. Even with demonstrable increases in opportunity and critical achievement, it is far too early to consolidate black experimentalism under the rubric of a movement. Its visual styles are too varied and unstable, the profile of its practitioners too heterogeneous and geographically dispersed. Moreover, it is evident that the recent flurry of film and video production is underwritten less by self-conscious adoption or endorsement of existing avant-garde practices than by the overarching failure of either conventional documentary or fictional cinemas to realize the imaginative scope of African American identity. In this sense, the affinities and linkages offered in the following discussions are heuristic; they are not dependent on familiarity by black artists with either the white avant-garde canon or its theoretical justifications (although greater enrollment of African Americans in film and art schools makes such familiarity more likely).

The primary evidence for an interweaving of nonmainstream sectors derives from institutional records and de facto policies, leaving little doubt that black experimentation has claimed a discernible place within prevailing channels of avant-garde funding, distribution, and exhibition.[5] Not long ago, the published rosters of grant recipients, in-person screenings, artists in residence, and nonprofit administrators were over-whelmingly white; now they are markedly more diverse. Further, as (mostly) young black media artists attempt to define alternative methods of visualizing their personal and social experience, their deployment of themes, materials, and formal strategies analogous to those already recognized in avant-garde circles has facilitated gestures of mutual accommodation. Black artists are afforded access to organs of publicity and a ready-made audience attuned to both the problematics of self-representation and the challenges of unconventional visual style. The avant-garde's willing incorporation of minority perspectives helps validate a heartfelt, if informal, multicultural agenda that serves to inoculate the established movement against twin accusations of aesthetic stagnation and ideological complicity. To be sure, the idea of an alliance founded on ex-plicit organizational goals and policies remains unlikely, yet advantages to both groups are at once relatively obvious and largely pragmatic.[6]

Devoid of a legacy of experimental achievement within their own community, black artists operate outside the web of intergenerational tensions, including competition for scarce resources, that continues to burden not only venerable subgeneric practices but feminist and queer initiatives as well. In this sense, de facto exclusion has resulted in a greater freedom to revisit older experimental styles and recruit elements from disparate mainstream genres. However, if their position as avant-garde neophytes exempts black artists from certain burdens of modernist succession, it can also engender pressures to which white experimentalists are immune. For instance, aesthetic postures of alien-ation or satirical detachment, which provided successive factions with clear signifiers of personal authenticity, are anathema to African American work. In consequence, the rich comedic traditions infusing avant-garde cinema and black culture alike remain largely untapped. Hence validation of black avant-garde production is in some sense tied to the seriousness of its engagement with aspects of racial, gender, or sexual op-pression. In short, the black avant-garde is assumed to be "political." An invidious spirit of exemplification binds artists to vexed standards of responsibility. And as is generally the case in marginal cinemas, the impulse toward cultural resistance is viti-ated by frequent suspicions of art-world elitism. Although manifest in myriad forms of personal and social expression, a version of Du Boisian double consciousness shrouds the trajectory of black experimental cinema. Marlon Riggs, in a deft commentary on contradictions between popular access and formal innovation, argues that a "new wave of media activism" should merge the realist prerogatives of documentary with the avant-garde's freewheeling subjectivity.[7] The crux of Riggs's proposal is the subversion of essentialist or exclusive components of social identity as projected through repre-sentational practices, in which a balance of radical individualism and recognition of shared histories would help obviate what he viewed as twin traps of reductivism and solipsism.

The avant-garde canon has frequently been chided by feminists and postmodernists as constituting a fringe bastion of conservative, idealist discourses.[8] What this line of criticism tends to ignore are deeply embedded identitarian impulses that form a scaffolding for contemporary multicultural energies. Over several decades, avant-garde film's insistence on self-representation, and on the ancillary documentation of sub-cultural activities and charismatic figures, resulted in the timely projection of Beat, hippie, punk, and queer oppositional styles.[9] Without repeating or appropriating previous micropolitical paradigms, black experimentalists have addressed omissions and distortions perpetrated by both Hollywood cinema and social documentary through formulas that parallel the pungent bricolage of post-1960s avant-gardists. At the risk of overgeneralizing a varied and complex field, a frequent vehicle for the concept of individual identity as fragmented and multiple—at once socially constructed and subjectively autonomous—involves assembling disjunct materials in a nonlinear, essayistic fashion in the treatment of autobiographical themes. Recurrent elements include archival footage and speech, talking-head interviews and pseudointerviews, pop music, spontaneous observation of quotidian domestic or street life, and sync-sound interludes of obliquely dramatic or outright symbolic performance. As distinct from practices in documentary and independent narrative, this discursive nexus is grounded in a first-person "voice" or source of knowledge that asserts the power of personal imagination as it fractures the illusion of unified subject position. Although particular features in this loose description are employed in a variety of contexts and combinations, in basic outline it is applicable to the majority of works discussed below.

Two points need to be made about the relationship between a segmented, collage approach and documentary practices. First, the avant-garde has in one sense edged closer to traditional documentary via its renewed interest in historical retrieval, the analysis and/or celebration of discarded episodes in the history of cinema or, alternatively, the examination of subjectivities suppressed by historical representation.[10] Second, the conventions of mainstream documentary have also shifted in the last decade or so—Michael Moore's *Roger and Me* (1989) is a convenient touchstone—to permit more personal, subjective interventions by filmmakers, whether in the form of voice-over narration, home movies, or onscreen appearances. Given these convergences, what are the grounds for insisting on critical distinctions between the two camps? Why shouldn't black experimentalism be considered a branch of the personal or essayistic documentary? An initial justification for inclusion in the avant-garde domain is, as I have suggested, institutional. Documentaries are funded, distributed, and exhibited to the public through networks different from those for experimental work. For instance, most documentaries are feature length, requiring appropriate levels of funding, and are presented as integral programs; the work considered here is, with several exceptions, much shorter and normally programmed in omnibus group shows. Despite recent revisions to protocols of objectivity, documentaries are nonetheless understood or "indexed" by viewers as placing special emphasis on informational or pedagogical functions rather than on visual tropes of expressivity.[11] The distinction is less a matter of theme or content than of *enunciation*. At least within the realm of circulation, documentary and avant-garde shows generate different sets of expectations and rely on separate modes of address. Irrespective of any shared commitment to a critique of social inequality or the redress of historical amnesia, experimental work differs also from documentary in the nature and degree of its insistence on direct, self-conscious participation in the events or situations represented. Further, autobiographical impulses in the work considered here limn an enunciative presence at once embodied in and mediated by a play of formal signifiers. While documentaries often portray marginal subjects as exemplary figures, as individual cases intended to illustrate a generalized group condition, the avant-garde tends to problematize perceptions of broader social truths as inextricable from individual consciousness. Refusing to posit an authoritative knowledge separate from that of personal experience, avant-garde film and video operate under an injunction to create aesthetic templates adequate to the presentation of inner, as well as external, realities, Its formal practices therefore constitute an implicit rejection of realist tropes of visual transparency, linearity, and closure—effects that even the recent "personal" documentaries of, say, Ross McElwee and Nick Broomfield are loathe to jettison. Not only is the documentary regarded by experimentalists, including Riggs, as colluding in the propagation of bourgeois values, but its conventional rhetorics of evidence, argument, and univocal explanation are deemed incommensurate with the exploration of identity as a bundle of multiple, overdetermined, and contradictory strands.[12]

A central, nearly ubiquitous feature of sixties avant-garde *and* documentary styles is found footage (including still photos, sound, and other artifacts). Here again, the recruitment of extant materials by black experimentalists has a stronger affinity with avant-garde usage than it does with documentary's inscription of archival images— typically used as visual accompaniment to and illustration of past events referenced by interview subjects or by a voice-over narrator. In both sets of practices, found footage may be assigned either a negative or a positive valence depending on a work's thematic orientation. It can become the target of ideological unmasking and/or comic inversion of its original contextual meaning, as is often the case with old materials gleaned from entertainment-industry sources or state-produced propaganda (e.g., instructions to schoolchildren on how to avoid an atomic bomb attack). Similarly, it can be seized upon as an instrument of remedial historical memory, as evidence of something spurned or suppressed (e.g., the lively frontier presence of black cowboys) because it calls into question an ingrained social truth.

In mainstream documentaries, regardless of political stance or method of selection and composition, found materials are adduced as direct, formally transparent signifiers of the Real. Footage may be edited into montage sequences juxtaposing disparate sources or production contexts—for instance, snippets from a Hollywood drama spliced to a newsreel scene—but such formal liberties rarely emphasize or substantially modify visual aspects of the original scenes. Their primary task is to advance expository or argumentative strands of narration. In the avant-garde, however, found footage is frequently denatured by optical printing, looping, changes in speed, and other techniques that can themselves be thematized around a blanket critique (e.g., looping of TV ads as a visual correlative of stultifying cultural repetition). When combined in complex montage patterns, recycled materials are made to yield not just a fresh set of image contents but stylistic qualities and a specter of production pointedly at odds with the artifact from which they were obtained. An additional effect of found images and speech, important to postmodern concepts of fragmented subjectivity, is the splitting or deflection of creative authority, the recognition that every text is in some regard a fabric of quotation. The underlying motives, as well as the tactics, of appropriation adopted by black experimentalists are hence more closely aligned with avant-garde practices than with documentary's evidentiary facade.

The ability to locate, duplicate, edit, and compositionally alter found footage has been considerably enhanced by recent video technologies. While 16mm film remains the standard gauge for feature-length documentaries—despite escalating production costs—video is clearly the principal format for nonmainstream black artists, a choice governed as much by aesthetic and social prerogatives as by economic criteria.[13] The combination of comparatively lower budgets, a factor in video's greater potential for public funding, and near-universal access to playback equipment allows for less rigid, localized strategies of circulation and reception. Lacking the mass appeal of Hollywood products, black experimental shorts are more easily assimilated into alternative settings such as college classrooms, music clubs, and community organizations. At the same time, desultory promises of wider exposure through public television and cable outlets have prompted some artists to adhere to broadcast requirements of length, image quality, and acceptable content. Yet frequently, an engagement with video elicits a self-conscious resistance to the middlebrow "public service" ethos of PBS. Nonetheless, as the history of avant-garde film has demonstrated, and the commodification of hip hop and rap music confirms, the flaunting of technical crudity or aesthetic alterity hardly ensures an oppositional cachet as "outsider art." As is true of the current white avant-garde, critical contestation by black artists of TV's dissemination of bourgeois ideology—in particular its racist, sexist, and homophobic underpinnings—is constantly in danger of being co-opted by the omnivorous, venal demands of mass culture itself.

The urgent dialogue conducted by black experimentalists with televisual languages, with news and other nonfiction discourses as well as with melodramatic spectacle, is the obverse of an equally persistent desire to mobilize more "organic," indigenous, or Afrocentric cultural idioms. As David James has suggested, micropolitical cinemas can validate their own sense of mission by transposing forms of art with which the producing group has a background of prior achievement. Just as earlier avant-garde coteries borrowed tropes from poetry and painting, black film and video adapts expressive and syntactic elements from jazz, blues, and other musics, as well as from dance, black poetry, and theater. According to James, nonmainstream minority movements "initially shape themselves by documenting practices in the earlier medium, and in the process develop ways of internalizing its aesthetic principles *filmically*, in their own form."[14] This insight helps clarify the distinction between black experimentalism and an adjacent mode of black "performance documentary" comprising ostensibly neutral transcriptions of performances or, alternatively, portraits of performing artists. To be sure, the quiddity of the work in question is at least partly defined through the interpenetration of vernacular, socially rooted aesthetic patterns and a modernist (or postmodernist) imperative to recalibrate noxious languages of mass culture.

Speaking in Tongues

Having argued for certain axes of connection to avant-garde cinema while acknowledging salient points of divergence from documentary, it is necessary to further annotate the formal and thematic vectors in which black experimentation parts company with other nonmainstream subcultures. This task is best realized through detailed descriptions and analyses of specific works. There is one area, however, that requires a bit of preliminary qualification. Despite a shared reliance on recycled materials as pretext and object of ideological critique, and despite the use of analogous formal devices, the recontextualizing impulse in black film and video proceeds from a rather different stance or body of rhetorical assumptions than those associated with avant-garde film. Simply stated, the relation of black artists to mass media representations indicates a level of disenfranchised hostility in which appropriated images are not just deceptive or alien but constitute part of an armature of determinate subjugation.

Both avant-garde and black practitioners tend to yoke claims for political efficacy to the exposure and interrogation of hegemonic visual discourses, especially those discourses that aid in the construction of social prejudice. Beginning with the work of Bruce Conner in the late 1950s, the avant-garde has doggedly pursued a strategy of mocking inversion of media images. As filmmaker Abigail Child describes her method, "I'm trying to dislodge, unearth, and subvert the image, exploring the limits of representation, asking how I can bring forward the contradictions in the image."[15] Similarly, Craig Baldwin asserts, "There's a political edge to it when you take the images of the corporate media and turn them against themselves."[16] Despite the yawning critical separation inscribed between original context and creative reordering of found materials, there is frequently a subtext of guilty pleasure in the selection and handling of such images, a hovering ambivalence stemming perhaps from connoisseurship or from a prior biographical stage of appreciation. Even as it registers malign effects of mass culture's ideological machinations, the avant-garde's approach to found footage often harbors a tenuous identification with the system producing this overly familiar material. A mixture of disdain and desire is evident as early as Conner's landmark *A Movie* (1958), in which cinema's propensity for violent spectacle is paralleled with our century's trajectory of mechanized disaster. Cinema is recognized as a public arbiter, as well as a recording instrument, of violent action; as such, neither the maker nor the viewer is entirely exempt from complicity in the synapse linking destruction and spectatorship.

In a eulogy for Marlon Riggs, Isaac Julien reminds us of the difficulty faced by black artists over "how to name yourself in a language that has named you as other."[17] The title of Riggs's best-known work, *Tongues Untied* (1989), hints at the double burden imposed by silence: the historical exclusion of black media artists from fashioning their own histories, and the accumulation of repressive languages by which entertainment industries "speak" for and to the social experience of minorities. The deployment of found materials by black experimentalists is underwritten by affirmative as well as nullifying impulses, an intersection of remedial historical representation with the intended creation of a new historical subject equipped with its own generative idioms. Operating

Tongues Untied by Marlon Riggs. Photograph courtesy of Janet Cutler.

beyond the limits of textual pastiche, the contestation of past images becomes inseparable from the struggle to directly integrate art into a praxis of everyday life. British artist
and theorist Kobena Mercer encapsulates the importance of found imagery as follows:
"At a micro-level, the textual work of creolising appropriation activated in new forms
of black cultural practice awakens the thought that such strategies . . . may be capable of
transforming the 'democratic imaginary' at a macro-level."[18] What counts as historical
evidence and the means by which evidentiary fragments are drafted into personal or
collective counternarratives are quandaries inflecting contemporary culture as a whole.
In the work of black film/videomakers considered here, the "evidence" of mass media
representation is entwined with and finally sublated by vernacular elements of voice,
music, and physical movement.

   The practice of recombining extant images into compilation films is nearly as old
as the cinema itself. Jay Leyda recounts how in 1898 Lumière cameraman Francis
Doublier constructed a version of the Dreyfus affair by connecting a series of generic
shots—an army parade, a street scene, a government building, and so on—none of
which actually referred to the "depicted" events.[19] It is possible to conclude from this
story that manipulation of found footage originates in a perceived absence, in the attempt to make visible an idea or meaning latent in the original material but to which
it is necessarily blind. A particular kind of absence, the socially conscious reception
of black viewers, is crucial to the compilation pieces of Tony Cokes. *Black Celebration*
(1988) brings together news clips of police and National Guard troops suppressing the

1967 uprisings in black urban ghettos. The visual text for this video, itself derived from an earlier gallery installation, is stripped of its familiar rhetoric by the use of repetition, slow-motion, and the superimposition of politically militant speeches. Following the corporate logo for "Universal Pictures," a matrix of shots of burning stores, soldiers on patrol, arrests, and confrontations between angry residents and occupying forces are shuttled into various configurations as printed titles and disjunctive voice-overs address the events as "A Rebellion against Commodity." Statements about the social effects of consumerism by artists such as Morrisey, Barbara Kruger, and Martin L. Gore, are initially heard as spontaneous voices of ghetto rebels, but as the tape proceeds they emerge as a highly diverse chorus challenging the unvoiced, official explanations of urban unrest.

The looping of scenes destabilized by the counterauthority of speeches (plus music) has a dual purpose. It demands that we "look again," re-viewing the coded media spectacle of "rioters" and "peace-keepers." It also summons an aesthetic awareness of the grim beauty of human suffering gathered in a rich video glaze of dark tones and ominous gestures. In addition, the formal rigor of repetition is freighted with larger implications of historical redundancy, the accumulating onslaught of racially reductive images, as well as brutal physical acts, and the simmering resistance they provoke. *Black Celebration* has a superficial resemblance to the avant-garde style known as structural film; however, its affect of barely suppressed rage against both social and image-making formations creates a marked separation from the latter's reflexive investigations of cinematic properties.

In *Fade to Black* (1991), Cokes again reworks scenes taken from mass media representations of African Americans through an overlay of printed statements, music, and speech. A chronological parade of demeaning Hollywood stereotypes and revisionist portrayals starts with *Uncle Tom's Cabin* (1903) and concludes with a swipe at Spike Lee's *Do the Right Thing* (1989), an image from which is juxtaposed against a subtitle claiming "I do not see the strong black women who raised me anywhere in this film." Hollywood's record of "framing" black characters is evoked and called into question in a tripartite visual field: shots seemingly recorded off a television screen are sandwiched between titles and dates at the top of the frame and printed first-person comments at the bottom. For example, brief prologue images from *Vertigo* are underscored by the question "What does this mean to me?" Later, a scene from *To Kill a Mockingbird* elicits the indictment "Chained? Framed? You know what I mean?" Cokes plays off cinema's capacity for multiple, discordant sources of knowledge—sound/image and text/image collisions—to "talk back" to commercialized representations of race.

On the densely textured soundtrack, music by N.W.A., Byrne-Eno, The Last Poets, and other groups is interspersed with textual excerpts from Jesse Jackson, Malcolm X, and Marxist philosopher Louis Althusser, who elucidates his concept of "hailing" or ideological interpellation. A summary statement of Cokes's polemic against the deceptions of Hollywood cinema, by black as well as white directors, appears near the end: "I ask why the discourse of my enemies should dictate my actions and perceptions." By including a postscript from Malcolm, "You'll be a slave as long as you're responsible and respectable," the videomaker challenges the usefulness of polite, distanced cultural analysis. His visual technique is insistently awkward, a low-tech history lesson that refuses the cloak of disinterested critique, substituting instead the perspective of an active, outraged subject of Althusser's "state ideological apparatus."

A more elliptical handling of found materials is offered by Lawrence Andrews in *An I for an I* (1987). Several shots from *Rambo: First Blood II* (1985) and a Leon Kennedy prison movie are wedged into a diverse orchestration of enacted scenes, interviews, and diarylike shots of domestic routines, buttressed by an assortment of sync-sound and contrapuntal sound units. Andrews makes a personal descent into the social mythology and pathology of male action tropes, with the role of black masculinity highlighted as simultaneous paradigm and demonized Other.[20] Icons of media violence are adduced as agents in an internalized regime of black machismo and internecine hostility. A jarring yet thematically coherent stream of vignettes assays linkages between the mass-cultural landscape of brutality, self-defeating standards of phallic toughness among black men, and the seepage of physical domination into erotic encounters. The most powerful image is a closeup of a man being repeatedly punched in the stomach over the spoken refrain, "Again; harder," the double-edged meaning of the act amplified by ambiguity over whether it is being performed in real time or looped in the editing room. A metaphor for inner-directed feelings of frustration and anger, meshed with a homoerotic attraction to physical pain, this image is posed rhythmically against unmistakably looped shots of Rambo wielding a machine gun cut against repeated shots of an explosion.

In another closeup, a kitchen knife is slapped again and again on a bare hand, recasting the punching episode into a grisly charade of sexual intercourse. Here as elsewhere, a pulsing exchange of diegetic movements and found footage expresses the distorted process of internalizing cultural definitions of self. Sensationalized models of male potency, through which and against which all men in our society define their outward demeanors, are addressed in their specific impact on African Americans. Andrews charts his own immersion in a realm of coded masculine images yet refrains from the fervid condemnations delivered by Cokes. As antidote, his elusive polyrhythmic editing of visual materials counters the dull thud of media bravado with brief moments of domestic and creative activity, including shots of cooking and a hand playing an African thumb piano. It is in such gestures, positioned as beyond the grip of prior, stultifying representation, that we glimpse a potential for individual resistance.

Subtitled "a personal journey through black identity," Marlon Riggs's *Black Is . . . Black Ain't* (1995) was shot and partially edited toward the end of his long battle with AIDS and was completed posthumously. Riggs's early films are relatively straightforward documentaries, and even after his formal breakthrough in *Tongues Untied* he continued to alternate between mainstream histories (e.g., *Color Adjustment*, 1991) and more experimental projects *(Non, je regrette rien*, 1992). *Black Is* is something of a hybrid, a documentary essay with avant-garde leanings, comparable in certain respects to Yvonne Rainer's feminist collage narratives. In a manner similar to that of Lawrence Andrews and others, Riggs gathers an array of disparate thematic elements and styles in exploring multiple, at times antithetical, views of African American subjectivity. Making common cause with an antiessentialist slant in recent cultural theory, he interrogates the notion of blackness as a transcendent, replete signifier of selfhood.[21] Through pointed juxtaposition of interviews, found footage, and dramatic or performative interludes, Riggs develops the idea that even as a historically specific response to racism, there can be no single "authentic" version or marker of black identity. He surveys a spectrum of individual components, from gender and sexual orientation to physical attributes (e.g., skin tone and hair texture), class divisions, and the cultural imperative of Afrocentrism—none of which, he maintains, deserves a privileged or unitary status in the calculus of identity. The argument is not solely or specifically with dominant social constructions but focuses on myopic exclusions or divisive myths nurtured by black communities.

In *Tongues Untied,* Riggs laments the secondary marginalization of gay men by the repressive sermonizing of fundamentalist churches, as well as homophobic stand-up comedy routines perpetrated by the likes of Eddie Murphy. Where *Tongues* employs a simple counterpoint of demeaning stereotype and queer self-assertion—provocation answered by artistic bonding—*Black Is* builds a complex and nuanced dialectic. For instance, Riggs rehashes the European tradition of depicting blackness as moral negation, then finds a putative response in the 1960s slogan "Black Is Beautiful." He then goes on to show how despite its emancipatory appeal, Black Power spokesmen marginalized women, as Angela Davis maintains, through "the rehabilitation of black patriarchy." Employing a similar tactic of admitting positive effects of liberatory movements then exposing their limitations, Riggs applauds the black church as instrumental in civil rights organizing but decries its homophobic policies, citing activist Bayard Rustin's concealment of his sexuality as a cogent illustration. This line of inquiry is then capped by a joyful gospel congregation in Los Angeles that welcomes homosexual parishioners, resolving in a historical montage the apparent contradiction between black religion and gay liberation.

In each miniessayistic sequence, Riggs is intent on creating connections between past and present that are grounded in the poetic retelling of his own life history. A schoolboy says in an interview that knowledge of history is overrated, that what counts are contemporary mass-mediated models of success. In its validation of historical continuity within diversity, *Black Is* rebuts the hedonism encountered in several street-hardened kids. As the title suggests, the dilemma of defining black identity—tied to but not synonymous with political empowerment—is rooted in discursive practices. If the problem of hierarchical conceptions of identity is compounded by divisive or exclusionary language (and visual representations), the solution is to forge a more heterogeneous, inclusive racial discourse. In *Tongues Untied,* the process of articulating twin markers of blackness and homosexuality was emblematized by subcultural idioms of vogueing and "Snap!" Here the master trope adopted by Riggs is the *gumbo,* a favorite childhood dish cooked up in brief segments over the duration of the work. In form as well as theme, *Black Is* embraces a host of different stylistic ingredients, economic and social as well as personal signifiers of identity. The gumbo metaphor embodies in a single, slowly evolving image a framework for the goal of "communal selfhood" advocated by Riggs. In this melding of form and didactic function, the familiar strategy of postmodern pastiche is invigorated, redeemed by a lucid, celebratory urgency.

What distinguishes *Black Is* from other recent personal documentaries—the films of Ross McElwee come to mind—is the profusion of cinematic roles Riggs is able to embody. Befitting his conception of fluid identity, Riggs switches from interviewer to interviewee, from performer (e.g., a wonderful, painful songfest of African American music) to commentator, anchoring individual sections with voice-over introductions and transitions. He casts himself as various literal and symbolic characters: artist, child, friend, scholar, PWA (person with AIDS). We see him in and out of the hospital and in and out of chronological time, gravely ill in one shot, cavorting in the woods in the following shot. Thus a personal horizon of mortality, and of autobiographical closure, haunts but also empowers the convergence of personal with social-historical problems. The film acquires a singular poignancy both in the recognition that its maker will not live to complete the work and that his ongoing creative labors are helping to keep him alive. Broached as an experimental investigation of the variables of self-naming, it stands as a last will and testament, a literal bequest whose generosity and communal spirit is, to say the least, inspirational.

Performing the Self: Allegories and Psychodramas

For artists such as Riggs and Lawrence Andrews, the use of visual and aural quotation and the dialogic splitting of sound/image unity is not, or not simply, a plank in the (post)modernist aesthetic agenda of fragmentation. Rather, quotation, repetition, and the preeminence of human speech in rhythmic structures are etched with affinities to non-European and indigenous black performance traditions. In a discussion of formal techniques in African American literature, James Snead points to the use of "circulative" iteration as derivative of African music and dance more than of modernist practices of repetition.[22] One can draw a similar inference from recurrent patterns in experimental film and video, where the emphasis is not on progressive development of phrases leading to a structural or thematic resolution but on a continuous texture of differing beats that together map a sequence of choral changes. Alternatively, visual systems governed by parallel editing can evoke an antiphonic call-and-response familiar to blues stomps and gospel music.

In the same vein, reworked quotations of found imagery can suggest culturally specific improvisational techniques having little to do with the aims of modernist collage—for example, the jazz soloist's treatment of standard melodies in a way that alters their original flow and, hence, their identification with sentimental platitudes. Leah Gilliam deploys clusters of jazzlike visual riffs in *Sapphire and the Slave Girl* (1995), a vibrant contribution to an emerging cinematic idiom of intertextual polyphony. Acted, spontaneously recorded, and recycled scenes are layered around a double exercise in urban detection. The crux of the enigma invoked by Gilliam is how women subjectively navigate a tough Chicago neighborhood and the liberating potential of female disguise.

Brief excepts from a 1959 British mystery film, *Sapphire*—about the murder of a young black woman passing for white in elite society—set off an intricate play of naming and concealment. "Sapphire" was a common appellation for mulatto women that figures obliquely in Willa Cather's 1940 novel, *Sapphira and the Slave Girl,* a romantic story with lesbian overtones about a jealous wife (Sapphira) and a light-skinned servant. Both the British film and the American novel turn on problems of assimilation and the "scandal" of interracial coupling.

Gilliam inverts while prismatically filtering the allegory of passing in white society to encompass transgendered as well as transracial social confusions. Variables of personal identity are thematized, displaced onto urban architectures—three sections are labeled "Networks," "Buildings," and "Open Spaces"—and mirrored in the formal design. As a TV voice-over complains, "Just tell me the name of the genre so I know the rules." The composite identity of "Sapphire" is assumed by five very different-looking women; the figure is at once an "undercover" agent gathering clues and the object of (self-)investigation. This elusive heroine oscillates in her relationship with the outside world between an alienated loner stuck inside a drab apartment and a member of a secretive cadre of streetwise, militant women.

At one point in her decentered trek through an inner-city neighborhood, she switches clothing in a narrow alley, assuming the costume of a businessman or 1940s private eye. The adoption of wigs and fashions from several decades, from Black Panther leather to call girl to bohemian, is animated by a soundtrack blending original jazz with excerpts from Latin American and other ethnic music. In a telling insertion of found footage, a white reporter tries to interview a black girl at a bus stop during the attempted integration of Little Rock Central High School. Her mixture of fear and defiance, positioned against the contemporary dilemma of women in a hostile environment, acts as both historical contrast and reminder of the power of silence as a form of masking. The uncertain focus of pursuit in Gilliam's video, coupled with its views of a deracinated urban landscape, hints at a feminist rereading of Poe's "A Man of the Crowd." It is as if Sapphire, the woman in the B-movie mystery whose romantic life (and death) hinged on a slippage in racial perception, had been transformed into a proactive version of the outcast woman.

Sapphire and the Slave Girl is one of the few experimental works that does not feature a strong vocal performance. In Gilliam's muted rite of female passage, musical improvisation and rhythmic movements of walking take on the subjective weight frequently accorded to speech. The significance of the artist's direct voice, or the voice of a surrogate figure, in black film and video cannot be overestimated. Although the technical and financial ease of video voice recording are clearly important, the centrality of spoken performance is rooted in populist oral traditions, in an aesthetic realm that in contrast to image composition appears less overdetermined by conditions of mass culture. In this sense, voice, and sound in general, is posed in virtual opposition to the cult of image "purity" maintained by earlier avant-garde initiatives. Thus the ideal of a silent cinema dedicated exclusively to visual cadence and affective qualities of the image, exemplified by the practice and writings of Stan Brakhage, appears irrelevant to black experimentalists. Silence, or for that matter subordinate musical accompaniment, does not seem a viable option insofar as it limits the expressive range and cultural specificity of self-inscription as realized in a variety of performative tropes.[23]

Black film and video's invocation of role-playing, verbal storytelling, song, and poetic recitation remains grounded in autobiographical impulses, the desire to re-create one's own story rather than rehearse the stories of others. Just as stress on vocalization in black cinema stipulates an embodied rather than an optical arena of subjectivity, an insistence on first-person narrative separates this work from the avant-garde's parodic engagement with Hollywood performance styles—as in films by Andy Warhol and George Kuchar. The prerogatives of autobiographical performance, especially its ability to juggle inner and external histories, are most clearly defined in a group of videos that reenact or allegorically portray childhood traumas of identity. In *Flag* (1989), Linda Gibson revisits the emotional disturbance produced by her early fascination with patriotic symbols and rituals. She assembles a patchwork of scenes around discrepancies between democratic rhetoric and the reality of racial exclusion, mingling a child's diary entries, stills and home movies, printed texts, street inter-views with people attempting to define the meaning of the American flag, and a med-ley of physical routines in which idiosyncratic dance movements collide with stylized variations on saluting. *Flag* flickers with the uncertainties of memory, the evocation of a child's credulous view of equality tempered by an adult knowledge of social hierar-chy and oppression. As in *Black Is,* Gibson formally renders the principle of collective correspondence within diversity, reclaiming the youthful vitality of unfettered toler-ance as an ideal of creative arrangement.

An adolescent's dawning awareness of class boundaries is rendered in Cheryl Dunye's wry memento, *Janine* (1990), about the videomaker's crush on a private school class-mate. The tangled desires of same-sex interracial romance are verbally recalled as catalysts of transformation, at once cause and effect of a crisis of identity (a similar di-lemma is probed from a male perspective in *Tongues Untied*). Dunye's anecdote unfolds in a playfully self-deprecating voice reinforced by stills, printed texts, and isolated shots of fetishistic objects such as candles and a carnival keepsake. As in *Flag,* subjectivity alternates between the emotional orientation of childhood and a more cautious, reflec-tive framework of social knowledge. What Dunye describes as a painful awakening is couched by her mother as a "problem" requiring medical intervention. Refusing to wallow in accusation or guilt, Dunye manages to at once lament the loss of naïve trust and reproach the exercise of class privilege.

The erotic psychodrama, in which the filmmaker, or an obvious stand-in, enacts a liberatory quest for sexual self-recognition, is among the earliest and most durable genres in American avant-garde cinema, connecting the groundbreaking films of Maya Deren and Kenneth Anger in the 1940s to contemporary practitioners such as Sadie Benning and Peggy Ahwesh.[24] Several formal and thematic aspects of the psycho-dramatic legacy have been revitalized in black experimental cinema as conduits for the statement and symbolic resolution of sexual anxieties as they intersect the social reckoning of otherness. Typically, a film/videomaker's revelatory self-exposure in front of the camera incites a double-edged confrontation with a prior moment of sexual confusion. Declarations of erotic longing are frequently visualized in metaphors of death and rebirth, in oneiric condensations of action, or in the magical display of threatening or benevolent supernatural figures.

Thomas Allen Harris's *Heaven, Earth and Hell* (1994), for example, embellishes an oracular journey of first love, rejection, and bereavement with costumed figures taken from African and Native American cosmologies. Harris himself assumes several mythic roles in a narrative fluctuating between autobiographical detail and dreamlike rituals. *Splash* (1991) has an even stronger affinity with the psychodrama's allegorical search for sexual meaning. Here Harris erects a fantasy of sadomasochistic frustration through a trope of entrapped desire, with the protagonist emoting from a literal cage. This externalized mechanism of sexual repression is traced by the speaker to society's compulsory standards of whiteness and heterosexuality.[25]

Although hardly the exclusive terrain of women and gay men, the psychodrama has proven an especially useful vehicle for questioning forbidden, or merely devalued, sites of social bonding. Zeinabu Irene Davis's *Cycles* (1989) and Julie Dash's *Praise House* (1991) share a similar regard for the significance of spiritual customs as consolation for the uncertainties and degradations of menial labor and domesticity. Davis draws from Caribbean folklore to inflect her protagonist's anxious anticipation of menses, an event made more acute by the possible abandonment of a romantic partner. The editing scheme juxtaposes talismanic objects with prosaic tasks of housecleaning and bathing, imbuing the female body's cyclical evacuation and regeneration with an aura of ancient fertility rites. Through the rhythmic alternation of enacted scenes of female isolation and solidarity, a secularized ordeal of ritual seclusion from the outside world is superimposed onto the modern subject's demand for change and self-definition.

Praise House, a collaboration with the performance group Urban Bush Women, lends a sinuous visionary stamp to an intergenerational parable of familial conflict, rebellion, and spiritual reconciliation. Abstracted movements of women's everyday work, shown in factory as well as domestic caretaking situations, are elaborated as the premise and processual backbone of creative expression. As women of various ages and attitudes filter in and out of a single communal dwelling, their brief exchanges of nurture and hostility are invested with wider significance by allusions to African and Southern ceremonial beliefs: corporeal inhabitation by spirits, the gift of "second sight," ecstatic gestures of flight and bodily yearning. The central relationship concerns a young girl's attachment to her dying grandmother and her refusal to accept the authority of a haggard woman, either an older sister or her mother. A fusion of dance, musical speech, and dramatic mime, *Praise House* unearths a rarely addressed internecine struggle for a balance between connexity and individual freedom.

Stylized performance as a natural product of female interaction is treated in a context devoid of unconscious or spiritual imagery in Cheryl Dunye's *She Don't Fade* (1991). In this reflexive gloss on how to filmically stage an explicit sexual encounter from a nonpornographic perspective, the psychodrama's ambivalent tracking of identity is transmuted into a playful round of personal confession, storytelling, and the mechanics of lesbian lovemaking. The actors, including Dunye herself, are understandably self-conscious about performing in semiscripted sexual scenes. The director does not try to hide but rather foregrounds this discomfort, exposing the mutual reticence that pervades any dynamic of sexual compliance and resistance, encompassing gnarly protocols and shifts of dominance otherwise known as the throes of seduction. The byplay between what is enacted on screen and how it is perceived, the slippage between "actor" and "spectator," mirrors as it displaces the groping of onscreen couples. The result is an incisive commentary on our multiple, attenuated expectations for sexual completion.[26]

Working once again in the gap between psychodrama and subcultural documentation, Dunye rehearses the issue of performance as vehicle of self-validation in *The Potluck and the Passion* (1993). Her explicit theme is group tensions and the personal disclosures unleashed by social role-playing. During a dinner party celebrating the anniversary of a lesbian couple, female guests improvise a series of conversations exposing unexamined attitudes toward friendship, jealousy, work, and interethnic identification. Romantic clichés and blind spots concerning lesbian relationships, prompted by a character's visual appearance or speech, are undercut by various instances of petty dissimulation. The dinner party begins to feel more like a skirmish than a sapphic idyll and, of course, that's the point. Held together by a series of comic vignettes featuring the entire party or pairs of guests, *Potluck* trips lightly through a minefield of submerged prejudice. By the end, this multiracial microcosm of assertive women has dredged up quite a bit of surprising psychic baggage. Direct talking-head interviews further annotate an individual character's possessiveness, diffidence, or smug assumptions of cultural cohesion. The interplay of fictive roles and fake cinéma vérité recording is further complicated by the insertion of found-footage fragments of a cartoon mammy and of Josephine Baker performing onstage—two disparate yet problematic versions of black female masquerade, at once images for potential identification and disavowal.

Cauleen Smith activates a very different approach to performance in *Sapphire Tape #1: The Message* (1994), a dramatized critique of ghettocentric images of black masculinity ("The Message" is also the title of an influential early hip hop record). A bare-chested man stalks around an apartment drinking and smoking, looking every inch the prototypical "gangsta." A woman's offscreen voice is attempting to direct and control, or perhaps simply describe, his movements while speculating on the theatricalization of male power and gender threat. The question of whether the man is acting or being recorded spontaneously is never fully resolved, but in either case the voice-over seems to emanate from a space outside the action. Hand-held camera movements caress the man's body, creating a dance of mutual attraction and withdrawal. However, a looped repetition of shots, poses, and glances undercuts both the ostensible unity of performance and the viewer's ability to sort out formal masks of dominance and submission.

Splitting voice from image, language from bodily performance, Smith inverts and destabilizes a common division in gendered authority: the male agent of knowledge versus the female object of scrutiny. However, in the context of black experimental cinema, her critical gesture of disarticulation also underscores the degree to which vocalization figures as an index of subjective presence. Frequently, the voice is presented as an instrument of abstract, rhythmic sound as well as semantic content, a necessary synthesis of body movement and language. The imagination of an aesthetic discourse in which speech, song, and musical sounds shift positions and overlap has been a focus of black American culture at least since the Harlem Renaissance, as demonstrated in the career of Langston Hughes. More recent, and perhaps more cogent, precedents for the use of musical speech in black cinema are the fusions of jazz and poetry promoted by the Black Arts Movement in the late 1960s and the related surge of singing and chanting in the cutting-edge music of Sun Ra, Cecil Taylor, and others. This legacy is particularly evident in the sound structures composed by Riggs, Cokes, Gilliam, and Lawrence Andrews.

In the loosely diaristic patterning of *and they came riding into town on BLACK AND SILVER HORSES* (1992), Andrews immerses the rhythmic qualities of African American vernacular speech in an ambivalent process of personal witnessing. A collection of what he refers to as "interchangeable verses" spirals outward from the testimony of a man who, by his own account, was wrongly convicted of a vicious mugging. Bracketing emotionally vexed verbal descriptions of crime with an officious talk on handgun safety, polemics on justice with poetic images of apocalypse, *BLACK AND SILVER HORSES* reminds us of the twin functions of testifying as personal expression and public evidence. The act of witnessing, removed from stock religious connotations of spiritual healing, dissolves in a tissue of negotiated truths in which the poisoned stream of commercial television simultaneously submerges and galvanizes memories of racial injustice (including references to dreams and textual citations from Aimé Césaire's "Notebook"). As Andrews bears witness to the unending conflation of black male experience with criminality, he transforms TV's official record by fragmenting, collaging, and condensing its repetitive messages; for instance, "Verse 12" delivers a skittering two-minute visual riff of "unedited" footage covering forty-eight hours of nonstop banality.

There is a final entry left in the catalogue of performance techniques and musical tropes employed by black experimentalists. The advent of hip hop culture in the early 1980s has furnished a major impetus for the structuring of sound—and to a lesser extent, visuals—in recent videos. The low-tech, improvised mixture of beats, street language, and sampling pioneered by Grandmaster Flash anticipates some of the effects of abrupt rhythmic and tonal shifts in the work of Riggs, Cokes, and especially Art Jones. In addition, the electronic sound mixing executed by rappers can be roughly analogized to graphic manipulations of video images by color solarization, split screen, and other denaturing devices. Jones's *Know Your Enemy* (1990) and *Knowledge Reigns Supreme* (1991) are, for lack of a better term, deconstructive music videos celebrating the second, politically militant phase of rap music. In *Enemy,* whose title makes a play on the overtly racist army indoctrination films of World War II and the Vietnam invasion, Public Enemy members Chuck D and Harry Allen are interviewed using a Pixelvision toy camera answering charges of anti-Semitic lyrics in their record "Welcome to the Terrordome." Jones studs their remarks with short excerpts from Malcolm X, Huey P.

Newton, Eldridge Cleaver, and Angela Davis, suggesting historical continuities between 1960s activists and current rap groups. The persistent question "Who is the enemy?" is framed within a dynamics of media distortion of black cultural politics. *Knowledge* is essentially a portrait of rapper KRS-One (Chris Parker) inveighing against the depredations of a Eurocentric educational system and racist news reporting. In both tapes, Jones employs an aggressively coarse visual style that undermines the polished look of commercial music videos. Reviving and totally subverting the tenets of spontaneous vérité documentary recording, he extends the arena of personal performance to embrace gritty textures and jarring movements of a defiantly untutored camera style.

Coda: Re-Taking the Past

By any measure, the career of William Greaves is nothing less than remarkable, and it has been remarkably undervalued. He began as a stage actor and was featured in several films made in the late 1940s by black directors; he also had a starring role in "March of Time" producer Louis de Rochemont's Hollywood "problem film," *Lost Boundaries* (1949). Sparked by the postwar social realism of semidocumentary productions—along with his disgust with the entertainment industry's exclusionary practices—Greaves moved to Canada where, from 1952 to 1960, he worked in several creative niches at the National Film Board on nearly eighty films, including the first North American cinéma vérité documentaries. Upon returning to the United States, he undertook an impressive series of nonfiction projects for various government agencies and public television. These include biographies of Frederick Douglass, Booker T. Washington, and Ida B. Wells. From 1968 to 1970, Greaves served as executive producer and cohost of NET's seminal series *Black Journal*. He went on to direct the controversial portrait *Ali, the Fighter* (1971).

In 1968, with money obtained from a private patron, he shot nearly seventy hours of footage for a projected five-part series of experimental narratives revolving around a single directorial provocation: the heated argument of a married couple over the husband's infidelity and their dimming prospect of having children. Five different couples, recruited from the ranks of seasoned New York stage actors, improvised their way through repeated takes of the same basic scene staged at different locations in Central Park. The premise was that not only the dramatic scenes but the filming process itself, complete with off-camera instructions and creative discussions, would be recorded and woven into the finished work. What emerged from this adventure in reflexivity and demystification was *Symbiopsychotaxiplasm: Take One*. Greaves screened an initial cut of the film for potential distributors, who were thoroughly perplexed, after which it was shelved. *Take One* was finally dusted off in 1991 for a retrospective of Greaves's work at the Brooklyn Museum of Art and has since played to receptive audiences and admiring reviews at film festivals and private screenings. In 1995, Greaves recut several sections, adding footage from other "takes."[27]

This brief note on the genesis of *Take One* omits two absolutely crucial details. Having assembled a racially diverse, mixed-gender crew of veteran documentary techni-

William Greaves on the set of *Symbiopsychotaxiplasm: Take One*. Photograph courtesy of the filmmaker.

cians, Greaves encouraged their collective creative input, an opening that resulted in what the director refers to as a "palace revolt." Frustrated over the progress of shooting and what they felt was a lack of coherent structure, the crew met privately to voice their discontent ("We're just sittin around here and are gonna just rap about the film"). Loose visual notes of several meetings were shown to Greaves, who then happily inserted them into the emerging design via parallel editing or split-screen effects. In addition to these sidebars, which nearly swamp the dramatic core, the crew shot spontaneous vignettes with assorted intruders and passersby, of which the most telling are a subdued confrontation with a cop demanding to see a city filming permit and the scatological ranting of a homeless denizen of Central Park. In a continuous series of slippages and outright abdications of creative authority, it is this figure, the thoroughly addled "Victor," who assumes the role of tertiary chorus, providing sly metacommentary on both the film's method of production and its dramatized battle of the sexes. In retrospect, the exchange of power is pure artifice, a function of discursive self-exposure; as Greaves puts it, "The film had to be chaos, but chaos of a very special character, *intelligible* chaos."[28]

As a summary restatement of the political and aesthetic ambitions of 1960s alternative cinema and street theater, *Take One* taps into utopian energies seeping from such signal interventions as Happenings, the ritualistic improvisations of the Living Theater, and the theatricalized spectacles of antiwar demonstrations (e.g., the attempted "levitation" of the Pentagon during the November 1967 March on Washington). There is as well a critical engagement with aspects of traditional theater, with roots in the sort of domestic drama associated with Ibsen or Chekhov but played out against the backdrop of countercultural imperatives of setting and theme. *Take One* refracts, and makes important contributions to, many of the period's leading cultural controversies: the philosophical dialogue between theater and cinema, between scripted and spontaneous behavior; the relationship of new forms of realism to stylized conventions; the inter-determining processes of individual and collective liberation. As in other late-sixties revisions of cinéma vérité performance, including *David Holzman's Diary* (1968) and *Gimme Shelter* (1971), Greaves ruptures the fiction/nonfiction dichotomy of means and terms of address. His scattershot yet rationalized dismantling of aesthetic boundaries propels *Take One* into the roiling climate of critique of power and repressive control, securing a place on the decade's roster of radical cinema alongside the work of Warhol, Godard, Jack Smith, Jacques Rivette, Chris Marker, and Dusan Makavejev. Interestingly, Greaves refers to his overall procedure as a "screen test" (the same term exploited by Warhol), understanding the offhand/directed uncertainties of his approach as encapsulating the era's rebellious attitudes toward authority.[29]

If *Take One* celebrates its historical moment in a clarifying jolt of invention, it also begs connection to a double trajectory pertinent to the primary concerns of this essay. Greaves's project can be construed as a bridge between the independent directorial tradition of Spencer Williams and Oscar Micheaux—directors often revered for their visual and narrative infractions of commercial codes—and a current generation of black experimentalists. By the same token, *Take One* underscores affinities between earlier modes of avant-garde cinema—spanning the metadocumentary excursions of Jonas Mekas and the self-destructing spectacles of Smith, Ron Rice, and George Kuchar—and the achievements of Riggs, Dunye, Andrews, and their cohort.[30]

Greaves's densely chaotic text is clearly prescient in its organization and production methods, but what makes the film a political beacon is the way in which its core social issues prefigure the current identitarian landscape. One of the first lines delivered by the character "Freddy," following a short precredit sequence, ignites an underlying tension: "You're telling me the name of the game is sexuality?" His wife, "Alice," accuses him of being a "faggot" because he won't fuck her in a "normal" way. Her comment sets in motion an intermittent series of accusations, confessions, and equivocations about sexual stereotypes that leaps from dramatic scenes to conversations between the actors and then with the director, finally resurfacing in the crew's private gripe sessions. This seemingly impromptu theme is finally reconfigured in the lewd spoutings of interloper Victor. A crew member expresses his disgust with what he views as the contrived nature of the enacted argument: "This isn't Edward Albee . . . This dialogue [about the nature of gender roles] is prescribed from birth." Reiterating the contention that sexuality is a function of nature rather than a social construct, another crew member blatantly reveals his homophobia during an exchange about whether Freddy could possibly be gay. Victor's final word on the topic of romantic attraction has a convoluted logic befitting the sexual ambiguity of his own outrageous performance: "Love is the feeling of a penis for a cunt."

Take One is organized like a hall of mirrors ("You know Alice, you're really talking in circles") with one level of filmic reality returning and intensifying cracks and contradictions evident in another level. As Victor puts it, "What is this thing? Oh, it's a *movie*... so who's moving whom?" Power relations veiled by personal prescriptions of gender difference, sexuality, and race are framed by psychodramatic excesses inherent in the original scripted scene. The film's thematic sinew is gathered around acknowledgment, dismissal, or casual denigration of human diversity. Without ever acquiring the thud of didacticism, this problem keeps pulsing near the center of every benignly corrective or irreducibly hostile confrontation. If the film maps an undulating terrain of inquiry enlivened by pressing controversies in our more recent social discourse, its unanticipated rescue from the coils of obscurity should remind us of the tasks still to complete in the effort to historicize an important body of work in black experimental cinema.

(1999)

8 | Bodies, Language, and the Impeachment of Vision: The Avant-Garde at Fifty

In memory of Margie Keller

OT LONG AGO, AS BABY JANE HOLZER BRUSHED HER TEETH for three minutes in luminous close-up, I had what felt like a revelation. The occasion was a screening by Peggy Ahwesh, a prominent member of the post-seventies avant-garde cadre. Into a string of Super-8 rolls and short studies, she wedged two wonderful and arcane 100-foot Warhol screen tests, circa 1964. Gorgeous and clearly intended as something of a critical intervention, they joined in a single stroke current creative emphases on historical retrieval, the elevation of the aleatory fragment, and the rediscovery of the filmed body. Bracing as this gesture was, it was only the backdrop to a murkier, more visceral flash of recognition. In truth I have had such moments in other Warhol films; at their best, they generate eerie occasions for the experience of corporeality as a continuous loop of presence and absence. Here then was the wide-eyed Ms. Holzer slowly massaging her mouth into such a grinning erotic froth that my own jaw became inundated with fluid and my gums ached with longing.

As is the case with most film viewers, my bodily sensations have been mobilized in various ways—separate parts under disparate circumstances across a range of tactile and internal organs—but this was a first: an originary brush with a Cinema of Salivation. I realized that aside from being further testimony to the massive orality in Warhol's production,[1] this fleeting cavity of perception could provide access to a wider enterprise to which avant-garde film has come to devote an increasing share of its most vibrant energies. That is, in headlong retreat from presumptions of mastery, monumentality, closure, expressivity (the disavowed agenda is finite and well known), recent practitioners have been mapping a representational "black hole" in which certain traditional, affective powers of the medium are eschewed in deference to all that is ontologically *beyond* the reach of the movie image, a bundle of impulses that together reveal deep uncertainty about the adequacy of film and that question the avant-garde's habitual recourse to the trope of vision as truth—regardless of the provisional or flagrantly subjective cast of such figurations. With fifty years of individual and institutional achievement under its belt, the recent avant-garde appears willingly, vigorously entrapped in a sort of liar's paradox, pursuing traces of desires which ipso facto cannot be realized or, for the viewer, satisfied in film (or for that matter, video). It is the burden of this essay to, as it were, flesh out a few of the conceptual arenas in which this strange dialectic has flourished.[2]

The (Postmodern) Body as Evidence

Poet Robert Kelly begins a 1963 essay in *Film Culture* by remarking that "all along the film has made little of the body." He goes on to chastise commercial cinema for its excessive use of close-ups as a "principal means of evasion." While finding some solace in the silent comedies of Chaplin and Sennett, and reason for hope in Brakhage's early work—especially its home-movie affinity with the body as "untrained, awkward, palpably *present*"—he rails against "film's insistence on the soul-body dichotomy, with synecdoche as its formal expression," as an "oppressive affliction of the human spirit. And of spirit's flesh."[3] What Kelly had no way of knowing was that the period in which be wrote in fact constituted a high point in the avant-garde's mobilization of the physical, performative image-self, as instanced in films by Jack Smith, Ken Jacobs, Ron Rice, Carolee Schneeman, and others.

With the rise of structural film in the late sixties the body all but vanishes as primary object or ground of camera vision, displaced by attention to the apparatus itself. In the elaboration of a general project of minimalist reduction and reflexivity, the body appears as no more than a bit player in a drama of formulaic procedures and their spectatorial decoding, suppressed along with "problematic" elements of subjectivity, poetic tropism, and moment-to-moment decision making.[4] It is as if the famous forward zoom that sweeps over a collapsed Hollis Frampton midway through Michael Snow's *Wavelength* (1967) dissolved in its wake the body's function as organic metaphor, as spontaneous index of worldly experience, or as bearer of allegorical meaning.[5] To be sure, the peripatetic Frampton occasionally revived the performative body along his trail of filmic ruminations (e.g., *Critical Mass,* 1971), as did Owen Land and, for that matter, Snow himself, in *Rameau's Nephew by Diderot (Thanx to Dennis Young) by Wilma Schoen* (1974) and elsewhere.

Yvonne Rainer's work, from *Lives of Performers* (1972) on, poses both a corollary and a feminist challenge to structural film's erasure of the body, and it is for this reason an important touchstone for younger filmmakers, especially women. Rainer, in effect, recasts the centrality of the body as a fulcrum operating between personal psychic identities and socially constructed roles. Yet corporeal presence in her work is held, as it were, at arm's length and becomes progressively disjunctive as voices, objects, and written texts infiltrate and inflect the spaces surrounding the body. When the body makes a full-blown return in avant-garde films of the 1980s, it appears in more direct, behavioral guises but retains some of the skeptical analysis of authenticity advanced by Rainer. And it is underwritten by some of the same intellectual and aesthetic currents: feminist theory, multiculturalism, psychoanalysis, postmodern performance.

Given the critical reclamation of the avant-garde sector Jonas Mekas called "Baudelairean," in tandem with broader cultural and political forces at work in the eighties, renewed passion for imaging the body hooks into a number of different prerogatives. It must be positioned alongside the profusion of body-centered painting and sculpture, the impact of queer theory and AIDS activism, and various feminist anti-antipornography initiatives.[6] In contrast to the philosophical crux of New Narratives, recent body films are more libertarian in their representational strategies and less concerned with reforming the apparatus of storytelling in its legacy of Hollywood production. The body is largely offered as a text whose "language" and surface features, as inscribed by a plethora of social-historical agencies, can be reread through cinematic exposure but, just as important, they can be rewritten by individual and subcultural practices, from body-building and prosthetic devices to sadomasochistic sex to tattooing and piercing—all of which have received at least some attention in avant-garde film and video.

Since the early eighties, Peggy Ahwesh has staked out self-avowedly slippery frontiers toward a new geography cum gendered ethnography of the body. Many of her films adopt the casual, handheld look of home movies or outtakes from cinéma vérité. One group seems rooted in familiar domestic environments in which their subjects perform personal rituals, improvised for and with the camera, that have the urgency of quotidian events pushed to the edge of breakdown. Several are built around someone's behavioral tics or narrated anecdotes, in which a form of direct-address complicity is established with the "social actors," acknowledging vulnerability and power on both sides of the lens. As Ivone Margulies has perceptively argued, "Ahwesh's proposition is two-fold: how to rearticulate the promise of filmic reality (and truth) entailed in the use of documentary modes and confessional address; and how to avoid the essentialist trappings of a psychodramatic narrative of the self."[7]

Her choice of subjects stems from personal relationships with friends and family, and what takes place onscreen often maintains an edge of creepy intimacy mediated by a more generalized sense of social determination: for instance, the family, as an institution for regulating the activity of the body, nonetheless generates under the auspices of "play," of temporary exchange and mutability of roles, the possibility of subversion. *Ode to the New Pre-History* (1984-87), *Martina's Playhouse* (1989), and *Scary Movie* (1993) depict children as partially imprinted products of extensive socialization, especially in their awareness of sanctioned codes of gender and sexuality, whose supposedly spontaneous patterns of speech and acting-out reveal aspects—however nondidactic or even inchoate—of our adult pretenses to order and self-control. There is a strong undertow of "regressive" liminality, of modern tribal rites of passage, nurtured in the charade of dressing up. An unhinged condition of disguise (at times verbal but more often physical) situates fashion, plus the seductive behavior sanctioned by clothing, as a pervasive sexual masquerade, and a trope for our mottled projection of idealized selves against which the idea of "transvestism" is little more than a particularly vibrant manifestation of widespread impulses. Thus Ahwesh's children are vehicles for the kinds of slippages, especially those of language and performance, she adduces as evidence of anti-essentialist resistance. Rather than being depicted as psychic wellspring of, or as corrective to, a more authentic and natural identity (as in segments of Brakhage's work), kids become welded into a continuum of role-playing that also features pompous male intellectuals and toy dolls.

Children and dolls are a virtual shibboleth in the recent avant-garde scene. Leslie Thornton's *Peggy and Fred in Hell* cycle (1984–92), perhaps the movement's signal achievement of the last decade, Julie Zando's video *Let's Play Prisoners* (1988), and Su Friedrich's *Sink or Swim* (1990) all forge links between children as bearers of social coding and feminist perspectives on family dynamics.[8] In a related vein, dolls have figured as surrogate adult bodies and means by which to deflect or undercut vocal (patriarchal) authority in the work of Todd Haynes, Luther Price, Joe Gibbons, and others.[9] Dolls and children as sources of renewed body imagery share telling aesthetic, as well as technical, limitations. They circumvent directorial problems of mimetic

Peggy and Fred in Hell by Leslie Thornton. Photograph courtesy of the filmmaker.

performance associated with New Narratives, to say nothing of affording "cheap labor"; at the same time, they foster an unselfconscious inscription of subjectivity that is exempt from burdens of motivation or unconscious repression. Capable of "spontaneous" displays of sexuality, they are at least putatively understood as beyond the boundaries of scopophilic consumption by viewers.

For Ahwesh in particular, the body as locus of representational play brings with it the shadows of decay and mortality. Children perform skits of mayhem in *Scary Movie,* while in the semiscripted *The Deadman* (1989, made with Keith Sanborn), Georges Bataille's story of bodily transgression and sacrament serves as pretext for a cinematic confrontation with the two human states most burdened by social signification, yet paradoxically liberated from the controlling clutches of rational thought and regimented identity (hence ultimately opaque to representation): death and fucking. *The Deadman,* then, helps clarify one vector in the avant-garde's resuscitation of corporeality. The realm in which the body perforce recognizes its own existence—tactility, physical pain and pleasure—is precisely a realm that the cinema, in its strident visuality, is least capable of rendering.[10] And just here the recovery of Warhol's early work, in its relentless, *impossible* exhibitions of eating, kissing, fucking, smoking, drug taking, and bondage, sheds a stony light on current proclivities. Caught in a prisonhouse of male narcissism, Warhol constructs a world, as Stephen Koch persuasively argues, in which "forbidden emotion is given permission to emerge by virtue of the falsity of the role. Yet it is real emotion."[11] The principal difference between Warhol and younger-generation filmmakers is twofold: for the latter, earlier avant-garde psychodramas and cinéma vérité documentary, rather than Hollywood melodrama, are crucial intertexts; and, second, the dichotomy of "false" roles and "real emotion" is rejected in deference to a postmodern discourse of multiple, fluid social identities. The current avant-garde is, in its celebration of the body as potential last frontier of noncommodification, distinguishable from Hollywood's recent imaging of the body as locus of taboo and revulsion. But it is almost equally distanced from Warhol's—and certainly Jack Smith's—profound suspicion of interpersonal pleasure, as evident in their elaborate figurations of sexual approach and withdrawal.

Several additional points need to be made about the overall (anti)romance of the body. First is that for a number of filmmakers, including Ahwesh, Price, Lewis Klahr, MM Serra, Pelle Lowe, and Greta Snider, the appropriation and reworking of actual images from pornography, or the restaging of its typical mise-en-scène, is a signpost for an erotics of "different desiring" as well as a jab of cultural resistance in a reactionary sexual climate.[12] Part of the attraction has to do with porn's status as marginal or "disreputable" genre, similar in effect to the recycling of obscure scientific documentaries in the work of Thornton, Julie Murray, et al. Explicit sexual acts serve as yet another paradigm of depsychologized, solipsistic performance. Commercial porn imagery may be set against personalized conditions of reception, as in Lowe's *nor* (1989), where a man shown masturbating in front of a cheap video is trapped in a weird triangulation of gazes—camera, actor, and TV image. Frequently, an underlying reproach of commercial porn's ideology of domination is introduced through recontextualization or aesthetic disruption. In Ahwesh's *The Color of Love* (1994), a piece of hilariously sadistic porn is nearly obliterated by chemical deterioration on the strip, summoning an unappetizing connection between the film's morbid body and that of its representational scene.

It should be stressed that, despite the impact of continental theory upon younger avant-gardists, the conceit of filmic apparatus as human body owes little if anything to the writings of Baudry, Comolli, and others; indeed, it might be better understood as an artisanal qualification of so-called apparatus theory in which sense organs and the responses they elicit occupy the position, held by academic theory, of psychoperceptual or unconscious processes.[13] Foregrounding the filmstrip as labile, quasi-organic material has historical loots in Brakhage's direct application of paint, dye, scratches, and so forth during the sixties. But unlike Brakhage's metaphors on vision, the tactics of filmmakers such as Ahwesh, Klahr, Phil Solomon, Roger Jacoby, and the silt collective are not geared to express inner subjective states but simply to mobilize sensory impressions through optical experience. Where structural film posed analogues for the filmstrip, camera aperture, or lens by recuriting images of nature or architectural form—e.g., in Paul Sharits's *S:TREAM:S.S.ECTION:S.ECTION:S:S:ECTIQNED* (1968–71), a running brook is posed as isomorphic with the mechanical flow of the projector—many recent films run the equation in the opposite direction. In Solomon's *Remains to Be Seen* (1989), personalized optical printing techniques transform the image surface into granular, reticulated clumps, suggesting properties of human skin, dried leaves, the undulating glaze of a wind-whipped lake. The celluloid skin is granted a "transparently" erotic dimension in Klahr's *Her Fragrant Emulsion* (1987), a found-footage portrait of actress Mimsy Farmer in which chemically altered and recombined shots from a semiexploitation movie seem to burst their confinement on the strip, creating a palpably heated dance of bodily image and mechanism.

Nowhere is the mining of the apparatus for tactile illusions more graphically or spectacularly realized than in Ken Jacobs's amazing "Nervous System" performances, especially *XCXHXEXRXRXIXEXSX* (1980) and *Two Wrenching Departures* (1989). Jacobs describes the basic method of these pieces as follows:

> two nearly identical prints on two projectors capable of single-frame advance and "freeze," turning the movie back into a series of closely related slides. The twin prints plod through the projectors, frame . . . by . . . frame, in various degrees of synchronization. Most often there's only a single frame difference. Difference makes for movement and uncanny three-dimensional space illusions.[14]

He goes on to define his pursuit as "poetry of motion, time/motion studies touched and shifted with a concern for how things feel, to open up fresh territory for sentient exploration." *XCXHXERXRXIXEXSX* transforms several minutes of a French porn short circa 1920 into a poundingly inclusive sex machine in which onscreen enactments are decentered and reciprocated by awareness of Jacobs's improvisations at the projector

Her Fragrant Emulsion by Lewis Klahr. Photograph courtesy of the filmmaker.

and by the wide latitude of effects (both optical and kinesthetic) available in individual viewer responses.

As in *Tom, Tom, the Piper's Son* (1969–71), the flipping or dissolution of figure/ground relationships unleashes latent shapes that suggest an entire inventory of Western painting styles, from van Ruisdael landscapes through Courbet, Impressionism, and Abstract Expressionism. But undeniably, this metahistorical romp is secondary to the mechanoerotic massage. The exchange of single frames is unveiled metaphorically as a copulation whose stuttering progression binds as it liberates one extended moment in continuous paroxysms of surprise, pleasure, and overstimulated irritation. In obliterating or radically retarding the already minimal masks of conventional temporality, character, setting, and event, Jacobs allows us to bask in the thumping heat behind every cinematic transaction.

The performative body is urged along a somewhat different circuitry in *Two Wrenching Departures,* a danse macabre conducted with and over "buried" footage of two deceased friends, filmmakers Jack Smith and Bob Fleischner. The exaggerated gyrations that Smith in particular, through the machinations of single-frame advance, is forced to execute tug in two directions simultaneously: a joyful reanimation of his charismatic spirit-as-flesh, and a brutally complicit puppetry that smacks of deep-seated personal ambivalence. The corrosive scent of morbidity, even necrophilia, that haunts nearly all found-footage projects is thickened here into breathtaking pall. As

XCXHXEXRXRXIXEXSX by Ken Jacobs. Photograph courtesy of the filmmaker.

Bruce Conner's *A Movie* (1958) amply demonstrated, the regurgitation of cinema's recorded history—whether personal history as home movie or the "universal" Silver Screen—is intimately connected with an imagination of apocalypse, the terminus of self or cinema in its "filmic phase," in Jacobs's term. It is no wonder, then, that so much of current avant-garde work has the aura of a "Nervous System."

Found Footage and the Lure of History

It is only an ostensible paradox that as cinema nears the end of its filmic phase, the avant-garde has adopted the inquest of history as one of its dominant projects. Although this topos had already surfaced by the early seventies, especially in the theoretical writings and films of Hollis Frampton,[15] it has gathered considerable momentum in the past decade or so, inflecting a disparate collection of styles, production modes, and political stances. Consciousness of a shared social past in interaction with individual experience has left its mark on the poetic lyric (e.g., Brakhage's *Murder Psalm*, 1981), New Narrative (e.g., Rainer's *Journeys from Berlin/1971*, 1980), diary film (e.g., James Benning's *American Dreams*, 1983), and the nonfiction essay (e.g., Thornton's *Adynata*, 1983).[16] It is, however, in the area of found-footage collage, easily the most ubiquitous practice of the last twenty years, that the full implications of a return to history can be assessed.

Roland Barthes's contention in "The Death of the Author" that writing is of necessity a "readymade" activity and that "the text is a tissue of quotations drawn from the innumerable centers of culture"[17] effects a kind of mantra for the anti-industrial practice of found footage. Bent in the crucible of montage (and other tactics of recontextualization), archival materials, along with Hollywood genres and star vehicles, and the detritus of mass culture such as TV episodes and advertisements, contribute to a postmodern aesthetic blueprint convened at the limits of standard representational channels. Making those limits visible and productive entails, among other functions, (1) the repudiation of the cult of originality by restricting authorship to a function of quotation and rearrangement; (2) leveling distinctions between "high" and "low" cultural forms; and (3) relocating knowledge as an effect of filmic organization, as situational, a byproduct of production-reception contexts and their critical collision through editing.

The origins of the compilation film are virtually coincident with the birth of cinema.[18] From the moment in 1898 when Lumière cameraman Francis Doublier assembled unrelated shots to simulate the arrest and trial of Dreyfus, found footage has been yoked to twin interests of economic conservation: fashioning new product from old with minimal cost to the maker; and historical (re)interpretation—recombining extant materials to reveal an underlying ideological slant. There is often an additional, compensatory thrust to the avant-garde's deployment of found footage. On a social or institutional level, the retrieval of images culled from cinema of the early 1900s (e.g., Ernie Gehr's *Eureka* [1979], Frampton's *Gloria!* [1979], Thornton's *Peggy and Fred in Hell*) establishes a spectral linkage between current work and modes of production operating beyond the constraints of classical narrative, thus offering a form of internal (historical) self-validation.[19] On the level of personal history, the use of childhood home movies (e.g., Marjorie Keller's *Daughters of Chaos* [1980], Nina Fonoroff's *A Knowledge They Cannot Lose* [1988]) or Hollywood fragments from the 1940s and beyond (Rainer's *The Man Who Envied Women* [1986], Esther Shatavsky's *Bedtime Story* [1981]) recalls a formative period in the filmmaker's early development, prior to the onset of creative commitment but propaedeutic to her or his current interrogation of socially constructed identity.

Regardless of the type of footage appropriated or the formal terms in which it is revived, subjectivity is pushed back at least one degree from direct camera confrontation with a profilmic reality. And it is implied that this removal, what I want to call an "impeachment of vision," is indicative of a widespread condition in contemporary critical consciousness.[20] There is another, equally potent charge attached to the use of found footage. Since in most cases the temporality of the film fragment is split between a present context and the shadow of prior production circumstances, the historical provenance of recycled images is never totally canceled. Rather, found-footage re-presentations work precisely because as viewers we grasp an ironic, impossible collision between successive phases of production and reception. Borrowed images are made to speak not only of a distant past and/or a "repressed" quotient of meaning but of manufacturing resources and protocols for the most part completely unavailable to avant-garde artists: film studio technical apparatuses or even the sync-sound rigs of documentary units. As Phil Solomon puts it:

> There are many stories I would like to tell (or re-tell). However, for me, the act of telling other people where to go ("marks"), what to do ("stage business"), how to feel ("acting"), and what to say ("script") is thoroughly embarrassing and rather silly. Most filmmaking of this kind is merely "execution."[21]

He might have added that apart from "silly," the economics of Hollywood production, traces of which inhere in every frame, bring to bear a set of social—as well as textual—relations heavily contested by avant-garde styles and institutions. The best found-footage exercises, in an arc that begins with Joseph Cornell's *Rose Hobart* (1939) and extends through Craig Baldwin's riotous *Tribulation 99: Alien Anomalies under America* (1991), simultaneously acknowledge complicity with an ideologically debased system of image making and promote critical attitudes toward that system.

It should be emphasized that found footage is related to, but diverges significantly from, practices of quotation, simulation, and ready-made fabrication in adjacent arenas of painting, photography, and assemblage. When Mike Bidlo copies a Picasso painting or Sherrie Levine rephotographs a Walker Evans print, the economic and social context for their work, and its conditions of reception, remain more or less commensurate with the canonical objects whose aura they are intent on puncturing; only observers already primed by art-historical knowledge are likely to "get" the pomo revisions. Although the objective is to raise issues of commodity status and authorship, in fact such art is usually shown in the same galleries, discussed in the same journals, and bought by the same patrons as those to which the reputations of Picasso and Evans are indebted. Of course, the same cannot be said about the avant-garde's "theft" of Hollywood product.

On the other hand, even if but a small portion of the original film is commandeered, and then altered in visual format, gauge, and so forth, it can still be regarded as an exact copy of an original whose exchange value rests only nominally in the uniqueness of the "original" (the film negative). The reuse of historical images does not "simulate" anything. Pieces of found footage are in essence tokens of a type, like identical playing cards from different decks or identical flags flying on different mastheads, for which there could be an infinite number of equally valid copies.[22] However invisible the differences may be between an original artwork and a Bidlo or Levine facsimile, the copies gain new status as types.

There is more to be said about the cultural politics of found footage, but a brief detour into one of the most accomplished—perhaps the most entertaining—films of the period is instructive. Morgan Fisher's *Standard Gauge* (1984) weaves together a number of thematic strands infusing not just the dominant styles of the past fifteen years but a significant swath of the avant-garde movement as a whole. Beginning in the late sixties, Fisher has methodically explored technical aspects of film production and exhibition processes through wry, conceptually nested short works; *Standard Gauge* bursts forth as his summa. It is both his longest and most explicitly autobiographical effort, and a belated response to Frampton's *(nostalgia)* (1973). Indeed, the two structural film pioneers have been compared in terms of their austerity, wit, and architectonic rigor. *Gauge* unfolds as a discursive history—annotated by Fisher's voice-over commentary and a long introductory factual title crawl—of 35mm film stock (the industrial standard), embedded in a personal account of the filmmaker's involvement in the Hollywood industry as an editor, stock footage researcher, bit actor, and movie spectator. In a long-take tour de force, Fisher builds a signature tension between a precisely calibrated structure and the variables of spontaneous performance, dragging strips of 35mm film—begged, borrowed, scavenged, or stolen—across a lightbox while momentarily freezing certain frames for visual or historical analysis or anecdotal exposition. In a production note Fisher states:

> The film combines two conventions usually held to be mutually exclusive, or even antagonistic: editing—the construction of a film through montage—and the long take, the impassive recording of a scene that has been arranged with some purpose in mind. Forced to the surface are antinomies between "amateur" and "professional" prerogatives, between material base and image, iconic images and printed language, touching and looking, still and moving, memory and presence, and so on.

These ostensible contradictions are interrelated and further expanded in an astonishingly dense web of associations that limn the very core of cinematic ontology and a stream of prominent theoretical positions organized around that ontology. Fisher deftly parodies aspects of formalism, apparatus theory, psychoanalysis, ideological critique, while his offhand yet carefully timed comments turn bits of "suppressed" material—color-correction inserts known as "China Girls," words and phrases printed on leader or slugs, such as "picture," "subject," "scene missing"—into dizzying puns. For instance, a scrap of dangling subtitle from Godard's *La Chinoise* (not coincidentally a notable instance of long-take/montage fusion) reads, "In the West the imperialists are still oppressing," a humorous precis of that film's content and a sly dig at Fisher's own complicity in Hollywood's international conquests.

Along with references to mainstream film, to Roger Corman (for whom Fisher once worked), *Detour,* Minnelli, and Hitchcock, there is a semiappreciative dialogue with several easily recognizable structural films, with Conner's *A Movie,* and once again, a thinly veiled historical dialogue with modernist painting styles, in particular the iconographic and compositional idioms of Johns, Rothko, Stella, Olitski, and others. On several levels, *Standard Gauge* is a "scholarly" achievement whose aesthetic conjunctions are never merely didactic but arise from a foundation of autobiographical retelling. It is, as well, an example of what I have elsewhere called "fantasies of un-power," in which an avant-garde artist thematizes his or her critical separation from, and indebtedness to, the engulfing effects of dominant cinema.[23]

If the relationship between corporate and marginal in Fisher's film is ambivalent, amiably self-deprecating as well as caustic, a more common stance in the recent deployment of found footage suggests something akin to a transaction between psycho-analyst and analysand—or at its most stridently adversarial, a campaign of guerrilla warfare. Nöel Carroll neatly summarizes the former position: "Once images are taken out of their original context . . . the image can be made to appear strange, and initially unnoticed features of it may be said to be unmasked."[24] For certain practitioners, the implicit purpose of appropriation is to *attack* a set of alien materials, marking above all the duplicity or inherent absurdity of their ideological address, and a reluctance to admit the possibility of affinity or interdetermination.[25]

In a more militant vein, the current rage for found footage invokes a significant European tradition of politicized collage that includes John Heartfield, George Grosz, Raoul Hausmann, and Hannah Hoch. According to their *Maschienkunst* ("machine art") aesthetic, journalistic photomontage held a promise of direct incursion into the public shaping of political consciousness, with the tactic of cutting and pasting popular images fostering a synecdoche for the rearrangement of relations of power in the social formation.[26] Nonetheless, discontinuities between these two cultural moments weaken any prospect for common cause. Aside from radically different historical conditions and conditions of reception—Heartfield's work appeared in workers' magazines, on book covers and public posters, a far cry from the avant-garde's cloistered screening spaces—Weimar collage was governed by commonsense metaphors and juxtapositions whose clarity in regard to their object of scorn was integral to the goal of accessibility. Too frequently, contemporary found-footage films traffic in ideological obscurity rather than risk a charge of overly partisan or "authoritarian" message-mongering.

A residue of photomontage's adversarial acuity is evident in Baldwin's *RocketKitCongoKit* (1986) and *Tribulation 99*, where a general desire to "take the images of the corporate media and turn them against themselves"[27] is ballasted by the send-up of specific geo-political episodes (African neocolonialism; U.S. foreign policy toward Latin America). Indeed, Baldwin poses Heartfieldesque conjunctions (e.g., Barry Goldwater/James Bond; Manuel Noriega/Wolfman) within a satirical framework that oscillates between rabid Right paranoia and Beavis and Butthead metacommentary. More typical of a growing faction is filmmaker Sharon Sandusky's contention that found footage is more or less automatically "analytical." Defining the so-called Toxic Film Artifact as a wellspring of media "brainwashing," she suggests the avant-garde "Archival Art Film" can constitute an effective antidote to public passivity:

> they have the ability to isolate a few images of interest and concentrate upon them; rather than permit an uninterrupted stream of someone else's image choices . . . it will not let go of the viewers until they receive the underlying message it represents. It is analytical because it understands that producers of the Toxic Film Artifact . . . fear that the audience will understand their machinations of deception and will not bypass critical awareness.[28]

Sandusky's strident found-footage manifesto is skeptical about the value of craft and renounces overly seductive effects of beauty and order, such as those found in films by Conner or Michael Wallin, valorizing instead the type of raw construction attributed to Greta Snider's *Futility* (1989). The notion that coherence might constitute a "problem," a tool of the mass media devil, seems widely shared among younger collage enthusiasts. A properly poetic evocation of this suspicion is provided by curator Mark McEllhatten in program notes to Julie Murray's *Conscious* (1994):

> Causality, Casualty, Depiction, Deception, Absence, Abscess. Slips of the tongue? *Conscious* should lead us to conclude that coherence is a lax convention, the lassitude that follows after logic is consummated. Coherence may be only incoherence struck senseless, a marriage of convenience, a shotgun wedding, the mortar that we believe holds things together, the connubial paste.

In this view, knowledge effects of filmic unity, clarity, and so forth become equated with bourgeois beliefs, something to be eschewed, one presumes, along with reifications of patriarchal discourse and the nuclear family (as a code secreted in the smooth "wedding" of disjunct images). The problem for *me* is that in many recent films the simple retrieval and display/recombination of images is construed as sufficient for the task of cultural critique; anything more elaborate borders on mental manipulation. Alternatively, inchoate or even manifest themes are subject in this work to continual qualification or obfuscation due to a refusal to provide enough clues to a given film's abiding principles of organization. Regrettably, films generated from such self-imposed constraints can register as unnecessarily hermetic, failing to move beyond the delectation of unquestionably "strange" images; such works resemble the aimless drift of proverbial "free-floating signifiers." More pointedly, they slide into a postmodern relativism characterized by Fredric Jameson as the "stylistic mask of pastiche, speech in a dead language"—heterogeneous heaps of intertextual fragments that deny historicism as they flaunt the collapse of temporal segmentation.[29]

A specific crisis in cinematic means is exposed by the tendency toward vague or paratactic structuring of found-footage fragments. It has to do with functions of editing or, more broadly, sequentiality. Having rejected both the avant-garde's poetic tradition of metaphor and formal association and the structural legacy of systemic design, filmmakers now find themselves in a dilemma whereby only loosely additive or "raw" connections can fulfill the negative obligation to withhold markers of personal expressivity, beauty, didacticism, and even technical virtuosity. Whether this dilemma can be understood as historically transitional, giving way to new patterns of editing and structuration, remains an open question.

Language and/as/versus Image

For nearly three decades the notoriety, and to some extent the achievement, of the North American avant-garde harbored as a major subtext the repudiation of language-based codes of visual representation. A concern with film as a medium that exceeds formal conventions of language is already apparent in the films and writings of Maya

Deren, especially in her well-known distinction between "horizontal" and "vertical" composition, and this imperative proceeds along a historical line that includes the lyrical elaborations of Brakhage and Baillie, the large-scale mythopoeic exfoliations of the 1960s, and structural film and its variants. Valorization of cinematic purity and "presence" is underscored by an animus directed at the discursive baggage of Hollywood narrative. In retrospect, however, it may be taken as less a verdict on narrative per se than a deep mistrust of the manner in which ideological and institutional mediations of visual experience corrupt meaningful exchanges with sensuous interior and outer worlds.

Over the past fifteen years, a fundamental commitment to vision has been downplayed or outright trampled on a number of fronts. A key index of vision's waning epistemological authority is a massive invasion of printed language or, more accurately, language-images—in the form of intertitles, textual crawls, sub- and overtitles—as a means of refracting, interrogating, and otherwise blocking identification between iconic images and the real.[30] An exploration of the background and implications of this aesthetic shift is necessary to any reckoning of the avant-garde's current aspirations.

The desire to avoid language formations peaked in the late 1960s, coextensive with a widespread cult of image immediacy and authenticity encompassing cinéma vérité documentary and more "experimental" precincts of commercial cinema (e.g., *Easy Rider* [1969]). The desire to enhance formal properties of the image as obstacle to the supposed linguistic domination of viewer perception fueled such practices as the absence of soundtracks and film titles, the preference for instrumental music or mechanical sounds over human speech, and the denaturing of photographic legibility through rapid editing, camera movement, superimposition, optical printing, and so on. To be sure, there were economic advantages to avoiding or marginalizing sound elements, but even a procedure like structural film's extension of duration through long takes conceals a logophobic undercurrent. Invited to focus for a considerable period on a more or less static visual field, our initial impulse of assigning conventional categories of reference— the names of things and their social contexts—is supplanted by a more active and reflexive process of apprehension. Filmmakers as disparate as Brakhage, Gehr, and Pat O'Neill have shared the aim of suspending or redirecting what Boris Eikhenbaum calls the operation of "inner speech" in cinematic discourse.[31] At the risk of oversimplifying a complex and controversial theory, a standard full-length shot of a dog is immediately translated as the verbal sign "dog," which is accompanied by a limited chain of modifiers such as "large," "brown," "furry." Masking or deflecting the initial "translation" through one or more formal devices encourages the viewer to arrive at, say, the percept "brown" without its normal categorical baggage.

By reducing the received denotative quotient of conventional signs, we might productively mistake the shot of the dog for that of a baby—or simply grasp the subject of a given image as a moving shape with this or that group of attributes. Thus we arrive at the threshold of Brakhage's vaunted "adventure in perception," the freeing of the film image from its ingrained residue of, and mental activity as, language. The key here is nontransparency, converting an automatic response into a less certain, vivifying "reading," the promotion of which is as crucial to structural film—albeit framed in a different mode of address (nonsubjective, mechanical) and offering different cognitive returns—as it is to *Dog Star Man* (1961–64).[32]

A countervailing axis in structural film's commitment to the unalloyed image surfaces by the early 1970s. The interest in the quasi-scientific organization of film structure through formulaic design proves to be fully compatible with an interest in visual analogues to formal language systems. The maintenance of a language/image dichotomy was breached and problematized, with a (previously disavowed) emphasis on words assuming a privileged place, in the careers of Snow, Frampton, Joyce Wieland, and Owen Land. This shift in avant-garde philosophy was bolstered by the infusion of academic, language-based film theory, such as that of Christian Metz, and in turn by word/image practices in other cultural arenas such as painting. And it gained further impetus from critical engagement with conceptual art. Although avant-garde film is at best a fellow traveler in a period redolent of what W. J. T. Mitchell, in another context, calls "linguistic imperialism,"[33] printed texts show up with increasing frequency by the early eighties and have since evolved into a familiar edifice on the avant-garde landscape.[34]

As part of a larger assault on myths of romantic authorship and originality, in which found footage is an apposite instrument of contestation, language-images have been employed as a means to disarticulate the immediacy and subjective motivation of iconic scenes. In Wieland's scandalously undervalued films—for example, *Sailboat*, *1933* (both 1967), and *La Raison avant la passion* (1968–69)—denotative or descriptive conventions implied in the relationship between photographed image and an overlay of commercial titling are ruptured, revealing a dense indeterminacy in the way words are used to fix the identity (or time or place) of an image. As Snow remarked in a note on *1933*, "You find out, if you didn't already know, how naming tints pure vision."[35] *Pierre Vallières* (1972) continues this line of inquiry, creating a triadic tangle of contradictions, slippages, and (mis)translations around the processes of hearing, seeing, and reading the same recorded event: a sync-sound speech by a Quebecois political activist shown in a long-take close-up of his mouth, accompanied by subtitles in English. Indeed, in this case the friction between the two languages literalizes the terms of a crucial debate in Canadian politics.

Owen Land has conducted perhaps the fullest—and most humorous—exploration of the slippery terrain of denotation and translation. Beginning with *Institutional Quality* (1970) and culminating in *On the Marriage Broker Joke as Cited by Sigmund Freud in* Wit and Its Relation to Time Unconscious, *or Can the Avant-Garde Artist be Wholed?* (1980), Land's work, like that of Wieland, anticipates many of the tropes of written language prevalent in current avant-garde practice. In contrast, however, to the rich sense of modernist irony and word play in these artists, younger makers seem to have adopted a more solemn and polemical approach to collisions between image and text. *Marriage Broker* and Snow's all-text extravaganza *So Is This* (1982) are pivotal in the transition to more theoretically inflected and overtly politicized uses of visual texts.

While it is utterly fruitless to attempt a synopsis of *Marriage Broker*'s convoluted anecdotes and interlocking system of iconic/verbal/formal puns, an indication of Land's

On the Marriage Broker Joke . . . by Owen Land. Photograph courtesy of Anthology Film Archives.

thematic obsessions will help frame a discussion of formal and theoretical features of language-images. Land's opus starts with a close-up of an Asian woman in the midst of ecstatic moaning caused by either an orgasm, a dream, or a spiritual revelation (and enhanced by the device of looping). In a set of nested narrational perspectives, the film begins again with a tacky TV children's show whose hosts are dressed as giant pandas: "Let's pretend we are avant-garde filmmakers making a film about marriage broker jokes." The notion of "structural" connections—the word itself is a source of multiple insider jokes on avant-garde figures—elaborated by Freud between jokes and dreams is relentlessly pursued through a disjunctive accumulation of nonsense verses, pseudo-scientific classroom lectures and recitations, quotations, textual overlays, and a pomp-ous hermeneutic unpacking of marketing techniques for jars of Japanese salted plums.

Three realms of personal desire and fulfillment—artistic, sexual, and religious—are intertwined in a revolving succession of displacements. At issue is the inadequacy of any secondhand representation—and behind that, of any articles of orthodox faith (e.g., Christianity) or intellectual discourse (e.g., psychoanalysis) or aesthetic theory (e.g., Sitney's account of structural film)—to truly register the convulsive jolt of transcendence available in sexual intercourse, artmaking, spiritual revelation, or the dreamstate. The core of this, and by implication every, film conceals a giant hole. What is absent, beyond the clarifying reach of language *or* image—yet presaged by their ill-fitting, impossible "marriage"—is what it means for consciousness to be "wholed," or alternatively, to "behold." Land attempts to parse out this absence, to hilarious ef-fect: films have sprocket holes; scribal errors open gaps in scriptural texts; sleep, like orgasm, functions as a pleasurable hole in daily routine. On the soundtrack and the printed image, words with long "o" sounds pile up. In the age of TV, an important organ in the production of hegemonic consumerism, the desire to "behold" a world beyond the two-dimensional image grows ever more mediated and experientially remote.[36]

What remains to be addressed are specific features or conditions of language-images that undergird their aesthetic currency. It should be stressed that visual texts usually appear in tandem with other materials and are embedded in a variety of stylistic and thematic arrangements. Moreover, not every text usage comports with every one of the propositions listed below, which are intended as descriptions of traits or symptoms of wider concerns. Although many films in which visual texts appear continue to be informed by earlier avant-garde paradigms, such as autobiography and trance film, many others are associated with a postmodern agenda of demystifying mass media codes in their policing of socially sanctioned identities.[37] Here, then, are nine possible reasons why texts fit so well into the avant-garde's reigning cultural politics:

> 1. They are not fragments of a larger photographed space. They *frame* nothing but themselves and thus resist any dynamic of mutual presence between subjective camera position and image. Moreover, they provide no clues as to perspectival distance or scale between camera and image-source (a factor exploited to humorous advantage in *So Is This*). When part of a diegetic ensemble, texts nonetheless fail to mobilize the viewer's figuring of offscreen space (Fisher's *Projection Instructions* is an exception).
> 2. Perceived as discontinuous with surrounding or adjacent representa-

Gently Down the Stream by Su Friedrich. Photograph courtesy of Anthology Film Archives.

tional images, visual texts disrupt the unity of a single optical or enunciative source (generally embodied by the combination of camera perspective and tropes of editing). When texts appear as intertitles, they can prevent shots on either side from entering into a visual bond or suture, thus underscoring the fragmentary nature of filmic units (Mary Filippo's *Who Do You Think You Are?* [1987] and Bruce Elder's *Illuminated Texts* [1982] are good examples). As Jean Epstein said of the intertitle debate in the 1920s, "It is first of all a rest for the eye, a punctuation mark for the mind."[38]

3. Since most language-images are produced by commercial processes outside the filmmaker's immediate control, they assume an anti-artisanal presence, interpolating an "other" space of production almost invariably in contrast to that of surrounding images, one that either recalls or satirizes standard—ideologically charged—functions of titles (e.g., Brady Lewis's *The Suicide Squeeze* [1989]; Janis Crystal Lipzin's *Other Reckless Things* [1984]). Their impersonality and frequent lack of bodily trace—who "speaks" the intertitle?—split the delegation of authorship even when the text itself is not a quotation.

4. Because they are often drawn from extant cultural sources, texts are allied with a widespread project of appropriation and intertextuality (e.g., Al Razutis's *Amerika* [1972–83]; Ken Kobland's *Landscape and Desire* [1981]).

5. To the extent that intertitles and crawls invoke the practice and historical lineage of silent films, they participate in the reabsorption of elements from film history that are outside conventions of classical Hollywood narrative.

6. Like the parodic, antidescriptive use of titles in films such as *Un chien andalou* and *Anemic Cinema*, recent films suggest a destabilization of potential truth value of the film image (e.g., David Goldberg's and Michael Oblowitz's *The Is/Land* [1981]; Bill Morrison's *Footprints* [1989]).

7. As opposed to the myth of universal perception attached to representational images, visual texts are of necessity addressed to or from specific cultural—and depending on idiom, historical—contexts. As art historian Ernst Gombrich said of the "Cave Canem" mosaic at Pompeii, "You will soon understand the radical difference between picture and text . . . To understand the notice you must know Latin, to understand the picture you must know about dogs."[39] Postmodernism seems to assume that the display of written texts, like the display of found footage, can reveal ideological pressures, such as the subordination of female subjectivity, which shaped their formation and original functions (e.g., Yvonne Rainer's *Privilege* [1990]); Lynne Sachs's *The House of Science: A Museum of False Facts* [1991]); Roddy Bogawa's *Some Divine Wind* [1989]).

8. Language-images can inscribe within a film what it cannot show directly through images, and they can do so without the technical devices

of diegetic characters or voice-over narration. In particular, factual statements, subjective feelings, and theoretical ideas can be inserted into visual
contexts for which they serve as elucidations, contradictory evidence, or
analytical conclusions (e.g., Su Friedrich's *First Comes Love* [1991]; Daniel
Eisenberg's *Cooperation of Parts* [1987]; Ahwesh's and Sanborn's *The
Deadman*).

9. Language includes the property of *deictics,* shifters such as "this,"
"now," "yesterday," which elude the photographic image (and in commercial films are conventionally established through fades, dissolves,
etc.). Temporal and spatial relations in the image can be reorganized via
this property, and tense and person can be indicated directly (*So Is This*
plays on the referential capabilities of deictics in a dizzying series of
permutations).[40]

In closing, there are several overarching considerations that while grounded in the immediate historical situation evince continuities with longstanding avant-garde themes
and styles. Leaving aside the use of texts as predominantly *graphic* elements adduced
as visual shapes or rhythmic corollaries (as in Peter Rose's *Secondary Currents* [1983]),
the introduction of language has had the paradoxical effect of reinvigorating the avant-
garde's compass of permissable imagery by adding both another facet and a tool with
which to interrogate, bend, or otherwise force new meanings onto diaristic or poetic
schema. It has, as well, responded to the perceived collapse of high art/mass culture
distinctions not, as in artworld settings, by rendering the distinction meaningless but by
critically blending syntactical structures of television and print sources with subjective
realms of experience characteristic of the postwar avant-garde movement as a whole.

In a similar vein, this practice has allowed access to pressing narrative conundrums
in and around cinema without having to resort to the model of semicommercial production adopted by so-called New Narrative features. While the latter explore some
of the same conceptual terrain, they have proved to be an economic albatross in the
careers of their adherents and have failed to attract the broader audiences necessary to
their social prospectus.

(1995)

9 | "I Just Pass My Hands over the Surface of Things": On and off the Screen, circa 2003

I N THE MID-1980S, some of the most ardent, persistent, and perspicacious champions of the American avant-garde—P. Adams Sitney, Fred Camper, Nöel Carroll, J. Hoberman—made declarations to the effect that the movement was in a state of profound crisis.[1] Supposed causes of the predicament were many and varied: skyrocketing costs of 16mm production; cutbacks in government and private-foundation funding; a paucity of fresh styles or ideas in the rising generation of film-makers; a corporately staged obsolescence of key equipment and film stocks; economic and aesthetic challenges posed by video; the negative impact of academic film theory. Debate on the dire state of avant-garde film culminated in 1989 in a large, well-funded, and suitably contentious "International Experimental Film Congress," held in Toronto, whose extensive screenings, panels, and informal events carried an unmistakably elegiac tone.[2]

A decade later the stream of grim assessments had evaporated, dismissed by some as stodgily alarmist and rebutted by the achievements of a vibrant cadre of younger artists and their return to the sort of vagrant, artisanal, trickle-up energies that had characterized the movement during prior moments of heightened creativity.[3] From a current perspective, there are several possible, not necessarily exclusive, reasons for the perception of "crisis" and its rapid reversal. Established critics and programmers might have been momentarily out of touch with grassroots, geographically dispersed factions at the forefront of change. Or perhaps avant-garde film is in *perpetual* crisis and pronouncements about its death form part of a self-validating ritual. A third option is that there was in fact a weakening of commitment but, phoenixlike, the movement revived itself in response to what, especially, younger makers saw as a cycle of overconsolidation and complacency—rather than slippage—from which they gleaned opportunities for localized intervention. Whatever the case, this intramural profile does not take into account additional factors such as the broader state of visual culture, including mass culture, and various pressures exerted by feminist, queer, and minority political initiatives.

Ironically, the upsurge of new figures, styles, and institutional strategies that began in the late 1980s, and continues more or less unabated, was informed by striking revaluations of older figures and by unanticipated aesthetic and/or technological breakthroughs by first-generation avant-gardists (that is, artists who entered the scene in the 1960s or earlier, most of whom are now at least in their sixties). Following years of general unavailability for public screening, posthumous programs of Andy Warhol's early films shown in 1989, and again in 1994, and their subsequent restored rental access had incalculable effects on younger filmmakers charged by the confluence of sexuality, Hollywood narrative, and gendered performance. The same can be said of the flurry of activity—screenings, a museum exhibition, book projects—around the films of Jack Smith after his death in 1989. In the early nineties, a traveling show of short "conceptual" or performance-oriented films by a truly contrarious band of sixties' Fluxus artists, including Nam June Paik and George Macunius, may also have contributed to a postmodern antimonumentalist, aleatory ethos in recent film/video.

In theory, it is imperative that all avant-gardes should devour their parents. Yet as the marginal, uniquely uncommodifiable wing of American alternative filmmaking lunges into its second half-century, a hearty core of early practitioners persists in stak-

Jack Smith. Photograph by Charles Allcroft; courtesy of Millennium Film Workshop.

ing out cutting-edge territory and in doing so challenges its own aesthetic progeny on the ground of innovation. Indeed, a remarkable, not widely appreciated aspect of the movement's history is deep continuities that obtain, amidst an aura of constant transformation, in the realm of production, distribution, and exhibition. Among tribal elders whose investigations of cinematic language have not only not diminished but, in certain cases, become more urgent and accomplished over the past ten years are Jonas Mekas, Ken Jacobs, Robert Beavers, Ernie Gehr, Gunvor Nelson, Nathaniel Dorsky, Michael Snow, George Kuchar, and the late Stan Brakhage. Although they comprise widely disparate visual and thematic approaches, the current appeal for younger adherents of the diary form, of anti-illusionist applications of video, of loosely accumulative imagistic structures, and of hand-tooled abstraction owes something to this group of stalwart experimentalists.

Despite the continuing, exemplary practices of canonical filmmakers, however, what defines the avant-garde today is neither an aesthetic stance toward formal inquiry—the residues of a modernist self-scrutiny—nor a collection of enduring themes (e.g., the vicissitudes of childhood) or idioms (e.g., the psychodramatic trance film). Rather, the most useful and, to my mind, least value-laden or partisan framework for understanding the movement is as a mesh of semistable funding sources, fixed channels of distribution and exhibition, and organs of publicity, along with material exigencies (e.g., budgetary and technological considerations) and shared elements of production (e.g., sub-feature length, unscripted, made by single individuals or two-person collaborations, predominantly in 16mm non–sync sound, and so on). In short, if it is financed like other works typically deemed avant-garde, if it is circulated through an established network of avant-garde venues, then by my reckoning it should be included in the category *avant-garde*. In the sections that follow I intend to provide something like an empirical "snapshot" of the movement's current institutional compass; my observations are provisional and pretend to neither comprehensiveness nor even-handed treatment. In the final section, I discard the mask of reporter and adopt the more familiar guise of critic in order to outline some heretofore unsounded visual and discursive issues infusing recent work.

In the Public Domain

The Avant-Garde in Print

It has been said that there are more people making more avant-garde films and videos than at any time in the past. What is less obvious is that more is being *written* about this field than in any previous period. By my admittedly unscientific count, in the past twelve years, 1991 to 2002, there have been twenty-three book-length studies devoted entirely or predominantly to avant-garde film, published in English from academic presses, more titles than in the previous two decades combined (excluding books on video art). An equal number of exhibition catalogues or chapbooks, containing substantial critical essays, have been issued under museum or gallery auspices—notably the Art Gallery of Ontario, the San Francisco Cinematheque, and Anthology Film Archives.[4] To be sure, academic film publishing in general has increased but that cannot fully explain the recent spurt of critical interest. The longevity of the movement and its backlog of critically underacknowledged masterworks may constitute one vector of engagement. The near exhaustion of signification by scholars of classical Hollywood genres and auteurist directors may slot avant-garde film into a kind of default position for younger scholars, but I doubt it. A more likely scenario suggests that, following decades of benign neglect or worse, avant-garde cinema has finally been placed on the agenda of "official" film history. To take one example, ten years ago only two commonly used introductory college textbooks offered more than brief mention of the American avant-garde. Now, prodded in part by David Bordwell and Kristen Thompson's efforts in their influential *Film Art: An Introduction,* every introductory text I've seen has at least a chapter subheading, if not a full chapter, on the movement (the quality of the scholarship is, however, another story).[5] In turn, it is probable that more of this work is being assimilated into basic college film courses, which magnifies possibilities for scholarly pursuit.

Leaving aside specialized journals whose dominant focus is the avant-garde, chiefly *Cinematograph* and *Millennium Film Journal,* a glance at wider-circulation film and arts periodicals such as *Film Comment, Film Quarterly, Afterimage, The Independent,* and *Art Forum* reveals that despite varied editorial policies, coverage of the movement has expanded considerably over the last ten years. Small journals with distinctly theoretical or historiographic slants—*Wide Angle, October, Persistence of Vision*—have chipped in with important pieces on avant-garde topics. On the other hand, there are decidedly fewer publications of the local or unsponsored variety that enlivened public discourse in the nineties; *Spiral, Spleen, The Squealer, Reversal, X-Dreams, Independent Eye, Film-Makers Coalition Newsletter,* and *Motion Picture* are all currently defunct. Journalistic reviews and feature stories in mainstream newspapers such as the *New York Times* or alternative papers like the *LA Weekly* have appeared with perhaps slightly greater frequency but coverage is, as always, constrained by the avant-garde's practice of screening new films once or twice instead of in extended runs.

Distribution

In the 1980s, nonprofit media arts organizations of different stripes found themselves in a surprisingly competitive fiscal climate, reliant on government grants and private donations. Many felt it incumbent to "professionalize" their staffs and governing or advisory boards with nonartists whose connections to the worlds of business and/or private philanthropy were supposed to produce new sources of revenue. For a number of groups, unearned income constituted nearly 50 percent of their operating budgets, and as funding for the NEA and other programs began to shrink, there were discussions concerning quasi-corporate management models, with distinct hierarchies and instruments for financial accountability. For the avant-garde's artist-run distribution cooperatives, such talk was faintly ridiculous, if also ominous. The Film-Makers' Cooperative in New York City and Canyon Cinema's distribution outlet in San Francisco, started in 1961 and 1966 respectively, have operated on or near the edge of financial disaster for the better part of forty years. In these organizations, usually staffed by one or two full-time salaried members who are also working artists, the intricate and time-consuming tasks of grant writing and fund-raising have often taken on an ad hoc quality. Nor are such efforts helped by avant-garde film's lack of cultural capital. Paradoxically, because unearned income has often accounted for only one-quarter of their tiny budgets (as low as $100,000 per year), they have proven less vulnerable to regulatory changes and cutbacks by state and federal agencies. Even with their print collections deteriorating at an alarming rate, MM Serra, director of the New York Co-op, reports that gross rental receipts in 2001 were the highest in nearly a decade, an unexpected spike given the downsized market for 16mm classroom rentals—as a majority of schools now show films largely on video or DVD.[6]

In contrast to nonprofit organizations in adjacent cultural arenas, including video art, avant-garde film distributors have several peculiar advantages. Among their bohemian keys to success, or more accurately, abject survival, is the fact that as artists and dedicated cinephiles, administrators tend to have strongly personalized stakes in the perpetuation of the movement, and many have enjoyed exceptionally long tenures.[7] Moreover, because the experimental film community is relatively small—the New York Co-op lists roughly 600 active members—and the horizon of financial reward for individuals is so meager, managers have been able to address short-term fiscal crises with maneuvers that larger, better-financed groups could never sanction. And despite adhering to founding policies of nonselective openness, and after many years of iconoclastic resistance by artists to "diluting" the power of the film image through video (or later, DVD) transfers, distributors now routinely rent or even sell tapes of films or video works prepared by the artists themselves. The dream of domestic consumption, embraced as far back as the 1960s by Mekas and Brakhage among others, now represents a small but growing market.

The avant-garde's tentative entry into digital circulation was nudged by two ancillary developments. First, other nonprofit and commercial distributors, in particular those catering to work by women, minority, and queer media artists, began to add avant-garde titles to their catalogues of documentaries and narratives: for example, Zeitgeist, Women Make Movies, Frameline, and NAATA. In addition, Arthouse, associated with Anthology Film Archives, has issued a video catalogue anchored by the work of Mekas and Brakhage, and in 2003 the DVD purveyor Criterion put out a lavish two-disk set of Brakhage films. In several cities, independent video stores have created sections of noncommercial, artist-produced tapes. Although it is not a panacea to the movement's endlessly vexing problem of expanding viewer access beyond offbeat urban screening rooms, there has been a belated acceptance of the role of digital technologies in bringing, especially, canonical films to a wider public.[8]

On another front, both the New York Co-op and Canyon Cinema have in recent years evolved strategies that might be referred to in the invidious corporate lingo of "synergy" and "diversification." Along with developing closer ties with, especially,

European museums and film festivals, a trend toward increased collaboration has resulted in joint film preservation or restoration projects with a number of well-heeled institutions, including the American Film Institute and the Warhol Foundation. It would be unwise to draw sweeping conclusions from scattered bits of information, yet the remarkable endurance and relative operational health of the avant-garde's two distribution mainstays, and the manner in which they now coexist with commercial outlets, can be attributed in part to a legacy of direct, democratic participation in processes of circulation.[9]

Exhibition

Electronic image transmission has, in the last decade or so, transformed possibilities for the display of avant-garde films in parallel fashion to the way video is changing the landscape for distribution; its arrival has been tardy, uneven, and received with an undercurrent of ambivalence. Nevertheless, a brief review of prominent exhibition forums evidences patterns of long-term stability that cannot be divorced from the movement's social, film-historical, even aesthetic meaning. A notable array of screening venues has recently celebrated twentieth or thirtieth anniversaries, albeit not usually in the same location. The list includes Anthology Film Archives, Museum of Modern Art's "Cineprobe" series, Art Gallery of Ontario, Pittsburgh Filmmakers, Black Maria Film and Video Festival, the "New American Cinema" series at the Whitney Museum, the San Francisco Cinematheque. Arguably the two most prestigious, economically powerful platforms for public exposure, the New York Film Festival and Whitney Biennials, revived commitments to experimental cinema that had wavered in the mid-nineties. When recent developments are factored in, such as the return of neighborhood club and storefront showcases, the advent of so-called microcinemas, and unprecedented broadcast opportunities on cable TV networks, there appear to be not only a greater number of potential venues than ever before but greater heterogeneity as well.

The burst of exhibition practices has been expedited in no small measure by the gradual erosion of boundaries separating film from video presentation, cinema from music and performance, the avant-garde from other nonmainstream genres, and the duties of programming from those of publicity and criticism.[10] A proliferation of gay and lesbian festivals, politically motivated didactic series, and meticulously researched historical retrospectives has substantially altered the perception of avant-garde shows as an isolated bastion of dry and "difficult" spectatorship imbued with mediumistic purity. As one element in a complex profile, a drift toward socially engaged quasi-narratives, along with tentative alliances to offshoots of the otherwise tepid "independent" narrative scene, has encouraged small theater exhibitors to showcase feature-length work by avant-garde makers. Whatever the reasons behind this phenomenon, since 1995 at least a dozen adventurous films, made by current or former avant-gardists, have received limited theatrical openings (typically one week in a single theater in a few major cultural centers) often followed by eventual cable broadcast. They include Craig Baldwin's *Sonic Outlaws* (1995), Jennifer Montgomery's *Art for Teachers of Children*

(1995), Alan Berliner's *Nobody's Business* (1996), Beth B's *Visiting Desire* (1996), Su Friedrich's *Hide and Seek* (1996), Yvonne Rainer's *MURDER and murder* (1997), Cheryl Dunye's *Watermelon Woman* (1997), Michael Snow's **Corpus Callosum* (2002), and Bill Morrison's *Decasia* (2002).[11] It is safe to assert that more avant-garde films are being shown in nonspecialized contexts than at any time in the past—including the New Narrative episode of the 1980s—and that continued growth of niche cable markets should only magnify this trend.[12] Moreover, it should be noted that recent forays into theatrical exhibition are markedly different from the migration of avant-gardists into the realm of industrial production in the sixties and seventies—beginning with Curtis Harrington and proceeding through Warhol, Robert Downey, Paul Bartel, and others—or, for that matter, similar incursions by British experimentalists Sally Potter, Peter Greenaway, Peter Wollen, Isaac Julien, and Derek Jarman.

Rather than addressing avant-garde exhibition in general, given its overall ductility and geographic differences, an alternative perspective suggests ways in which screening practices have been shaped by social conditions in particular cities. To this end, thumbnail sketches of three cities will be useful, although it should be clear that they do not exhaust the range of options found in other North America enclaves.[13]

One might presume that with its dense population of college students, its abundant art schools and cultural traditions, the Boston area would be rife with avant-garde film activity, but that is not entirely the case. Unlike San Francisco, Chicago, or smaller cities, there is not one or a couple of dominant venues to which a majority of aficionados will flock on a regular basis. Operating on a miniscule budget, the Film Society of the Massachusetts College of Art has for thirty years consistently shown a broad menu of nonmainstream films as a supplement to its instructional classes. Harvard Film Archives and the Boston Museum School have showcased the avant-garde since the 1960s, but in recent decades their programming has been sporadic, dependent upon individual administrators or curators such as Harvard's Bruce Posner. The Brattle Theater in Cambridge, a venerable art house, has presented selected features from Warhol's oeuvre, while an innovative series at the suburban Coolidge Corner Theater has allowed outside curators to program new work in regular monthly screenings. Along with the expected effusion of gay/lesbian and related festivals, an assortment of clubs, bars, and art galleries have given intermittent support to avant-garde film.

According to Adam Hyam of the Los Angeles Filmforum, "I don't know if anything really works in LA. The city is simply too big." That is, the time it takes to get from one section of LA's sprawling basin to another, in tandem with a paucity of state or municipal funding, has been an obstacle to building broad-based, coordinated screening venues. On a scale not apparent in other cities, LA has engendered a loose network of *neighborhood* groups hosting local, often unadvertised or floating events that segue avant-garde films with performance, music, and/or art. In some instances, programming is organized around identity affiliations—punk, Chicano, Asian and Pacific Islander, gay/lesbian/transgender—and geared toward the promotion of artists from their own communities. NewTown, located in the San Gabriel Valley, is decidedly resistant to the avant-garde's enshrinement by academia and the media arts "establishment," preferring such strategies as mobile outdoor projections and screenings tied to barbeques and block parties. Another group without a fixed screening space, Flicker, serves the Echo Park neighborhood by presenting work in bars and storefronts. Film and video nights are also held in the Expresso Mi Cultura bookstore in Hollywood and The Smell, a downtown indie music club; the multimedia LA Freewaves Festival, celebrated at various locations throughout the city, has been an important forum for new video since 1990. The oldest and perhaps most dedicated venue, Filmforum, has been in operation since 1975, but due to the overhead costs of maintaining a permanent site has recently piggybacked onto two more affluent facilities, the Hammer Museum and the American Cinematheque.[14]

Aside from New York, the San Francisco Bay Area undoubtedly has the richest and most sustained history of avant-garde film activity. Since the early eighties, four preeminent exhibition venues, each with its own philosophy, have assayed nearly every facet of the (international) movement. At the ripe age of forty, the San Francisco Cinematheque is by any standard a remarkable organization, and its ability to adapt to new filmmaking cadres and new audiences is equaled only by its penchant for pioneering trends in presentation. Balancing in-house and guest curators, local and nonlocal artists, traditional formats and "expanded" or paracinematic modes, the Cinematheque under the leadership of Steve Anker has also participated in monumental collaborations, one of which, "Big as Life: An American History of 8mm Film," ran in weekly installments for two years in San Francisco and at the Museum of Modern Art in New York.[15] A second major institution, the Pacific Film Archive in Berkeley, revived its sagging involvement to the avant-garde in 1983 with the curatorial appointment of Kathy Geritz and has since been instrumental in putting together large-scale historical surveys and career retrospectives.

In 1982, a group of filmmakers disaffected with institutional programming policies started a grassroots cinema in an industrial garage that they dubbed "No Nothing"—renamed "New Nothing" when it was forced to relocate. Its guiding philosophy echoed the kind of funky anarchistic spirit that has inflected Bay Area culture since at least the 1960s: no money changes hands (no admission fee or artist's honorarium), publicity is mostly word of mouth, and events become occasions for raucous socializing, not worshipful study. Two years later, in 1984, filmmaker and media activist Craig Baldwin founded the series "Other Cinema," housed in a storefront under the aegis of Artists Television Access and dedicated to all manner of politically pungent moving pictures, from hokey fifties newsreels to work by emerging artists of color. Finally, it is impossible to ignore a short-lived but surprisingly influential venue, David Sherman's and Rebecca Barton's Total Mobile Home Cinema. Erected in the storage area of their basement, this original "microcinema" gave new meaning to the notion of home movies with a schedule that included both avant-garde work—including their own—and independent features. Their model has spread across the country, adopted by younger artists and cinephiles in cities that had previously demonstrated little interest in exhibiting nonmainstream genres.[16]

It is possible to draw a few provisional conclusions from this admittedly scattershot report. Perhaps most saliently, the stability of a set of core exhibition venues and pro-gramming conventions (in-person appearances, thematically organized group shows, and so on) over the last three decades has allowed—in certain instances, provoked—the eruption of what might be called a new underground administered by younger film- and videomakers often connected to wider creative communities. Specific practices associated with this initiative—where and how work is presented, in addi-tion to preferred stylistic idioms—include bypassing established channels of funding and publicity. Ensconced in clubs, basements, hand-built pocket theaters, and the like, these venues serve as spaces for localized social interaction and transmedia exchange. While still sustained by the energies of charismatic individuals, the new underground exudes a casual attitude toward public recognition, preservation, and consolidation of artistic advances. Moreover, since their adherents no longer have to, or care to, contest through exclusion the hegemony of Hollywood product, they happily embrace the most disreputable genres from the past, such as educational and exploitation films.

The desire to summarize programming tendencies and de facto policies is fraught with at least two problems. First, simple empirical methods of classification can mask as much as they disclose; for instance, noting the number of films or videos by women implies something about the politics of that work which is potentially misleading. Second, since many innovative venues are either transient or leave little in the way of a paper trail, the easiest survey targets may also be the most conservative in terms of what they present. Nonetheless, a look at the screening schedules of four impor-tant venues—Millennium Film Workshop, the San Francisco Cinematheque, the Art Gallery of Ontario, and Filmforum—over the last six years confirms a number of commonsensical patterns. Despite the persistence of the one-person show, the vast majority of programs were arranged into short-form anthologies. Nearly 40 percent of the artists shown were women, of whom more than 70 percent had their first public screen-ings within the last fifteen years. Less than 10 percent of the total roster were artists of color (I suspect that this figure actually represents an increase over previous periods); unlike, say, social documentary, the avant-garde remains a preserve of the white middle class. In keeping with larger shifts in cultural perspectives, a sizable portion of descrip-tions for individual programs pointed to political analyses, many pertaining to femi-nist and gay/lesbian agendas. This was so despite, or perhaps because of, a proliferation of queer cinema festivals. Film and video were freely intermingled and the use of live performance elements and installations has become increasingly popular.[17]

One institution deserves further commentary, the Whitney Biennials. In the 1980s, Whitney programming, under John Hanhardt, arguably established itself as the pre-miere North American showcase for avant-garde work. Its mandate, then as now, was to locate cutting-edge aesthetic ideas and present them on a highly visible cultural stage that attracted national reviews, ongoing international exposure through traveling Biennial packages, and, anecdotally, increased leverage with funding sources. Although today the Whitney venue registers as somewhat peripheral to the gritty populist im-pulses of the new underground, in recent editions it has added performance sidebars, reversed an earlier policy barring Super-8, and fostered a seamless integration of film and video. Discernible changes since 1979 in the style, artistic provenance, and format of selections are, in a limited way, indicative of transformations in the movement as a whole.[18]

The number of participating film- and videomakers has been relatively stable, averaging about twenty-five per Biennial. Predictably, the number of women has risen from one in 1979 to four in 1981 and 1983 to nine—or roughly half—in 1985. After 1993, the percentage of women dropped to around one-third. By the same token, the number of first-generation makers began to decline in the late eighties from a clear majority to less than a quarter in any given year. The amount of feature-length narrative work remained quite low—two or three per exhibition—until 1987 when, somewhat behind the curve, the Whitney began to highlight the accomplishments of New Narrative. In 1993 a dozen features were presented, some of which had little or no connection to avant-garde traditions. Another spurt of "indie" narratives, this time produced in the industry standard of 35mm, appeared in 1997. In two subsequent Biennials, this trend has fortunately subsided. Finally, where early Biennials were stocked with artists from the New York area, in the last fifteen years the Whitney has been more inclusive of West Coast and regional artists.

Contingencies of Production and Discourses of Contingency

Andy Warhol, whose pale but flagrant shadow now lurks in every corner of avant-garde activity, confessed in 1967 that "I see everything that way, the surface of things, a kind of mental Braille. I just pass my hands over the surface of things."[19] Whether or not my observations in this essay constitute a kind of critical or historiographic Braille, they are clearly intended as synoptic, as probative trails to be followed or diverted by future scholars. Two rather different trajectories define the current state of production: the economic or material conditions under which films are made, and the emblematic styles or discursive strategies of the present moment. Providing an account of the former is relatively straightforward since, with several noteworthy exceptions, the avant-garde's characteristic methods of image-making have changed only slightly in the last two decades. Consideration of the latter is of necessity less settled and direct.

Perhaps the most telling technological change is that the ballyhooed antagonism between the aesthetic prerogatives of film and video has been rendered moot, except as a subject of academic theory. Although frequently deployed as an adjunct to or transposition of an artist's signature filmic concerns, a large contingent of first- or second-generation former defenders of the celluloid faith have completed work in video; this group includes Ken Jacobs, Michael Snow, Gunvor Nelson, Ernie Gehr, Jonas Mekas, Bruce Baillie, Barbara Hammer, Andrew Noren, Peter Hutton, Peter Rose, and Vincent Grenier. They join younger makers such as Peggy Ahwesh, Scott Stark, Leslie Thornton, Tony Cokes, Abigail Child, and Keith Sanborn, for whom material differences between the formats were from the start not just elided but understood as a site of diacritical elaboration. That is, as projects such as Thornton's multipart *Peggy and Fred in Hell*

(1984–92) indicate, designed slippages from film to video and back again can cue potentially explosive confrontations between commercial and artisanal visual languages.

The operational fluidity obtaining between film and video extends to disparate levels or protocols of production. As already noted, many older as well as younger makers have oscillated between feature-length and short form. In the last decade, industry directors such as Todd Haynes, Elias Merhige, and Julie Dash made seemingly irreversible transitions from avant-garde to Hollywood or indie production, while others such as Guy Maddin and Gus Van Sant have staged sporadic returns to the avant-garde's institutional terrain. Indie directors such as Michael Almereyda and Richard Linklater, neither of whom really participated in the movement, have tapped younger avant-gardists like Lewis Klahr and Jem Cohen to create short self-contained sequences for use in longer, more conventional features (Klahr and Cohen are also among a group of makers to have fashioned MTV-style music videos). Yet another faction has produced personal documentaries, often with experimental leanings, on subjects ranging from draft resistance in the sixties to dissident music bands of the nineties; avant-documentarists include Cohen, Hammer, Lynne Sachs, Alan Berliner, Jack Walsh, MM Serra, and Thomas Allan Harris.

To be sure, documentaries, music videos, and piecework on indie narratives are funded through different channels, completed according to different criteria, and circulated via different venues from those associated with the avant-garde. Nonetheless, despite budgetary fluctuations in federal and state agencies, and fitful attacks by reactionary politicians and pundits, levels of private foundation funding for avant-garde work have remained relatively steadfast in the last ten years—and judging from acknowledgments at the end of recent films and videos, the pool of potential funding sources has grown. To take but two examples of prominent foundations, during the 1990s an average of five to eight yearly recipients (from a total of 150) of Guggenheim Foundation fellowships were avant-garde film- or videomakers; from 1988 to 2002, roughly one-fifth of nearly 200 Rockefeller Foundation Media Arts fellowships had the same affiliation.[20]

A remarkably persistent infrastructural support system, in concert with the revitalized energies of veterans like Mekas, Jacobs, Snow, Robert Beavers, and Nathaniel Dorsky, helps to illuminate a related phenomenon in which themes, iconographic motifs, formal vocabularies, and subgeneric categories, coined during the movement's initial period of development, are recast by a new generation according to contemporary aesthetic and political desiderata. Indeed, in an updated chapter to the latest edition of *Visionary Film*, Sitney claims that "in the end, every apparently massive reorientation of direction and style culminated in a reaffirmation of the fundamental continuity of genres and themes that have shaped this cinema since the Second World War."[21] This may be an exaggeration, as I will argue shortly, but the premise is sound. Take for example the way in which an early fascination with sexually charged dream states—as conveyed by Deren, Kenneth Anger, and Curtis Harrington—infuses the recent work of Lewis Klahr, Eve Heller, David Sherman, and Janie Geiser. The invocation of the unconscious by younger makers often implies that dreams are colonized by mass-cultural detritus or, to put it differently, that an individual's subjective experiences and fantasies are less determinate than second-order relationships with Hollywood or TV images. A related theme involves the psychosexual dynamics of childhood, a signal concern, say, of Brakhage films of the sixties, addressed by contemporary makers through optics mediated by feminism or Lacanian psychoanalysis. Childhood as a state of *partial* socialization is prominent in the work of Klahr, Ahwesh, Nina Fonorof, Erin Saks, and Su Friedrich, among others.

Revisions of the diary genre, inscribing larger questions about the status of autobiography, suggest something of the dilemma faced by postmodernist practitioners, whose rejection of the imperatives of a unified, coherent self and its rhetorical trappings of sincerity, expressivity, and directness contradicts basic tenets of the diary. On the other hand, the diary allows for the fulfillment of crucial contemporary ideals: veneration of the fragmentary and discontinuous; a stance of antimastery rooted in low-tech production skills and moderate costs; a casual attitude toward structure (as Jonas Mekas likes to say, "I don't make films, I just film"); an emphasis on voice and language; the play of presence/absence, private/public, and indexical/symbolic in the presentation of everyday images. In this sense, the diary as revamped by Ahwesh, Joe Gibbons, Mark LaPore, Anne Robertson, and others inherits as much from the observational tactics of Warhol and Kurt Kren as it does from Mekas.

In 1987, Yvonne Rainer contended that a new generation of avant-garde makers prioritizes the "unmasking and reassessing of social relations, rather than overturning previously validated aesthetic positions."[22] Sitney would concur, citing what he calls a "relentless politicization" and "an insatiable desire to unmask ideology."[23] Undoubtedly, the movement's most telling discursive shift during the eighties and early nineties was away from personal or reflexive concerns to social issues of gender roles, media vernacular, and political oppression. However, rather than serving as incentive to invent a fresh set of generic options, this shift ironically wound up elevating—in both qualitative and quantitative terms—previously recessive, hybrid idioms of the sixties and seventies. One strand in this development is the avant-garde essay film, or what Sitney prefers to call "Menippean satire,"[24] a heterogeneous blending of materials and voices often staged at the intersection of personal and social histories. Pioneered by Rainer, James Benning, and Bruce Elder, essay elements have been enhanced by a group that includes Trin Minh-ha, Craig Baldwin, David Gatten, and Kerry Laitala.

A second revival has taken place around notions of poetic ethnography. Earlier filmmakers such as Baillie, Chick Strand, Peter Hutton, and Peter Kubelka represented their experiences in other cultures through avant-garde tropes like the abstract patterning of color and shape, discontinuities of image and/or sound, or solipsistic modes of camera address. More recent ethnopoetic practitioners have utilized found footage, printed texts, narrative enactments, and voice-over narration in order to critique the privileged position of tourism and undercut the impulse to exoticize Others. Trinh, Thornton, LaPore, Robert Fenz, Jose Rodriguez, Sharon Larkin, and Larry Gottheim have made idiosyncratic contributions to this category.[25] LaPore's *The Five Bad Elements* (1997), part of a series of disturbing studies of non-Western societies, constructs a radical, if

politically ambiguous, version of *depaysement*. A succession of compositionally aus-
tere, long-take sync-sound tableaux, shot in different countries, are arranged without
attributions of time, place, or human activity. Lacking clues with which to adduce
any broader social context or meaning, the viewer is cast adrift amidst a mysterious
physicality of bodies performing banal, repetitive tasks: cans are filled with milk or are
flooded with water from a pump; hands exchange bills and coins across a wide table. In
other scenes, tension between the inchoate facticity of abject peoples and the entropic
flow of time yields a creeping voyeuristic dread. When LaPore's hand-held camera gently probes the features of a corpse (his favorite motif is the sleeping body), its absolute
inanition becomes a mirror for the unseen camera presence, and by extension for the
viewer as well.

A third, nearly ubiquitous practice involves the archeological or demystifying recontextualization of found footage, what might be regarded as the preeminent gesture in
postmodern aesthetics. The impetus for collecting and reworking extant images begins
with Joseph Cornell, Bruce Conner, and Arthur Lipsett but it also draws sustenance
from didactic structural exercises of the 1970s. A variety of factors contribute to the
immense popularity of found-footage critique: archival material is easy to obtain and
cheap to work with; it celebrates the fragment, confounds romantic residues of originality or individual genius; and it solicits an *automatic* connection with history (either
mainstream Hollywood or fringe, non- or anti-industrial artifacts such as pornography
and early cinema). A list of current disciples of recycled footage, virtually coextensive
with the domain of avant-garde cinema itself, would serve little purpose here. Instead,
a brief description of a single work by a young filmmaker points both to continuities
with older practices and to what is distinct about recent cinematic approaches. Michelle
Smith's two-hour collage *Regarding Penelope's Wake* (2002) is at once outsized in scale
and physical labor and modest in thematic ambition. Employing a frame-by-frame
polyvalent editing scheme that is augmented by hand-painting and scratching the
film surface, Smith jams together alternating shots from multiple sources, including
8mm stag films, an instructional tract on public speaking, *The Frog Prince*, a biography
of van Gogh, science fiction, a B-movie mythological epic, home movies, and crude
educational training shorts. A variety of recurrent motifs feature women in physical
danger, magical transformations, and situations of humiliation and repression, but it is
difficult to locate internal principles of development or an overarching narrative. The
effect is that of an intricately designed New England quilt stitched together from worn
scraps of material whose intrinsic features and social provenance are submerged in an
all-over pattern.

Smith's achievement attests to a symptomatic yet paradoxical generation gap in the
manner in which it negotiates the avant-garde's imposing history of found-footage manipulation. In visual density and temporal demands, it begs comparison with Jacobs's
Tom, Tom, the Piper's Son (1969) or Jack Chambers's *The Hart of London* (1968–70). Yet
it lacks Jacobs's reflexive historical exhumations or Chambers's apocalyptic conflation
of metaphoric figures; that is, it lacks not coherent strategies but allegorical meaning. In
Tom Gunning's useful sense of a "minor cinema," *Penelope's Wake* "assert[s] no vision

of conquest, make[s] no claim to hegemony," flaunting an indifference to aesthetic closure or technical perfection. Moreover, as he puts it, "image, rather than the Self, domi-
nates."[26] In the epistemology, as it were, of found footage, Smith and her cohort signal
a displacement of previous (erotic) identifications of cinema-as-body, of the apparatus
as corporeal trope and object of either expressive or logical articulation.[27] And it is on
this ground that the dismembering of found footage and contemporary doctrines of
performance meet.

There are at least three separate precincts or paradigms of performativity currently
in vogue: enacted performance *in* film, performance *with* a filmic or protofilmic apparatus, and performance directly *on* film by painting or related noncamera procedures.
It should be emphasized that these processes are not mutually exclusive, even within a
single work, and that in each case various precedents and canonical influences obtain.
Significantly, all three types understand the body as a nexus of nonsubjectivized, non-
rational idiolects of production. In other words, the imprint of corporeality, regardless
of the degree to which physicality is deflected or sublimated within a given enterprise,
constitutes a shared aesthetic mediation.

Warhol and Jack Smith, with a nod to George Kuchar, underwrite the legacy of
improvised, dispassionate, anecdotal play-acting that governs the current avant-garde's
rhetorics of the human image. It is surely no accident that the most viable traditions
are those of gay male impersonation and self-exposure, closely linked to postmodern
concepts of multiple, fluid identities. First-person films or videos in which the artist
is a central character tend toward psychodrama or self-portrait; practitioners include
Gibbons, Luther Price, Brian Frye, and Bradley Eros. The use of third-person stories,
skits, jokes, and parodies informs the work of Ahwesh, Pelle Lowe, Abigail Child, and
others. Frye, an administrator and critic as well as a filmmaker, neatly summarizes the
appeal of ironic, nondidactic performance strategies: "My favorite way to talk about
Warhol films is that they don't tell you to do things, they just ask you. They invite you
in, giving you a space to immerse yourself in."[28]

The roots of paracinematic performance are even deeper and more expansive,
and once again they spring from the loam of sixties cultural upheaval. The desire to
break out of the narrow material limits of flat screen animated by projected stencils
of light is spread across a landscape of countercultural initiatives, from rock music
light shows to gallery installations to theatricalized film screenings. By 1967, Carolee
Schneeman, whose career in performance-oriented art equals her accomplishments
in film, was using her body as a live element in combination with moving images.
Robert Whitman, Jud Yalkut, and Aldo Tambellini were engaged in similar pursuits.[29]
Structural filmmakers Paul Sharits and Barry Gerson—both trained in painting and
sculpture—performed with or built environments for projected images that reversed
the expressionistic "mind-trip" excesses of earlier approaches. British structuralists
Malcolm LeGrice, Anthony McCall, and Annabel Nicholson fabricated striking performance pieces in established avant-garde screening venues. Ken Jacobs began giving
3-D shadow performances in the mid-sixties, followed in 1975 by the initial stirrings
of his amazing "Nervous System" improvisations for dual projectors. Of special note is

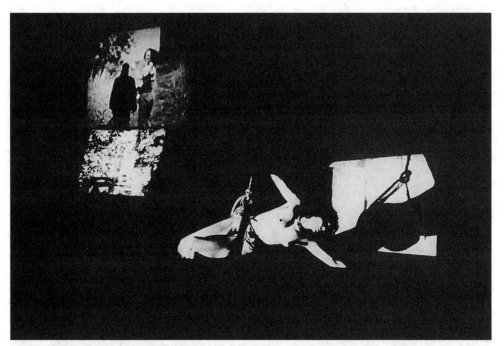

Carolee Schneeman, from a performance/installation of *Kitch's Last Meal*. Photograph courtesy of Millennium Film Workshop.

Fluxus devotee Tony Conrad's hilarious glosses of both expressionistic and minimalist cinematic ontologies. In his cooking shows of 1972–73, Conrad displayed film rolls as "objects" that had been pickled, deep-fried, electrocuted, and rendered otherwise un-projectable; he also stir-fried film strips in a wok along with vegetables, then tossed the concoction at a blank screen in a semblance of a Jackson Pollock "action" movie.

After a hiatus of nearly a decade, cinematic performance and installations resurfaced as a regular attraction in the mid-eighties, cohering especially around younger artists showcased at the San Francisco Cinematheque and at Bay Area events cosponsored with festivals or galleries. Today's "expanded cinema" enthusiasts engage a wide range of practices, and I can do no more in this space than tender a haphazard inventory. Luis Recoder uses live bi-packed projection loops and standard reels, injecting an element of chance image conjunctions into recycled footage. Bradley Eros and Jeanne Liotta create sensuous dance/music/light extravaganzas with mystical overtones. Janie Geiser works with puppets and moving images. Zoe Beloff has made stereoscopic projections. Joel Schlemowitz has shown scroll-like "cine-paintings" and customized image apparatuses in gallery settings. Richard Lerman does sound-loop pieces and the collective Kino-Sonic performs agitated demolitions of commercial movies employing up to six film and video projectors. Other notable artists in this incursion are Bruce McClure, Steve Polta, Scott Stark, Chuck Hudina, Gregg Bierman, Cade Bursell, and the collectives silt and Wetgate. Their commitment is to an ethos of spontaneity, if not a site-specific ephem-erality, that ruptures the privatized and quietist dynamics of avant-garde presentation linking static spectators to a static screen. Therefore even when overt political discourse

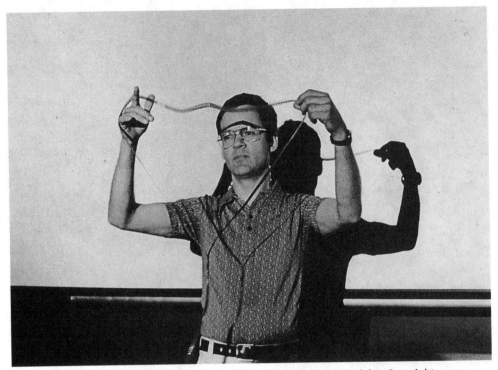

Tony Conrad in a film performance, circa 1978. Photograph by Bruce Meisler. Copyright 2003 Millennium Film Workshop.

is absent, rebellious or communitarian aspirations fuel the bulk of paracinema. As is only partly true of Warholian performance strategies, what is at stake is a repudiation of the absolute autonomy of the movie image—and its complicity in exploitative corporate systems of mechanical reproduction—along with a deferral of semiotic closure. In this sense, live performance is always a "work in progress," courting contingency rather than laboring under the (mostly elusive) promise of commodified dissemination.

In a 1969 issue of *Film Culture*, P. Adams Sitney begins what is perhaps his best-known and most controversial essay with a declaration: "Suddenly a cinema of structure has emerged." He goes on to state that it represents an unexpected and puzzling divergence from a developmental history of increasingly complex forms—which he boasts as the defining aesthetic trajectory of the avant-garde movement.[30] Nearly thirty-five years later, it is tempting to make a complementary declaration: "Suddenly a cinema of *surface* has emerged." The problem is that the emergence of this cinema, in truth a wing of the performative triad, has not been sudden and, despite an ample trail of progenitors, it cannot be read as another reaffirmation of "fundamental" continuities of genre and theme but as a refusal of the crux of Sitney's Herculean critical enterprise.

A prime inspiration, and in turn a prime target of revision, is the brand of hand-crafted images and image-overlays produced by Brakhage, following the lead of Len Lye, in the sixties. At the heart of every attempt by Brakhage to scratch, paint, bleach,

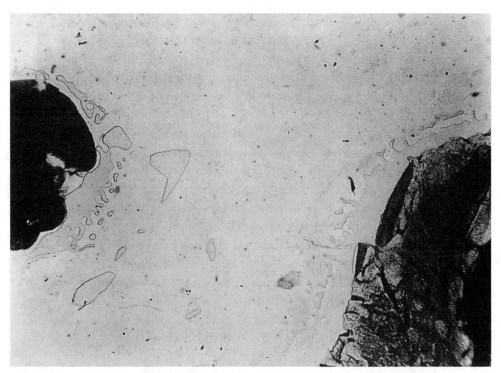

Mothlight by Stan Brakhage: a progenitor of the new cinema of surface. Photograph courtesy of Anthology Film Archives.

bake, encrust, and otherwise intervene in the process of mechanized imaging is the simulation of some mode of internal vision, from "closed-eye" abstractions (created by rubbing your fingers against lowered eyelids) to presleep hypnagogic reveries to actual dreams and fantasies. There are, however, several less commanding precedents to the recent obsession with visual textures. Schneeman dyed and baked film for her erotically ebullient *Fuses* (1968). Films by Marie Menken such as *Go! Go! Go* (1962–64) and *Notebook* (1962) provide an apposite model of speed-driven textural rhythms seemingly impervious to narrative or symbolic development. The same can be said of Harry Smith's *#14 (Late Superimpositions)* and the rediscovered *#15: Untitled Seminole Patchwork Film* (both circa 1964–67, although dating Smith's work is notoriously difficult).[31]

Another sinew of connection for proponents of manual or "environmental" denaturing of the photographic comes from the German group Alter Kinder, whose members began exposing found or unprocessed film to external elements by burying rolls or hanging them outside, or by treating celluloid strips with chemicals. Earlier filmmakers had hand-processed or "weathered" film stock—including Baillie, Schneeman, Roger Jacoby, and David Larcher—but younger European artists such as Jurgen Reble and Matthias Muller were among the first to fuse denaturing impulses with a metathematic contemplation of cinema as organic loop of transformation, deterioration, and revival. Short-circuiting at least two conventional stages in the litany of production—photography and industrial processing—a varied cadre of American artisanal image-makers have embraced what is essentially a decorative ideal, color and texture without apparent overall shape, drained of subjective or expressive cues, immune to internal metaphor, and oblivious to rigorously predetermined designs.

Generating film images becomes for this group a matter of performance in the sense that a particular procedure may be executed over a more or less unbroken expanse of time—as when a roll is buried for a set period—and often involves a combination of uncontrolled or chance operations along with direct manipulation. Among individual and collective adherents to this composite approach are Frye, silt, Peter Herwitz, Jennifer Reeves, Stom Sogo, Glen Fogel, Lee Krist, Mary-Beth Reed, Izabella Pruska-Oldenhoff, and Mark Street. In Bruce McClure's lyrical scratch epic *Indeterminate Focus* (1999), lengths of black-and-white and color stock were abraded with sandpaper that was applied with differing amounts of pressure for variable periods of time. This technique produces swirling filigrees of color or line that build and recede, but there is no feeling that such developmental cues can be translated into nonliteral meanings, allegories of emulsion grain or microcosmic worlds (*Focus* has also been presented in live projector performances). Although wary of what is traditionally deemed "content," reflexive insights or conceits about the nature of the medium are occasionally distilled in the experience of such work: the filmstrip as living flesh, or the image per se as a palimpsest of physical interruptions. Yet to make the point again, the cinema of *surface* eschews the didactic, self-congratulatory, and at times monumentalizing agendas characteristic of the structural moment. It pays to give the final word to a vital cog in the onrush of original, or perhaps merely rekindled, vocabularies of performance: "The films I see myself and a lot of younger filmmakers are making seem concerned with the medium, yes, but not in the same way. You're not trying to assert yourself over the film: instead you try to tease out a paradox."[32] Paradox is also an apt term for an avant-garde faction that is still trying to "make it new" but is no longer committed to remaking cinema in its own image.

(2003)

Appendix
Lines of Sight (A Travelogue)

THE SOCIAL HISTORY OF AMERICAN AVANT-GARDE FILM presents a rich and almost completely uncharted terrain. Not surprisingly, the wave of film studies in the past twenty years organized around conditions of exhibition and reception—especially as manifested in early cinema—bypassed noncommercial arenas. Despite a reputation for eccentricity on and off the screen, the omission of avant-garde practices can hardly be attributed to the anarchic elusiveness of the filmmakers or a paucity of primary materials. The movement continues to be relatively self-contained, and its network of institutional support has been remarkably stable and internally monitored. Documents such as screening schedules, attendance figures, budgets, and overhead—routine items in grant applications and annual reports—coexist with a wealth of still photography, organizational correspondence, and newsletters, to say nothing of an oral tradition replete with cherished anecdotes.

In 1988, while a member of the board of directors of the Film-Makers' Cooperative, I was awarded a grant to study patterns in avant-garde film distribution. Intellectually ill-equipped to perform the kind of empirical analyses that the project required, I was nonetheless able to copy a substantial portion of the Co-op's handwritten ledgers, meticulously kept by its secretary, Leslie Trumbull, and briefly indulged my fascination with where avant-garde films are seen, when, by whom, and in what types of situations. My intuition was that they have enjoyed a more diverse audience than is commonly assumed, and that in certain periods the circulation of popular titles rivaled 16mm rentals of Hollywood movies. Several years ago, I selected a "test group" of five well-known films of various styles, lengths, and origins, and then mapped their itineraries over a span of eleven years.

Unfortunately, the temptation to extrapolate geographic or temporal or social tendencies from these lists proved unfeasible. The same titles were simultaneously distributed by Canyon Cinema or by commercial outlets, and individual filmmakers often forwarded prints on their own. Entries of films sent to individuals rather than to institutions were deleted, and for reasons of economy I list only the first rental by a given site during the prescribed time frame (universities frequently rented the same film as part of cyclical course offerings). Moreover, a given booking provides no indication of the setting or purpose of a screening, or of other films that appeared on the same program. Caveats aside, the spectrum of places in which avant-garde films have been shown, especially the number of private and public high schools, still seems impressive. Why certain titles were chosen by organizations such as libraries, church groups, and medical associations remains a genuine enigma, but a very pleasant one. What follows is offered in anticipation of more sweeping and savvy future inquiries.

Little Stabs at Happiness, Ken Jacobs (1959–63, 15 minutes)

1963   Blecker Street Cinema; Cornell University; Experimental Cinema Group (University of Colorado); Gramercy Arts Theater; *TV Guide* press preview; Royal Films Archives (Brussels); Canyon Cinema.

1964   San Juan Arts Center (Puerto Rico); Washington Film Society; SUNY New Paltz; Canadian Federation of Film Societies; Museum of Modern Art (New York).

1965   *New York Times* preview; Washington Gallery of Modern Art; University of Toledo (Ohio); The Bridge Cinema Group; Paradox Lost (New Jersey); University of Wisconsin; Milwaukee Arts Center.

1966   Janus Film Society; Haverford College; Firehouse Films; Pratt Institute (New York City); SUNY Buffalo; Gold Coast Film Society (Davis, California); Seventh Ward DFL Club (Minneapolis); Cinematheque 16 (Los Angeles); St. Eric Foundation; The Happening Art Club; Philadelphia Arts Council; Walker Art Center (Minneapolis); Elmira College (New York).

1967   Art Institute of Chicago; Lynn Co. TV preview; Rosary Hill College (New York); Mount Holyoke College; Movies Round Midnight; Cinema Psychedelica (California); The Danforth Foundation (St. Louis); Antioch College.

1968   The Alumni Club of Chicago; ACLU, Manhattan chapter; Smithsonian Museum preview; Lotus Film (Atlanta); *Life Magazine* preview; Wayne Ave. Playhouse (Philadelphia).

1969   South Shore Community Arts Council (New York); Harpur College; Japan
       Coop (Tokyo); Southwestern College (Kansas); Anthology Theater (New York
       City); University of Pennsylvania; University of Vermont (Norwich); American
       International School (New Delhi); Oberlin College; St. John Fisher College;
       University of Alaska; Sonoma State College (California); Fort Wayne Unitarian
       Congregation.

1970   University of Illinois (Chicago); Scarsdale Adult School; New York University.

1971   Contemporary Arts Center (Ohio); Anthology Film Archives; Queens
       College CUNY; Lawrence Academy (Massachusetts); Hampshire College
       (Massachusetts).

1972   SUNY New Paltz; School of the Art Institute of Chicago; Yale University;
       Vancouver Art Gallery; Madison Art Center (Wisconsin).

1973   Columbia University; Rhode Island School of Design; Indianapolis Museum
       of Art; Boston College; Contemporary Arts Museum (Houston); University of
       Oklahoma; Harvard-Epworth Church.

Castro Street, Bruce Baillie (1966, 10 minutes)

1968   Wichita State University; New York City Community College; Cambridge
       Center for Adult Education (Massachusetts); Yale University; Freedom Forum;
       White Plains High School (New York); Newark State College; Mount Holyoke
       College; Southwest Texas State Museum; Friends of the Whitney Museum;
       Southwestern College (Kansas); Cornell University; Aardvark; Allegheny
       College Union (Pennsylvania); SUNY Cortland; New Jersey Institute for
       Film Art; Crack of Doom (Baltimore); Fieldston School (New York); Apple
       Farm Art and Music Center (New Jersey); Quinnipiac College (Connecticut);
       University of Washington; Montgomery County Schools (Pennsylvania);
       Moderna Museet (Stockholm); New College (Florida); Wayne Ave. Playhouse
       (Philadelphia); Smithsonian Museum preview; Flaherty Seminar; Central
       Missouri State College; Brown University.

1969   University of Iowa; Anthology Theater; New York Cinematheque; Vanderbilt
       University; New York University; McPherson College (Kentucky); United
       Ministry in Higher Education (Milwaukee); Jewish Museum (New York City);
       University of North Dakota; St. Joseph's College; College of New Rochelle
       (New York); College of the Virgin Islands; Loyola University; Mount Hermon
       School (Massachusetts); Colby College (Maine); Independent Film and Multi-
       Media Coop (Wisconsin); Rhode Island School of Design; Manhattanville
       College; Tennessee Fine Arts Center; USIA; Aspen School of Contemporary

Art; Ohio State University; Manheim High School (Pennsylvania); Collegiate School (New York City); University of Illinois (Chicago); Center for the Eye (Aspen); New York Film Festival; University of Pennsylvania; Fairleigh Dickinson University (New Jersey); Bard College; Massachusetts Institute of Technology; University of Illinois Medical Center (Chicago); University of Maryland; Mount Sinai School of Medicine (New York City); Wadsworth Atheneum (Connecticut).

1970   Wells College (New York); Ulster County Community College (New York); University of Wisconsin; University of South Carolina; Philadelphia College of Art; Kent State University; Newton College of the Sacred Heart (Massachusetts); Whitney Museum preview; Antioch College; Waukegan Township High School (Illinois); University of Florida; Maryland Institute; Harpur College; University of Delaware; Hudson River Museum; Colorado College; Temple Buell College (Colorado); Dartmouth College; Long Island City High School; Central Michigan University; Harvard University; Ivy School of Professional Art (Pennsylvania); University of South Florida; Boston University.

1971   Providence Art Directors' Club; Dana Hall Schools (Massachusetts); Loomis School (Connecticut); Slippery Rock State College (Pennsylvania); University of California, Santa Barbara; University of Minnesota; Kalamazoo College (Michigan); Trinity College (Connecticut); Wesleyan University; Museum of Fine Arts (Boston); Lawrence Academy (Massachusetts); Hampshire College (Massachusetts); Birmingham Art Association (Alabama); Edinboro State College (Pennsylvania); University of Virginia (Charlottesville).

1972   Eastern Washington State College; St. Cloud State College (Minnesota); Museum of Modern Art (New York); Thomas More College (Kansas); First Methodist Church (Philadelphia); Brotherhood-In-Action (New York City); Jersey City State College; Hiram College (Ohio).

1973   Northern Illinois University; Rockford Art Association (Illinois); Miami-Dade Junior College (Florida); Illinois State University; Triton Regional School (Massachusetts); Temple University; Brandeis University; Vassar College; University of New Mexico; Mt. Hood Community College (Oregon); Albright College (Pennsylvania); Queens College CUNY; Upsala College (New Jersey); Habonim Camp Tel Ari (New York); Spence School (New York City); Walker Art Center (Minneapolis).

1974   Skidmore College (New York); Wright State University (Ohio); White Ox Films at RPI (New York); Prince George's Community College (Maryland); American Film Institute (Washington, D.C.); Sangamon State University (Illinois); Corpus Christi School (Maryland); University of Pittsburgh;

Villanova University (Pennsylvania); Norwalk Community College (Connecticut).

1975   Pittsburgh Film-Makers; New Orleans Public Library; Upstate Films (New York); Moore College of Art (Philadelphia); Colgate University; Detroit Society of Arts and Crafts; Cleveland State University; Ramapo College Media Center (New Jersey); Lewiston State Arts Park (New York); University of Oklahoma; College of Marin (California); SUNY Purchase.

1976   University of Kentucky (Lexington); Adelphi University (New York); Lake Placid School of Arts (New York); New Baltimore Independent Film Museum; William Paterson College (New Jersey); Emerson College (Massachusetts); Clark University (Massachusetts); Vermilion Community College (Minnesota); University of Rhode Island; St. Lawrence University (New York); University of Missouri (Columbia); Boulder Public Library; Oberlin College; McNay Art Institute (Texas); Bradley University (Illinois); University of Michigan (Ann Arbor); Philbrook Art Center (Tulsa); Cayuga County College (New York).

1977   Peters Township High School (Pennsylvania); Robert Morris College (Pennsylvania); Kirkland College (New York); Hotchkiss School (Connecticut); Arrowmont School of Art (Tennessee); Thomas Jefferson College (Michigan).

1978   Virginia Polytechnic Institute; School of Visual Arts (New York City); New Trier High School (Illinois); Wilmette Park School District (Illinois); Lake Michigan College (Benton Harbor); Community College of Allegheny County (Pennsylvania); Junior College of Albany (New York); Florida Atlantic University (Boca Raton); Visual Studies Workshop (Rochester); Stanford University; Compass Film Association (New Haven); State University College of Brockport (New York); La Guardia Community College (New York City); Maumee Valley Country Day School (Ohio).

FUSES, Carolee Schneeman (1964–68, 22 minutes)

1971   Northwestern University; University of New Hampshire (Durham); University of California (San Diego); University of Texas (Austin); Ohio University; Dickinson College (Pennsylvania); Middlebury College; University of Colorado (Boulder); Festival of Women's Films (New York City); Virginia Commonwealth University (Richmond).

1972   Magic Lantern Society (Chicago); Brock University (St. Catherines, Ontario); Washington University (St. Louis); Castleton State College (Vermont);

University of Minnesota (Minneapolis); Pacific Film Archive; University of Bridgeport (Connecticut); Southern Methodist University (Dallas); Santa Barbara City College (California); American University (Washington, D.C.).

1973   California Institute of the Arts; Miami-Dade Junior College (Florida); Williams College; Pratt Institute; University of Maryland (Baltimore); Syracuse University; Albright College (Pennsylvania); SUNY Binghamton; Pennsylvania State University; University of California (Berkeley); SUNY Buffalo.

1974   University of Massachusetts (Amherst); Portland Community College; USIA; Bard College; Queens College CUNY; Boston College; Philadelphia Museum of Art; Massachusetts Institute of Technology, Center for Advanced Visual Studies; Kalamazoo College (Michigan); Bucks County Community College (Pennsylvania).

1975   SUNY Purchase; Cedar Crest College (Pennsylvania); University of Wisconsin (Madison); Art Institute of Chicago; Cornell University; Southern Illinois University.

1976   Denver Free University; University of Rhode Island; Goucher College (Maryland).

1977   Colby College (Maine); Southeast Masschusetts University (North Dartmouth); Welles College (New York); University of Delaware; Kansas City Art Institute.

1978   Rochester Institute of Technology; Michigan State University; Emory University (Georgia); Jersey City State College.

1979   Water Street Arts Center (Milwaukee); Collective for Living Cinema (New York City).

1980   Eastern Illinois University; Merzaum Collection (Baltimore); Wayne State University (Detroit); Pasadena Film Forum (California); Film in the Cities (Minnesota); Massachusetts College of Art; University of Iowa Film Festival.

1981   Northwestern University; Massachusetts College of Art Film Society; Hamilton College Library (New York); Institute for Art and Urban Resources (New York City); Ithaca College (New York).

Window Water Baby Moving, Stan Brakhage (1959, 12 minutes)

1976   Gustavus Adolphus College (Minnesota); Ithaca College (New York); SUNY Utica; New School (New York City); University of Massachusetts (Amherst);

University of Wyoming; Indianapolis Museum of Art; Lyndon State College (Pennsylvania); Pitzer College (California); Brooklyn College; University of North Carolina (Chapel Hill); Purdue University; Daniel Boone Regional Library (Missouri); Northwestern University; Harvard University; Colgate University; Wright State University; White Ox Films; St. Lawrence University; Walker Art Center (Minneapolis); SUNY Buffalo; Dartmouth College; Temple University; University of Hartford; Northern Illinois University; Boston College; University of Delaware; Center for the Living Force (New York); University of Rhode Island; University of Texas (El Paso).

1977   Westover School (Connecticut); Museum of Modern Art (New York); Salesian High School (California); Rhode Island School of Design; SUNY Agricultural and Technical College (Cobleskill); Lincoln Land Community College (Illinois); Thousand Eyes Cinema (New York City); Hiram College (Ohio); Art Institute of Chicago; Kansas City Art Institute; University of Maine (Portland); Central Michigan University; Hanover School (Massachusetts); Scarsdale Board of Education (New York); Collective for Living Cinema; Skidmore College (New York); St. Olaf College (Minnesota); Grand Valley State College (Michigan); Princeton Public Library; Hunter College; SUNY Empire State College (Suffern); Cooper Union (New York City); Hobart and William Smith College (New York); Genesee Community College (New York); Cleveland State University; New Trier High School (Illinois).

1978   Bethany College (Kansas); University of South Florida (Tampa); Cornell University; Ball State University (Indiana); American University; University of Toledo; Stockton State College (New Jersey); Visual Studies Workshop (Rochester); Massachusetts Institute of Technology; University of California (San Diego); Edinboro State College (Pennsylvania); Film Society, West Allas (Wisconsin); St. John Fisher College (New York).

1979   University of New Mexico; University of Kentucky (Lexington); Columbia University; Middlebury College; Vassar College; Ramapo College (New Jersey); Film in the Cities preview (Minnesota); New Mexico State University (Las Cruces); Denison University (Ohio); South Dakota State University (Brookings); La Guardia College CUNY; Long Island University (New York); Ohio State University (Columbus); St. John's University (New York); Cayuga Community College (New York).

1980   Otis Art Institute (Louisiana); University of Kansas (Lawrence); North Carolina Museum of Art (Raleigh); University of Wisconsin (Madison); School of Visual Arts (New York City); Southern Illinois University; Wesleyan University (Connecticut); University of Southern Maine; Hampshire College (Massachusetts); Macalester College (Minnesota); University of California (Santa Barbara).

1981   Bard College (New York); University of Oregon; Old Dominion University
        (Virginia); Contemporary Arts Center (New Orleans).

1982   School of the Art Institute of Chicago; Virginia Commonwealth University
        (Richmond); Drew University (New Jersey); Colgate University; Hamilton
        College (New York); Mothering Publications (New Mexico); New York
        University; University of Pennsylvania; Bucks County Community College
        (Pennsylvania).

1983   Amherst College; Quinnipiac College (Connecticut); Miami University
        (Ohio); Sacred Heart University (New Jersey); Upper Valley Development
        and Training Center (New Hampshire); Yellowstone Art Center; University
        of Colorado; New York Public Library, Donnell; Minneapolis Society of Fine
        Arts; Princeton University.

1984   Hitchcock Clinic (New Hampshire); Whitney Museum; Media Study Center
        (Buffalo); University of California (Los Angeles); Sarah Lawrence College;
        College of Mount St. Vincent (New York); SUNY Purchase.

1985   University of Maryland; Minnesota College of Art and Design; New Canaan
        High School (Connecticut).

1986   Rice University (Texas); The Kitchen (New York City); Hofstra University
        (New York); Texas State University (Denton); Miami-Dade Community
        College; University of Arizona (Tucson); University of Illinois (Champaign-
        Urbana).

Zorns Lemma, Hollis Frampton (1970, 60 minutes)

1970   New York Film Festival; University of Iowa; Union College (New York);
        Contemporary Arts Center of Ohio; Canyon Cinema; Yale University; New
        York University; New England College (New Hampshire).

1971   Museum of Fine Arts (Boston); P. A. Foundation (New York City); University
        of Rochester; University of Colorado (Boulder); SUNY Buffalo; Hansen Fuller
        Gallery (San Francisco); Guggenheim Foundation; Ohio University; Museum
        of Contemporary Art (Chicago); Cooper Union (New York City); University of
        Hartford; USIA.

1972   Pratt Institute (New York City); South Dakota State University (Brookings);
        Pacific Film Archives; Rhode Island School of Design; Hunter College CUNY;
        Bard College; Harvard-Epworth Church; Museum of Modern Art (New York);
        Philadelphia Institute of Cinema.

1973   University of Pennsylvania; Colby College; Northwestern University; University of Maine (Gorham); Hampshire College (Massachusetts); University of New Hampshire (Durham); Moorhead State College (Minnesota); Spence School (New York City); Antioch College; Kent State University; University of Pittsburgh; University of Oklahoma (Norman); Boston College; Queens College CUNY; University of Texas (Arlington).

1974   University of California (San Diego); San Francisco Art Institute; Art Institute of Chicago; Portland Community College; SUNY Purchase; Dartmouth College; Colorado College; Wright State University; Center for Visual Studies, Massachusetts Institute of Technology.

1975   Anthology Film Archives; St. John Fisher College (Rochester); Colgate University; Purdue University; School of Visual Arts; Brooklyn College CUNY; Oberlin College; University of New Mexico; Nassau County Library System (New York); University of Illinois (Chicago); Princeton University.

1976   University of Wisconsin (Oshkosh); California Institute of the Arts; Ramapo College (New Jersey); Stockton State College (New Jersey); Utica College (New York); Harvard University; Southern Illinois University; St. Norbert College (Wisconsin); Syracuse University; Wesleyan University.

1977   University of the South, Sewanee (Tennessee); Ohio State University; Idaho State University (Pocatello); Johnson Museum (New York); Virginia Polytechnic Institute (Blacksburg); Indianapolis Museum of Art; SUNY Plattsburgh; University of Wisconsin (Milwaukee).

1978   School of Visual Arts (New York City); Whitney Museum Downtown; IBM Corporation (New York); SUNY Binghamton; Independent Film Oasis (Los Angeles); Wilmette Park School District (Illinois); Sarah Lawrence College.

1979   University of California (San Diego); Middlebury College; University of New Mexico (Albuquerque); Institute of Contemporary Art (Boston); Denison University (Ohio); Chatham College (Pennsylvania); Southern Illinois University; San Francisco Art Institute; Segue Foundation (New York City); Occidental College (California); Rhode Island School of Design.

1980   Carleton College (Minnesota); Hofstra University (New York); Independent Media Arts (Atlanta); University of Wisconsin (Stout); University of Iowa; University of California (Santa Barbara); Otis Art Institute (Los Angeles); Drexel University; Rochester Institute of Technology; Brown University.

(2000)

Notes

Introduction

1. Kelly's sinuous meditation on the visual dynamics of a small house, with copious footnotes, was published as *Sparrow* 20 (May 1974): n.p. I met Kelly in the early seventies during a teaching stint at Bard College, have used his title on two other occasions, and appreciate his forbearance in letting me riff on it one more time.

2. The two preeminent books in the field, Sitney's *Visionary Film: The American Avant-Garde, 1943–2000* (New York: Oxford University Press, 1974/2002) and David E. James's *Allegories of Cinema: American Film in the Sixties* (Princeton: Princeton University Press, 1989), are built around in-depth discussions of leading filmmakers, along with theoretically nuanced accounts of major styles or modes of organization. Scott MacDonald's three volumes of interviews, *A Critical Cinema,* published by the University of California Press in 1988, 1992, and 1998, contain extensive information on the production contexts and ideas behind individual films. I have undertaken a series of career overviews intended for general film viewers with limited knowledge of the avant-garde. See: "Qualities of Light: Stan Brakhage and the Continuing Pursuit of Vision," *Film Comment* (September–October 1995): 68–76; "Creating Spectacle from Dross: The Chimeric Cinema of Ken Jacobs," *Film Comment* (March–April 1997): 58–63; "Dancing on the Precipice: Warren Sonbert," *Film Comment* (March–April 1999): 46–51.

3. As someone who is hardly an important player in the movement, I have followed the examples of Brakhage, Mekas, Saul Levine, Ken Jacobs, Chick Strand, Bruce Baillie, Marjorie Keller, and others in taking on a succession of roles: besides writing scholarly and journalistic commentaries, I have curated programs for several conferences; coedited two journals, *Motion Picture* and *Millennium Film Journal*; served on the boards of directors of several screening and/or production facilities, as well the board of the Film-Makers' Cooperative; evaluated

grant applications for private foundations; and of course lectured and taught courses on the avant-garde. I have also completed twenty films in various avant-garde idioms. The point is that my résumé is far from unusual. Indeed, it is possible that *most* makers, past and present, have involved themselves in nonfilmic arenas of administration, writing, and promotion. There are a number of possible explanations for this fluidity: the community is relatively small, concentrated in a handful of urban centers, and has a long history of resisting internal hierarchies; economic rewards are tiny or nonexistent, thus decreasing internecine competition; for those who came to maturity in the cauldron of sixties upheavals, organization building has served as a form of activism.

4. I have more or less cribbed—perhaps bowdlerized—this account of editing paradigms from Sitney's *Visionary Film,* as informed by James's later commentaries in *Allegories of Cinema.*

5. There are a number of interesting versions of the "poetic vs. structural" debate. Although not as easily accessible as some, a heated and informative confrontation is transcribed in "Stan Brakhage and Malcolm LeGrice Debate," *Criss-Cross* 6 (March 1978): 42–56.

6. For a useful analysis of Deren's extrafilmic career, see Lauren Rabinowitz, *Points of Resistance: Women, Power and Politics in the New York Avant-Garde Cinema, 1943–71* (Urbana: University of Illinois Press, 1991), 49–91.

7. Mekas, *Movie Journal: The Rise of a New American Cinema, 1959–1971* (New York: Collier Books, 1972), 183–84, 329–32.

1. Routines of Emancipation

1. A metaphoric relation between a spiritual journey, especially one involving cross-country travel, and cinematic narrative is a key premise of Ken Kesey's "Merry Pranksters" episode as celebrated by Tom Wolfe in *The Electric Kool-Aid Acid Test* (1968) and figures as well in Allen Ginsberg's collection *The Fall of America* (1972) and Don DeLillo's novel *Americana* (1971). For more on the conflation of movies with altered consciousness, see David E. James, *Allegories of Cinema: American Film in the Sixties* (Princeton: Princeton University Press, 1989).

2. During this period, Hollywood was the beneficiary of a new crop of writer-directors, many of whom had made amateur movies as children and gone on to train in then-proliferating university film programs. A small number of independent filmmakers (John Cassavetes, Robert Downey, Curtis Harrington, Andy Warhol) made the difficult transition to commercial feature production. Conversely, the "liberated" film studios of the late sixties tapped both formally and informally into the visual innovations wrought by avant-garde makers. On the relationship between amateurism and the period's movie mania, see Patricia R. Zimmerman, "Hollywood, Home Movies, and Common Sense: Amateur Film as Aesthetic Dissemination and Social Control, 1950–1962," *Cinema Journal* 27, no. 4 (summer 1988): 23–44.

3. Annette Michelson was among the first to connect the avant-garde's diffusion of movie technology to a "radical aspiration": "One rejoices in the promise of . . . the generation of little Americans making science-fiction films after school in those backyards." "Film and the Radical Aspiration," in *Film Culture Reader,* ed. P. Adams Sitney (New York: Praeger, 1970), 409. Another version of this common scenario is found in Ernest Callenbach, "Looking Backward," *Film Quarterly* 22, no.1 (1968): 8. Accepting many of the premises of Marshall McLuhan's then-influential theories, promoters of independent film invariably stressed the conjunction of amateurism with resistance to political domination, a basic motif in Jonas Mekas's private diaries, stored in the library of Anthology Film Archives in New York City. In what follows, I

quote extensively from these (unpaginated and at times undated) volumes. All citations appear in parentheses within the body of the text. As well, I frequently cite Mekas's collection of newspaper columns, *Movie Journal: The Rise of a New American Cinema, 1959–1971* (New York: Macmillan, 1972). Once again, references to this text are included in parentheses. Finally, I conducted an interview with Mekas on April 14, 1990, quotations from which are also indicated internally.

4. *"Easy Rider* and Its Critics," in *Mass Culture Revisited,* ed. Bernard Rosenberg and David Manning White (New York: Van Nostrand Reinhold, 1971), 244.

5. Reprinted in James Miller, *"Democracy Is in the Streets": From Port Huron to the Siege of Chicago* (New York: Simon and Schuster, 1987), 329.

6. Calvin Tomkins, "All Pockets Open," *New Yorker* (6 January 1973): 36.

7. James, *Allegories of Cinema,* 100.

8. Todd Gitlin, *The Whole World Is Watching* (Berkeley: University of California Press, 1987), 6.

9. Miller, *"Democracy Is in the Streets,"* 83–84.

10. It is a pleasure to report that in 1990 the New York Co-op is alive and well, continuing to operate according to the precepts of openness and direct participation on which it was founded. For the record, I am on the board of directors and am a past president of that oversight body.

11. For Mekas's early condemnation of American experimental film, see "The Experimental Film in America," *Film Culture* 3 (autumn 1955): 15.

12. The best accounts of this galvanizing incident are in Mekas, *Movie Journal,* 111–15 and 172, and Tomkins, "All Pockets Open," 36–38.

13. Mekas, *Movie Journal,* 319.

14. In 1960 C. Wright Mills, who helped provide the New Left with its theory of power, urged intellectuals to "make the mass media the means of liberal—which is to say, liberating—education." He set an example by publishing a defense of Castro's revolution in a cheap, mass-market paperback. Debates over the potential to mobilize or affect public consciousness through channels of mass communication raged from the beginning to the end of the decade. At one extreme is the Yippie assertion that the TV image is the very site of revolutionary work because that medium unavoidably transmits the values it records; see David Armstrong, *A Trumpet to Arms: Alternative Media in America* (Boston: J. P. Tarcher, 1981), 118. With equal conviction, the founder of a radical video group cited by Armstrong argues that "no alternative cultural vision is going to succeed . . . until it develops its own alternate information structures, not just alternative content pumped across existing ones" (132). Despite the dominance of a type of Frankfurt School analysis of mass culture, there were continuous efforts at alliance even from those most instrumental in building alternative institutions.

15. Gitlin, *The Whole World Is Watching,* 157.

16. Hoffman, cited in *The Sixties Papers: Documents of a Rebellious Decade,* ed. Judith Clavir Albert and Stewart Edward Albert (New York: Praeger, 1984), 417–28.

17. Tomkins, "All Pockets Open," 37. There is insufficient reason here to examine the intricate history of personal friction between Mekas and Vogel, except to say that the tenor of Vogel's attacks was often that of traditional Old Left politics railing against the younger generation's lack of discipline and focus.

18. P. Adams Sitney, "Introduction: A Reader's Guide to the American Avant-Garde Film," in *Film Culture Reader,* 9.

19. Susan Sontag, "Jack Smith's *Flaming Creatures,*" *Against Interpretation* (New York: Delta Books, 1964), 228.

20. Mekas's diaries mention similar accusations by other Co-op members and by Canyon Cinema members who screened their films under Mekas's auspices. It appears likely that rentals and box-office receipts were at times handled in a loose fashion, but it is inconceivable that improper personal gain was the motive or outcome.

21. The legend of Smith's missing negative is another turbid story not, in this context, worth trying to reassemble. According to Mekas—and confirmed by others—the negative was salvaged from a film-lab trash heap many years later and returned to Smith.

22. David Ehrenstein, *Film: The Front Line* (Denver: Arden Press, 1984), 29.

23. Ibid., 15–34. David Ehrenstein, to his discredit, repeats and even enhances Smith's charges without a word of skepticism or qualification, in order to bolster his own misguided campaign against Mekas and the "avant-establishment."

24. Jack Smith, "Uncle Fishhook and the Sacred Baby Poo-Poo of Art," *Semiotext(e)* 3 , no. 2 (1978): 192.

25. Ibid., 194.

26. Ibid., 198, 202, 203, respectively.

27. Mekas was adept at turning his self-evident passion for collecting and preserving into a politically correct course, as in the following passage: "Who started the idea that the new, revolutionary, radical, underground culture is diametrically opposed to the old? I think the idea was invented by the enemies of processes of change . . . Revolutionaries and the underground are really restorers of culture, they are attacking the vulgarizations and misuses of culture, art, etc." *Movie Journal*, 400.

28. See Todd Gitlin, *The Sixties: Years of Hope, Days of Rage,* (New York: Bantam Books, 1987), especially 237–40, 338. Gitlin's detailed account of factional conflicts within SDS is in many ways comparable to countercultural clashes between advocates of unconstrained, isolated activity and the strategic management of mass-movement dynamics. By the late sixties, at the apogee of SDS's power, a younger core of spokespersons from various ideological factions sought to discredit the original leadership base through accusations of "revisionism," "popularization," careerism, and counterrevolutionary policies. See also Miller, *"Democracy Is in the Streets,"* 238–40.

29. "When the Left Was New," in *The Sixties without Apology,* ed. Sohnya Sayres, Anders Stephanson, Stanley Aronowitz, and Fredric Jameson. (Minneapolis: University of Minnesota Press, 1984), 33.

30. Gitlin, *The Sixties,* 26–27, 84–85; See also Miller, *"Democracy Is in the Streets,"* 146–48. There has been considerable discussion of the literary and intellectual roots of New Left writing.

31. Entreaties such as Timothy Leary's "Get out of your mind and into your senses" are indicative of a broad tendency in regard to traditional rules of argument and exposition (logical sequence, evidence, appeals to authority) as aligned with established structures of power and repressive of the individual's firsthand experience. The animus against formal language is reflected by such diverse phenomena as lyricless rock music, the near-muteness of much experimental theater, and avant-garde film's almost complete severing of the image from human speech.

32. "On Making a Perfect Mess," in Albert and Albert, eds., *The Sixties Papers,* 405.

33. Quoted in Gitlin, *The Sixties,* 134.

34. A similar spirit inflected other precincts of the counterculture. *Rolling Stone* magazine founder Jan Wenner spoke for what he imagined was the "purity" of rock music at exactly the moment of its increasing politicization and interpenetration with mass protest: "Rock wants no part of today's social structure, especially in its most manifestly corrupt form, politics, even 'new left' politics." See Armstrong, *A Trumpet to Arms,* 124

35. Eventually, the avant-garde became almost synonymous with "art" in Mekas's politico-

aesthetic pronouncements, and all art was inherently revolutionary in its "betterment of man, wakening up of his humanness . . . Art is always anti-status quo, anti-imperialist, anti-capitalist, anti-dictatorship, and anti-private property" (Diaries, May 1970).

36. Another avant-garde filmmaker who braided liberationist ideology with the prospect of aesthetic renewal was Saul Levine, at one time a prominent member of the national leadership of the SDS and an editor of the organization's newsletter, *New Left Notes*. In an interview for a campus newspaper, Levine defended Brakhage's work as the most radical filmic contribution to social change: "The kind of film I'm interested in is unmanipulative. It teaches people to be free." "Interview," in *The Book of Saul*, ed. Marjorie Keller (New York: Collective for Living Cinema, 1976), n.p.

37. The equation of improvisational performance with a political ideal of direct confrontation is a common rhetorical figure. For example, Ernest Callenbach praises cinéma vérité documentary for its refusal of an omniscient, authoritarian camera address in "Looking Backward," *Film Quarterly* 21, no. 1 (spring 1968): 7. Leo Braudy goes even further in an assessment of early Newsreel work: "The non-sync film becomes more radical than the sync because the sync suggests easy solutions, the effortless marriage of word and image." Newsreel, he maintains, proposes a "more open-ended" political result via the "radicalizing of aesthetic responses." "Newsreel: A Report," *Film Quarterly* 21, no. 2 (winter 1968–1969): 48–49. One of Mekas's earliest and most comprehensive treatments of the link between spontaneous form and emancipation is found in "Notes on the New American Cinema" *Film Culture* 24 (1962): 6–16.

38. Armstrong, *A Trumpet to Arms*, 120.

39. Herbert Marcuse, *One-Dimensional Man* (Boston: Beacon Press, 1964), 250.

40. Fredric Jameson, "Periodizing the Sixties," in Sayres et al., eds., *The Sixties without Apology*, 184.

41. See Mekas, "A Call for a New Generation of Film-Makers," *Film Culture* 19 (1959): 3.

42. Endorsing in 1964 the New York League for Sexual Freedom, Mekas demanded "respect for individual liberty" and the repeal of laws restricting what is done "voluntarily by adults in private" (Diaries, 24 March 1964).

43. Again, David James supplies a thorough and authoritative analysis of the confluence of Beat and underground film cultures: *Allegories of Cinema*, 85–102.

44. Miller, *"Democracy Is in the Streets,"* 147.

45. "Rock and the Politics of Memory," in Sayres et al., eds., *The Sixties without Apology*, 65.

46. Hebdige, *Subculture: The Meaning of Style* (London: Methuen, 1979), 49.

47. Gary Snyder, "Buddhism and the Coming Revolution," in Albert and Albert, eds., *The Sixties Papers*, 432.

48. The opening statement by SNCC proposed that "the redemptive community supersedes immoral social systems," in Albert and Albert, eds., *The Sixties Papers*, 113. This vision is one source for subsequent demands by African Americans for "community control" and autonomy within economic, political, and cultural spheres. For a powerful example of this commitment, see Malcolm X, "The Ballot or the Bullet," Ibid., 126–32.

49. Gitlin, *The Sixties*, 107.

50. Quoted in Miller, *"Democracy Is in the Streets,"* 239.

51. *The Sixties*, 262.

52. Victor Turner, *The Ritual Process* (Chicago: Aldine, 1969), 143–48.

53. Victor Turner, *Dramas, Fields, and Metaphors* (Ithaca: Cornell University Press, 1974), 231–70.

54. Ibid., 266.

2. Identity and/as Moving Image

1. Gerald Mast and Bruce F. Kawin make a similar point about this scene as home movie in *A Short History of the Movies* (Boston: Allyn and Bacon, 1996), 26. In Sarah Moon's omnibus tribute film to the centenary of cinema, *Lumière* (1995), Spike Lee "remakes" *Le Déjeuner* using a Lumière camera to capture his young son enjoying an outdoor meal.

2. See Patricia Zimmerman, "Hollywood, Home Movies, and Common Sense: Amateur Film as Aesthetic Dissemination and Social Control," *Film Journal* 27, no. 4 (summer 1988): 23–44.

3. The original version of this essay surveys documentary as well as experimental works; see "No Longer Absolute: Portraiture in American Avant-Garde and Documentary Film of the Sixties," in *Rites of Realism: Essays on Corporeal Cinema,* ed. Ivone Margulies (Durham: Duke University Press, 2003), 93–118.

4. Jerome Hill titled his important autobiographical work *Film Portrait* (1970). A similar slippage is evident in Judy Collins's and Jill Godmilow's documentary *Antonio: A Portrait of the Woman* (1974), a straightforward feminist biography.

5. Wendy Steiner, *Exact Resemblance to Exact Resemblance: The Literary Portraiture of Gertrude Stein* (New Haven: Yale University Press, 1978), 2.

6. Although this may seem obvious, making a *film* portrait typically requires the explicit knowledge, presence, and participation of the subject, whereas paintings, drawings, and literary portraits can be created in their subjects' absence. A counterexample, which had a significant impact on postsixties styles of avant-garde portraiture, is Joseph Cornell's great found footage tribute, *Rose Hobart* (1939).

7. André Bazin, "The Ontology of the Photographic Image," *What Is Cinema?,* trans. Hugh Gray (Berkeley: University of California Press, 1967), 16. Picasso's 1939 version of this dictum is cited by William Rubin in "Reflections on Picasso and Portraiture," in *Picasso and Portraiture: Representation and Transformation,* ed. Rubin (New York: Museum of Modern Art, 1996), 18: "photography has arrived at a point where it is capable of liberating painting from all literature, from the anecdote, and even from the subject."

8. Rubin, "Reflections," 9.

9. Cesare Zavattini, "Some Ideas on the Cinema," *Sight and Sound* 23, no. 2 (October–December 1953): 225.

10. P. Adams Sitney gives the best account of this cultural influence in *Visionary Film: The American Avant-Garde, 1943–2000* (New York: Oxford University Press, 2002), passim.

11. "Richard Leacock Interviewed by Mark Shivas," reprinted in *Imagining Reality: The Faber Book of Documentary,* ed. Kevin Macdonald and Mark Cousins (London: Faber and Faber, 1996), 257.

12. Cited in David E. James, *Allegories of Cinema: American Film in the Sixties* (Princeton: Princeton University Press, 1989), 67.

13. Jonas Mekas, "Sixth Independent Film Award" (1964), in *Film Culture Reader,* ed. P. Adams Sitney (New York: Praeger, 1970), 427.

14. Patrick S. Smith, *Andy Warhol's Art and Films* (Ann Arbor: UMI Research Press, 1986), 154–56. In addition, Smith quotes Warhol's instructions to playwright and scenarist Ronald Tavel for one of several separate films titled *Screen Test*: "Sit and ask him questions which will make him perform in some way before the camera . . . The questions should be in such a way that they elicit, you know, things from his face, because that's what I'm more interested in rather than in what he says in response" (159).

15. Gisele Freund, *Photography and Society* (Boston: David Godine, 1980), 40–41. See also Beaumont Newhall, *The History of Photography* (New York: Museum of Modern Art, 1964), 50–53.

16. A summary statement of portraiture's enduring humanistic appeal is offered by E. H. Gombrich, describing the effect of a Rembrandt painting: "We feel face to face with real people, we sense their warmth, their need for sympathy and also their loneliness and suffering"; *The Story of Art* (New York: E. P. Dutton, 1972), 332.

17. James, *Allegories of Cinema*, 69. James takes issue with the yoking of Warhol and documentary, claiming that "far from affirming the possibility of cinema verite, Warhol mordantly exposes the fallaciousness of both the social psychology on which its assumptions are based and the cinematic codes produced to implement them" (68).

18. The critical literature on Warhol's films is quite extensive yet, significantly, very little of it is devoted to issues of portraiture. I trace some additional implications of Warhol's ironic treatment of painterly codes in "Flesh of Absence: Resighting the Warhol Catechism," in *Andy Warhol Film Factory*, ed. Michael O'Pray (London: British Film Institute, 1989), 149–52.

19. Mekas, *Movie Journal: The Rise of a New American Cinema, 1959–1971* (New York: Macmillan, 1971), 158.

20. Rubin, "Reflections on Picasso and Portraiture," 13.

21. Cited in Wendy Steiner, *Exact Resemblance*, 183. Stein was acutely aware of correspondences between her method and ontological properties of cinema: "I was doing what the cinema was doing, I was making a continuous succession of the statement of what a person was until I had not many things but one thing" (176).

22. As Sitney astutely observes "the form of the portrait radiates through the *Songs*," *Visionary Film*, 245. His exemplary discussion and formal analysis of the cycle has been crucial to my understanding of Brakhage's stake in portraiture.

23. Until the late 1980s, Brakhage continued to make sporadic portraits and self-portraits.

24. Cited in P. Adams Sitney, "Autobiography in Avant-Garde Film," reprinted in *The Avant-Garde Film: A Reader of Theory and Criticism*, ed. P. Adams Sitney (New York: New York University Press, 1978), 208.

25. Sixties guru Theodore Roszak summarizes the countercultural agenda as "the effort to discover new types of community, new family patterns, new sexual mores . . . [and] new personal identities on the far side of power politics," *The Making of a Counter Culture* (New York: Harper and Row, 1968), 31.

26. John Welchman, "Face(t)s: Notes on Faciality," *Artforum* 27, no. 3 (November 1988):131.

27. It is important to stress the generative relationship between Super-8's democratic, low-tech ethos and the elevation of post-sixties portraiture.

28. See Keller's study, *The Untutored Eye: Childhood in the Films of Cocteau, Cornell, and Brakhage* (Cranbury, N.J.: Associated University Presses, 1986).

29. By far the best reckoning of Mekas's diary project is by David E. James, "Film Diary/Diary Film: Practice and Product in *Walden*," in *To Free the Cinema*, ed. David E. James (Princeton: Princeton University Press, 1992), 145–79.

30. It can be argued that the "sketches" mode in *Diaries, Notes, and Sketches* is already implicit in the satirically static group portrait *Award Presentation to Andy Warhol* (1964) and again in *Report from Millbrook* (1966), a somewhat jumbled encounter with Timothy Leary.

31. Although a discussion of portraiture's artworld cachet during the late seventies and eighties is outside the boundaries of this essay, it is worth mentioning such figures as Chuck

Close, Cindy Sherman, Bruce Nauman, Lucas Samaras, Nan Goldin, Robert Mapplethorpe, and Adrian Piper, each of whom maintained some sort of involvement with experimental film and/or video.

32. Scott MacDonald, "Peggy Ahwesh," *Millennium Film Journal* nos. 39/40 (winter 2003): 5.

33. Although she addresses the aesthetics of portraiture only in passing, Alex Juhasz provides an important overview of AIDS media in *AIDS TV: Identity, Community, and Alternative Video* (Durham: Duke University Press, 1995).

34. *Canyon Cinema Catalogue #6* (San Francisco: Canyon Cinema, 1988), 55.

3. The Redemption of the City

1. Since 1991, when an earlier version of this essay was published, there has been a hopeful ripple of scholarly interest in cinematic urbanism, and in geographical approaches to cinema in general, yet the field remains woefully underdeveloped. See for instance, Stuart C. Aitken and Leo E. Zonn, eds., *Place, Power, Situation, and Spectacle: A Geography of Film* (Lanham, Md.: Rowman and Littlefield, 1994); also David B. Clarke, *The Cinematic City* (New York: Routledge, 1997). Several important essays by leading film scholars are featured in two linked journal issues edited by Clark Arnwine and Jesse Lerner: "Cityscapes I," *Wide Angle* 19, no. 4 (October 1997); "Cityscapes II," *Wide Angle* 20, no. 3 (July 1998). Examinations of the relationship between American avant-garde cinema and urbanism are, however, virtually nonexistent. Symptomatically, James Sanders's massive *Celluloid Skyline: New York and the Movies* (New York: Knopf, 2001) devotes less than a page to consideration of the New York avant-garde. On the other hand, David E. James lends a typically agile theoretical perspective in "Toward a Geo-Cinematic Hermeneutics: Representations of Los Angeles in Non-Industrial Cinema—*Killer of Sheep* and *Water and Power*," *Wide Angle* 20, no. 3: 23–53. Scott MacDonald's recent study of place in independent cinema, *The Garden in the Machine* (Berkeley: University of California Press, 2001), contains many informative discussions of avant-garde city symphonies.

2. See Berman, *All That is Solid Melts into Air: The Experience of Modernity* (London: Verso, 1982), 16–19. William Sharpe and Leonard Wallock provide an effective summary of cultural discourse on modernity and the city in "From 'Great Town' to 'Nonplace Urban Realm': Reassessing the Modern City," in *Visions of the Modern City,* ed. Sharpe and Wallock (Baltimore: Johns Hopkins University Press, 1987), 1–50. Burton Pike frames a similar discussion in *The Image of the City in Modern Literature* (Princeton: Princeton University Press, 1981), esp. 58–106.

3. See Sharpe and Wallock, "From 'Great Town' to 'Nonplace Urban Realm,'" 36–37. The notion of "intelligibility," of strategies that condense complex physical or social arrangements into easily recognizable sites or images, was first elaborated by Kevin Lynch in *The Image of the City* (Cambridge: MIT Press and Harvard University Press, 1960). By 1938, Lewis Mumford had already diagnosed a crisis in the city's loss of form: "No human eye can take it in; no single gathering place can hold its totality." *The Culture of Cities* (New York: Harcourt Brace Jovanovich, 1938/1970), 543.

4. This well-known idea is expounded in Leo Marx's *The Machine in the Garden: Technology and the Pastoral Ideal in America* (New York: Oxford University Press, 1964). As it pertains to avant-garde film, the specter of industrialism is certainly as potent as the locomotive that rumbled past Thoreau's pond.

5. It is no accident that the cities referred to here are the preeminent locations for avant-garde activity in America, New York and San Francisco. Nevertheless, a number of important

filmmakers have explored the unique attributes of Los Angeles (Pat O'Neill), Boston (Saul Levine, Pelle Lowe), Pittsburgh (Peggy Ahwesh), Chicago (Tom Palazzolo), Akron (Richard Myers), and London, Ontario (Jack Chambers).

6. For an overview of the antiurbanist bias in American thought, see Morton and Lucia White, "The Intellectual Versus the City: The Outlines of a Tradition," in Paul Kramer and Frederick L. Holborn, eds, *The City in American Life* (New York: Capricorn Books, 1970), 243–54.

7. In 1928 industry director and moonlighting avant-gardist Robert Florey made *Skyscraper Symphony,* a film that unfortunately I have been unable to see.

8. Although this topic somewhat exceeds the limits of the present essay, what I have in mind is the delicate balancing of formal and sociological elements in Feininger's "Coenties Slip" (c. 1940) or Lisette Model's "Times Sq." (1940–41).

9. The sublime and obsessive cataloguer of New York underground society in the sixties is of course Andy Warhol, whose serial "action" films like *Kiss* (1963) and *Couch* (1964) and composite portraits like *The Thirteen Most Beautiful Women* (1964) can be read as deadpan celebrations of urban eccentricity. See chapter 2 for a discussion of his largest and most comprehensive project, the "Screen Tests."

10. Perhaps the closest analogy in the social sciences to Gehr's admittedly noninstrumental methods is Erving Goffman's social proxemics as elaborated in *Relations in Public* (New York: Basic Books, 1971). Goffman, like other sociologists, analyzed filmed sequences and his work became popular during the period of structural-minimalist aesthetics.

11. In *Film-Makers' Cooperative Catalogue No. 7* (New York: New American Cinema Group, 1989), 272.

12. Scott MacDonald, "Interview with Jonas Mekas," *October* 29 (summer 1984): 88.

13. Michel de Certeau, "Practices of Space," in *On Signs,* ed. Marshall Blonsky (Baltimore: Johns Hopkins University Press, 1985), 78–96.

14. MacDonald, "Interview," 95.

15. Walter Benjamin makes this assertion in *Charles Baudelaire: A Lyric Poet in the Era of High Capitalism* (London: Verso, 1973), 36.

16. Steven Marcus, "Reading the Illegible: Some Modern Representations of Urban Experience," in Sharpe and Wallock, eds., *Visions of the Modern City,* 240.

17. See William H. Whyte, *City: Rediscovering the Center* (New York: Anchor Books, 1988), 7; and Richard Sennett, *The Conscience of the Eye: The Design and Social Life of Cities* (New York: Knopf, 1990), 58.

18. Fredric Jameson, "Postmodernism, or the Cultural Logic of Late Capitalism," *New Left Review* 146 (July–August 1984): 72.

4. The Resurgence of History and the Avant-Garde Essay Film

1. This phrase is from P. Adams Sitney, *Visionary Film: The American Avant-Garde, 1943–2000,* 3rd ed. (New York: Oxford University Press, 2002).

2. A telling sidebar to this anxiety is evident in Peter Kubelka's proposal to have the written "score" to his absolute flicker film, *Arnulf Rainer* (1960), carved in marble so that it could be reproduced in as-yet unimagined mediums by future generations.

3. Yvonne Rainer is one of the best and most prolific artist-spokespersons for this position, and for the primacy of analyzing social relations in avant-garde idioms. See, for example,

"Beginning with Some Advertisements for Criticisms of Myself, or Drawing the Dog You May Want to Use to Bite Me With, and Then Going on to Other Matters," *Millennium Film Journal* 6 (spring 1980): 5–7.

4. The relative dearth of critical commentary on the essay film is surprising, especially given its contemporary influence and unquestionable record of achievement. Two useful introductions to this genre are Michael Renov, "History and/as Autobiography," *Frame/Work* 2, no. 3 (1989): 6–13; and Phillip Lopate, "In Search of the Centaur: The Essay-Film," in *Beyond Document: Essays on Nonfiction Film*, ed. Charles Warren (Hanover, N.H.: Wesleyan University Press, 1996), 243–70. In a recent essay, I attempt a broad historical overview of the Essay and its theoretical underpinnings; see "Essay Questions," *Film Comment* 39, no. 1 (January–February 2003): 58–63.

5. Cited in Christopher Williams, ed., *Realism and the Cinema: A Reader* (London: Routledge and Kegan Paul, 1980), 34.

6. Hayden White, "The Value of Narrativity in the Representation of Reality," *Critical Inquiry* 7, no. 1 (autumn 1980): 5–28.

7. Ibid. What White finds appealing in these early records is in part their lack of symbolic hierarchies, and their disinterest in narrative mechanisms of anticipation, retrospection, and dramatic closure.

8. See, for example, Michel Foucault, "Two Lectures," *Power/Knowledge: Selected Interviews and Other Writings, 1972–1977,* ed. Colin Gordon (New York: Pantheon Books, 1980), 88–90.

9. Quoted in Emmanuel Le Roy Ladurie, "History That Stands Still," *The Mind and Method of the Historian,* trans. Sian Reynolds and Ben Reynolds (Chicago: University of Chicago Press, 1981), 21.

10. Leo Tolstoy, *War and Peace,* ed. George Gibian, trans. Louise and Aylmer Maude (New York: Norton, 1966), 1256.

5. The Last of the Last Machine?

1. Raymond Williams designates "flow," as opposed to film's mechanical intermittence, as the ontological benchmark of TV: *Television Technology and Cultural Form* (New York: Schocken Books, 1974), 88–99. Jane Feuer offers a useful perspective on relations between flow and segmentation in "The Concept of Live Television: Ontology as Ideology," in *Regarding Television,* ed. E. Ann Kaplan (Los Angeles: American Film Institute, 1983), 12–22.

2. Many of TV's syntactical features derive from radio broadcasting of the late 1930s and the programming practices of theatrical cinema by which newsreels, trailers, advertisements, and cartoons were played prior to dramatic features in a highly interchangeable sequence.

3. In a recent review of the Whitney Museum of American Art Biennial, Kim Levin describes the dominant trope of the picture plane in cutting-edge painting as a surrogate TV screen: "It's art that counts on a 30 second attention span, switching channels constantly, and suffering from and making the most of information overload"; *Village Voice* (26 April 1983): 108. The conceit of channel switching has also been a mainstay in performance art and experimental theater. Calling new Hollywood releases bloated music videos or extensions of half-hour sitcoms has become a journalistic cliché.

4. P. Adams Sitney, *Visionary Film: The American Avant-Garde, 1943–2000* (New York: Oxford University Press, 1974/2002), 106–10, 189–97.

5. Avant-garde exceptions to the avoidance of TV include Bruce Conner and, especially,

Stan Vanderbeek. Surprisingly, several Brakhage films, notably *23rd Psalm Branch* (1966–67), incorporate TV as a repository of antidomestic or alien imagery.

6. A growing number of filmmakers in Los Angeles and, to a lesser extent, New York are not only assisting but directing music videos. Exciting visuals for this form have been produced under the auspices of John Whitney's Digital Productions.

7. The New York Film-Makers' Cooperative and Canyon Cinema's distribution arm were founded within several years of each other. It is difficult now to adequately capture the extent of their impact. See, however, the "Editorial" at the beginning of *Film Culture* 46 (autumn 1967): 5.

8. During this period, the Whitney Museum began showcasing avant-garde films in their New American Cinema series; Sitney delivered three important lectures at the Museum of Modern Art; *Artforum* published a special issue devoted largely to structural work; and filmmakers discovered an unprecedented receptivity on the part of funding agencies such as the Ford Foundation.

9. See, among a batch of optimistic prognoses, Patricia Mellencamp, "Receivable Texts," *Wide Angle* 7, nos. 1, 2 (spring 1985): 74–91; and Peter Wollen, "The Two Avant-Gardes: Europe and America," *Studio International* 190, no. 978 (November–December 1975): 171–76.

10. See, for example, Constance Penley and Janet Bergstrom, "The Avant-Garde: Histories and Theories," *Screen* 19, no. 1 (autumn 1978): 112–28. More recently, Peter Lehman renews the call for historical revision: "For Whom Does the Light Shine?," *Wide Angle* 7, nos. 1, 2 (spring 1985): 68–73. In the same issue, focusing on avant-garde controversies, see Peter Wollen, "Popular Culture and Avant-Garde," 102–3. From a very different critical angle, Fred Camper argues for critical parity between Hollywood and avant-garde modes, "Two American Cinemas," *Spiral* 4 (July 1985): 52–66.

11. Without belaboring the point, certainly Penley, Bergstrom, and Lehman all count themselves in the antiformalist camp. In an otherwise quite encouraging initiative, Jonathan Rosenbaum's *Film: The Front Line, 1983* (Denver: Arden Press, 1984) and David Ehrenstein's *Film: The Front Line, 1984* (Denver: Arden Press, 1985) generate auras of critical "independence" by railing against what they see as an academic power elite twisting avant-garde history to suit narrow, reactionary ends. Both argue for new methodologies to expand the scope of meaning available to this discourse. The ridiculous charge of a "Sitney-Michelson" conspiracy—neither has written much of late on the avant-garde; Anthology Film Archives has been inoperative for years; Michelson was never a member of the Anthology selection committee; etc., etc.—is by Rosenbaum (212), who might do better looking at a few more films than engaging in faux-leftist name-calling. For the record, I studied with both Sitney and Michelson at NYU.

12. Since the original publication of this essay, the need for a full-scale theoretically informed revision of avant-garde film studies has been amply fulfilled by David E. James in *Allegories of Cinema: American Film in the Sixties* (Princeton: Princeton University Press, 1989). Conversations with the author during the preparation of his book greatly influenced my methodology and choice of topics.

13. Much has been written on the movie industry's drive for middle-class respectability. Robert Sklar provides useful information in the early chapters of *Movie-Made America: A Cultural History of American Movies* (New York: Random House, 1975). A more recent and more detailed account is found in Tom Gunning, *D. W. Griffith and the Origins of American Narrative Film* (Urbana: University of Illinois Press, 1991).

14. P. Adams Sitney, in his original declarations in "Structural Film," *Film Culture* 47 (summer 1969): 1–10, suggests that the movement's basic procedures had been latent in the careers of

many earlier filmmakers. Although he does not fully develop this insight, it is indeed useful to think of this style not as a sudden eruption but as a constant dialectical option.

15. For a belated attempt to reposition the critical underpinnings of structural film, see my "Structural Film: Revisions, New Versions and the Artifact: Part Two," *Millennium Film Journal,* nos. 4, 5 (fall 1979): 135–44.

16. It is important to note a broader category of Anglo-European "experimental" narratives dubbed "The New Talkie." Its practitioners include Peter Wollen and Laura Mulvey, Sally Potter, Valie Export, and Rosa von Praunheim. An initial elaboration of this inclusive phenomenon is in *October* 17 (summer 1981); see especially the essays by Wollen, Hollis Frampton, and Yvonne Rainer. Nöel Carroll offers insights into the American avant-garde branch in "Interview with a Woman Who . . . ," *Millennium Film Journal,* nos. 7, 8, 9 (fall 1980–winter 1981): 37–68.

17. Gary Doberman, "New York Cut the Crap," *The Cinemanews* 79, nos. 5, 6 (spring 1980): 23–27. Quotes from this article appear in parentheses in the body of the text. Accompanying Doberman's essay are two absurdly vicious letters to the editor that codify a bitter East-West avant-garde rivalry (28–30).

18. For a sampling of local attitudes by filmmakers concerning the putatively unequal distribution of power in the avant-garde, see the "Point of View" forums in the journal *Spiral,* especially nos. 1 (October 1984), 4 (July 1985), and 6 (January 1986).

19. Peter Gidal's lonely and curiously heroic resistance to the mixed conditions of cinematic reference/representation are expounded in "Theory and Definition of Structural/Materialist Film," in *Structural Film Anthology,* ed. Peter Gidal (London: British Film Institute, 1976), 1–21; and perhaps most convincingly in "The Anti-Narrative," *Screen* 20, no. 2 (summer 1979): 73–93.

20. There have been scattered observations on the reciprocity between avant-garde and documentary forms. See, for example, Bill Nichols, *Ideology and the Image* (Bloomington: Indiana University Press, 1981), 233–36. It is also pertinent to mention the extent to which Snow and Frampton, among others, reject the notion that their work is devoid of social reference. See, for example, "Ten Questions to Michael Snow," in Gidal, ed., *Structural Film Anthology,* 34–36; Snow's response to Gidal's critique of *Back and Forth* (1968) appears in the same volume, 50–51.

21. Farber, *"Wavelength,"* reprinted in *Movies* (New York: Hillstone Press, 1971), 250.

22. Michelson, "Toward Snow," *Artforum* 9, no. 10 (June 1971): 30–37.

23. This "restoration" of narrative forms the crux of Teresa de Lauretis's feminist position in "Oedipus Interruptus," *Wide Angle* 7, nos. 1, 2 (spring 1985): 34–41. Although she writes within the terms of psychoanalytic theory, she seems to reject the situation and functions secured by women filmmakers outside of narrative film production. See also Laura Mulvey, "Afterthoughts on 'Visual Pleasure and Narrative Cinema' Inspired by *Duel in the Sun,"* *Framework* 15/16/17 (1981): 10–17. Linda Dubler is optimistic about the unproblematic relation between feminist themes and appropriated narrative codes in *"Variety,"* *Film Quarterly* 38, no. 1 (fall 1984): 24–27, and Bette Gordon herself has discussed the need to build narrative models of female pleasure in an interview with Coco Fusco, *Idiolects* 14 (spring 1985): 61–66. Peter Gidal, as expected, adopts a hard line against the infiltration of avant-garde work by narrative: "The Anti-Narrative," *Screen* 20, no. 2 (summer 1979): 73–92.

24. The list of filmmakers working entirely or frequently in narrative modes includes Richard Myers, Paul Bartel, Jim McBride, James Broughton, Steve Dwoskin, Storm de Hirsch, and Walter Gutman.

25. Jon Jost, a veteran avant-gardist and leading proponent of a hybrid approach, takes a refreshingly pragmatic stance in two separate interviews on avant-populist dreams: see "Money

and Art," *Wide Angle* 3, no. 3 (1979): 28–33; and "Interview with Jon Jost," *Framework* 13 (autumn 1980): 29–31. English independent and avant-garde filmmakers are not only better organized politically than their American counterparts, they have subjected the issues of government funding and avenues of distribution to more rigorous discussion. For examples of how economic realities can inform theoretical debate, see Jonathan Curling and Fran McLean, "The Independent Film-Makers' Association Annual General Meeting and Conference," *Screen* 18, no. 1 (spring 1977): 43–48. See also Richard Woolley, "The Facility to Unite," and Sue Aspinall, "The Space for Innovation and Experiment," both in *Screen* 25, no. 6 (November–December 1984): 19–23 and 73–87 respectively.

26. Of roughly a dozen established filmmakers with whom I spoke in preparation for this essay, nearly half—including Pat O'Neill, Warren Sonbert, and Morgan Fisher—reported they were engaged in feature-length projects.

27. An example of this line of attack is in Mellencamp, "Receivable Texts," 76–78. More obliquely, Lisa Cartwright admonishes the entire "male-dominated" avant-garde system in "The Front Line and the Rear Guard," *Screen* 25, no. 6 (November–December 1984): 60–62.

28. Using an admittedly very crude instrument of measurement, in the 1979 *Film-Makers' Cooperative Catalogue,* with listings on nearly six hundred makers, only fifty-five were women (including male/female collaborations). In the 1976 Whitney Museum's *New American Film-makers* catalogue, representing the more than one thousand films screened at the museum between 1970 and 1975, seventy-five artists are male while seventeen are female. Similarly, the American Federation of the Arts' "History of the American Avant-Garde Film" traveling series features twenty-seven men and three women. A cursory examination of film schedules over the last five years published by the Whitney Museum, Filmforum in Los Angeles, and the San Francisco Cinematheque suggests that a much larger number of women are now making films, or perhaps just getting them shown.

29. Jarmusch's film has grossed over $1.6 million and reached as high as 32nd place on *Variety's* chart. It reportedly cost around $120,000 to produce.

30. "Independent Filmmaking in America," *Journal of the University Film and Video Association* 35, no. 2 (spring 1983): 4–16. In the same issue, see Betsy McLane's "Domestic Theatrical and Semi-Theatrical Distribution and Exhibition of American Independent Feature Films: A Survey," 25–33.

31. For a fascinating exchange between Jonas Mekas and Jim McBride on the vicissitudes of independent distribution, see "Interview," *Motion Picture* 1 (spring–summer 1986): 16–17. Mekas's passionate defense of the co-op system takes on added validity for the current scene.

32. This is more or less the contention of Yvonne Rainer in "More Kicking and Screaming from the Narrative Front/Backwater," *Wide Angle* 7, nos. 1, 2 (spring 1985): 8–12. Although I disagree with what she says, I also understand her tone and comments on the cultural domination of narrative forms as a useful intervention.

6. The Western Edge

1. Bertolt Brecht, "Hollywood Elegies," *Poems: 1913–1956* (New York: Methuen, 1976), 380.

2. To cite a single example of this critical gambit in film discourse, complete with high-academic imprimatur, see Alan Spiegel, "American Film-Flam," *Salmagundi* 41 (1978): 153–69. For an introduction to the LA/NYC rivalry, see Peter Schjeldahl, "L.A. Demystified," reprinted

in *Journal: Southern California Art Magazine* 28 (winter 1981): 21–25. There has been a considerable amount written about the culture of LA since the publication of this essay, at least some of which would inflect any current assessment of the avant-garde scene. Of particular note is David E. James, "Hollywood Extras: One Tradition of 'Avant-Garde' Film in Los Angeles," *October* 90 (fall 1999): 3–24. Although it addresses cinema primarily in its industrial, mythmaking capacity, Mike Davis's *City of Quartz: Excavating the Future in Los Angeles* (New York: Vintage Books, 1992) is essential to urban theories of the region. An equally cogent model of urban discourse is tendered by Edward Soja in *Postmodern Geographies: The Reassertion of Space in Critical Social Theory* (London: Verso, 1989). For perspectives on alternative cultural movements that overlap or parallel those of avant-garde film, see David E. James, ed., *The Sons and Daughters of Los: Culture and Community in L.A.* (Philadelphia: Temple University Press, 2003). I examine the relationship between urban dynamics and Hollywood's postwar crime films in "LA as Scene of the Crime," *Film Comment* (July–August 1996): 21–26.

3. David Curtis, *Experimental Cinema: A Fifty-Year Evolution* (New York: Dell, 1971), 164. Curtis's label was picked up in subsequent accounts. For a helpful historical and aesthetic summary of regionalism in art, see Donald Kuspit, "Regionalism Reconsidered," *Art in America* (July–August 1976): 42–51.

4. I attempt to read Welles's masterpiece through a lens of avant-garde film aesthetics in "Out of the Depths: *Citizen Kane,* Modernism and the Avant-Garde Impulse," in Ronald Gottesman, ed., *Perspectives on Citizen Kane* (New York: G. K. Hall, 1996), 367–82.

5. The early experiments of Fischinger and the Whitneys are described in William Moritz, "You Can't Get Then from Now," *Journal: Southern California Art Magazine* 29 (summer 1981): 27–40.

6. A prime intersection between art and the Hollywood industry was Choinard Art School, set up as a trade school yet employing such influential artists as Larry Bell and Robert Irwin. For a while it served as an apprenticeship system for Disney animators, industry set painters, and designers. For a particularly scathing account of the Art and Industry phenomenon, see Max Kozloff, "The Multimillion Dollar Boondoggle," *Artforum* 10, no. 2 (October 1971): 31–36. A defense of alliances with big business is offered by curators Maurice Tuchman and Jane Livingston in their introductions to *Art and Technology* (Los Angeles: LA County Museum, 1971), n.p.

7. For a rough overview of avant-garde exhibition in LA, see Samir Hachem, "Now You See Them, Now You Don't: Exhibition and Distribution of Avant-Garde Film in L.A.," *Journal: Southern California Art Magazine* 29 (summer 1981): 59–64.

8. See Richard Armstrong, "Sculpture in California, 1975–1980," *Journal: Southern California Art Magazine* 28 (September–October 1980): 85–94.

9. In personal conversation with the filmmaker, 20 March 1982.

10. For a more detailed discussion, see my "Tom Leeser: Coming into View," *Journal: Southern California Art Magazine* 29 (summer 1981): 43–46.

11. Included in this group are virtually all of Jordan Belson's films, Scott Bartlett's *Moon 69,* Tom DeWitt's *Fall* (1971), Bartlett's and DeWitt's *Offon* (1968), Larry Jordan's *Our Lady of the Sphere* (1969), and Dennis Pies's *Luma Nocturna* (1973).

12. Nöel Carroll provides a persuasive account of relations between horror and sci-fi in *The Philosophy of Horror, or Paradoxes of the Heart* (New York: Routledge, 1990). I discuss Hollywood's recent sci-fi allegories of technology in "The Four Last Things: History, Technology, Hollywood, Apocalypse," in Jon Lewis, ed., *The End of Cinema as We Know It* (New York: New York University Press, 2001), 242–55.

13. Relevant films in this group include Bruce Conner's *A Movie* (1958), Bruce Baillie's *Quixote* (1964–65), and Stan Vanderbeek's *Newsreel of Dreams* (1963–64).

14. Although the trend away from realism and its emphasis on verisimilitude and narrative plausibility is difficult to quantify, Academy Award winners for Best Picture during the seventies remained firmly committed to realist formulas (from 1970 to 1980, only Woody Allen's *Annie Hall* falls outside the parameters of realism). On the other hand, the majority of recent box-office champions, from *Jaws* (1975) to *E.T.* (1982), are exemplars of technological excess.

15. I learned of the interest in avant-garde work by founders of Industrial Light and Magic during several conferences with Dykstra and others in 1980 related to an ill-fated Hollywood project for a 3-D animated "head-trip" feature.

16. In a well-known essay written after the initial publication of this article, Tom Gunning provides rich analysis of the use of pure spectacle in early movies: "The Cinema of Attractions: Early Film, Its Spectator, and the Avant-Garde," reprinted in *Early Cinema: Space, Frame, Narrative*, ed. Thomas Elsaesser (London: British Film Institute, 1990), 56–62.

17. Fredric Jameson makes some interesting comments about the suppression of work, and of filmic production, in fifties sci-fi: *Marxism and Form* (Princeton: Princeton University Press, 1971), 405–8.

18. Grahame Weinbren and Christine Noll Brinckman discuss O'Neill's subversive rendering of the laws of physics as embodying a kind of American pioneer spirit. See "The O'Neill Landscape: Four Scenes from *Foregrounds*," *Millennium Film Journal* 4/5 (summer/fall 1979): 101–16; and "Selective Transparencies: Pat O'Neill's Recent Films," *Millennium Film Journal* 6 (spring 1980): 51–72. My analysis shares various assumptions, and I am indebted to their fine descriptions. I am in obvious disagreement, however, with their assertion that a concern for "surface" in O'Neill is naïve and critically obtuse.

19. See, for example, Carey McWilliams's 1946 study, *Southern California: An Island on the Land* (Santa Barbara: Peregrine Smith, 1979).

20. *Larry Bell: New Work* (Yonkers, N.Y.: Hudson River Museum, 1980), n.p.

21. Leo Marx provides an excellent overview of this seminal theme in *The Machine in the Garden* (New York: Oxford University Press, 1964).

22. O'Neill has published several (partial) versions of, and notes around, the film's script: see "*Water and Power*: A Fragmentary Synopsis," *Motion Picture* 3, nos. 1–2 (winter 1989–90): 19–20; also "*Water and Power*," *Millennium Film Journal* 25 (summer 1991): 42–49.

7. Springing Tired Chains

1. Frequently lauded for their poetic imagery and infractions of narrative convention, the "race movies" of Oscar Micheaux and, especially, Spencer Williams's 1941 *Blood of Jesus* were rediscovered in the late 1960s, receiving regular screenings at avant-garde showcases such as the Collective for Living Cinema in New York, along with other obscure examples of ethnic filmmaking. However, to the extent that they were appropriated by the white avant-garde as part of a project of retrieving noncommercial artifacts, these works were still largely unknown to the first wave of African American media artists. The best account of the politics of 1960s underground film is in David E. James, *Allegories of Cinema* (Princeton: Princeton University Press, 1989), esp. 85–119.

2. On Locke's assessment of modernism, see *The New Negro* (New York: Atheneum, 1968). See also Ralph Ellison, "The Art of Romare Bearden," *Going to the Territory* (New York: Random

House, 1986), 227–38. The irrevocable split between modernist tendencies and 1960s black radicalism is amply documented in Addison Gayle, ed., *The Black Aesthetic* (Garden City, N.Y.: Doubleday, 1971). Essays in this volume by Hoyt W. Fuller, Ron Karenga, and Larry Neal are especially cogent in their rejections of "European" aesthetics. As Neal puts it, "The Black Arts Movement is radically opposed to any concept of the artist that alienates him from his community" (273).

3. The New American Cinema Group, formed in 1960 as a loose alliance for the production and publicity of independent features and documentaries, included several black members. The first catalogue of the Film-Makers' Cooperative, an artist-run distribution collective with a policy of open submissions, lists a half dozen films made by or with black artists.

4. The LA Rebellion was grounded in a curious hybrid of realist baggage and experimental impulses. Although its adherents produced perhaps a half-dozen films reasonably classified as avant-garde, their primary aim, as I understand it, was the revision of narrative structures and social protagonists via the example of European New Wave and Latin American Third Cinema; see Clyde Taylor, "The LA Rebellion: New Spirit in American Film," *Black Film Review* 2, no. 2 (1986): 9–16; also Ntongela Masilela, "The Los Angeles School of Black Filmmakers," in *Black American Cinema,* ed. Manthia Diawara (New York: Routledge, 1993), 107–17. With a few exceptions, the aesthetic orientation and institutional parameters of the LA School are markedly different from the work central to this essay. Although possible points of convergence are of interest, space does not allow me to address them here.

5. The degree to which black experimental media have been incorporated within avant-garde circles is evident in, for example, catalogue listings of distributors such as Film-Makers' Cooperative, Electronic Arts Intermix, Frameline, and Women Make Movies. Of course, other criteria for institutional inclusion such as gender or sexual orientation are also relevant. There is a comparable crossover effect in the broadcast schedules of the PBS series "Independents" and screening schedules of major venues, including the San Francisco Cinematheque, Filmforum in Los Angeles, various gay and lesbian festivals, and the Whitney Museum of American Art's influential Biennial programs of film and video. For instance, in the 1997 Biennial, five of twenty-five chosen media artists were black, more than the total for all previous exhibitions combined. Unfortunately, critical organs specializing in avant-garde cinema such as *Millennium Film Journal* have yet to acknowledge the burgeoning significance of African American work. *The Independent* and *Cinematograph* have done a slightly better job. For reasons that remain murky, this connection has also been ignored by media publications dedicated to minority artists—*Black Film Review* and *Visions* are two examples. *Black Face,* an organ of the Black Filmmaker Foundation, has provided some superficial coverage.

6. The relationship between black British and African American experimentalists, for which Isaac Julien is a pivotal figure, is instructive if somewhat peripheral to my concerns. It is sufficient to note that the emergence of the Black Audio, Sankofa, and Ceddo collectives was underwritten by both a level of political activism and a theoretical sophistication unknown in the United States. In addition, governmental and communal structures of organizational and financial support encouraged black artists to form semiautonomous channels of production and distribution rather than become assimilated into the—admittedly small and desultory—British avant-garde movement. For an overview of the black British movement in film and video, see Jim Pines, "The Cultural Context of Black British Cinema," in *Blackframes: Critical Perspectives on Black Independent Cinema,* ed. Mbye B. Cham and Claire Andrade-Watkins (Cambridge: MIT Press, 1988), 26–36.

7. "A Snap! Queen Deliberates: 'Reading' the Media," *Video* (November–December 1991):
8. Not surprisingly, the debate around audience expectations and the institutionalization of
black experimental film and video has received a more intensive exploration in England; see,
for example, Judith Williamson, "Two Kinds of Otherness—Black Film and the Avant-Garde,"
Screen 29, no. 4 (autumn 1988): 106–13.

8. One of the earliest attacks is by Constance Penley and Janet Bergstrom: "The Avant-
Garde: History and Theories," reprinted in *Movies and Methods*, vol. 2, ed. Bill Nichols (Berkeley: University of California Press, 1985), 287–300.

9. For a recent rereading of 1960s underground cinema through a grid of gay subcultural
identification, see Juan A. Suarez, *Bike Boys, Drag Queens, and Superstars* (Bloomington: Indiana University Press, 1996).

10. On the resurgence of historicity in the avant-garde, see chapter 4.

11. Nöel Carroll has a useful discussion of "indexing" as a categorical tool bypassing questions of style or theme: "From Real to Reel: Entangled in Nonfiction Film," *Theorizing the Moving Image* (New York: Cambridge University Press, 1996), 231.

12. The post-sixties brief against documentary's rhetorical structures comprises diverse
charges leveled by disparate creative and theoretical factions, including feminists, poststructural-
ists, community activists, and minority artists. Riggs cites the "disempowering" effects of "non-
participant" documentaries in "A Snap! Queen Deliberates," 8. For a collection of broadsides by
academic commentators, see essays by Brian Winston, Bill Nichols, Jay Ruby, and E. Ann Kaplan
in *New Challenges for Documentary*, ed. Alan Rosenthal (Berkeley: University of California Press,
1988). For analysis of how the traditional documentary constrains minority perspectives, see
Trinh T. Minh-ha, "Documentary Is/Not a Name," *October* 52 (spring 1990): 87–94; also Kobena
Mercer, "Diaspora Culture and the Dialogic Imagination," in *Blackframes*, 50–61.

13. Although cognizant of significant divergences in the historical development and formal properties of video and film, I often conflate the two formats in discussions that follow,
since previous institutional and production dichotomies have been largely eroded and since
the video practices of black artists are roughly compatible with those of a dominant faction
in avant-garde film. The high-modernist reflexivity of the movement referred to as "video
art," pioneered by Nam June Paik, Bruce Nauman, Peter Campus, and others, has had no real
counterpart in black experimentalism.

14. David E. James, "Hollywood Extras: One Tradition of 'Avant-Garde' Film in Los Angeles," *October* 90 (fall 1999): 4–5.

15. Cited in William C. Wees, *Recycled Images* (New York: Anthology Film Archives, 1993), 74.

16. Ibid., 81.

17. "Black Is . . . Black Ain't," *Sight and Sound* 4, no. 7 (July 1994): 22.

18. "Diaspora Culture and the Dialogic Imagination," in *Blackframes*, 59. In a similar vein,
Pratiba Parmar concludes that "it is these politicized appropriations of dominant codes and
signifying systems which give us powerful weapons in the struggle for empowerment": *Queer
Looks: Perspectives on Lesbian and Gay Film and Video*, ed. Martha Gever, John Greyson, and
Pratiba Parmar (New York: Routledge, 1993), 11. Although no one working in American experimental cinema has offered such cogent and sweeping claims for the effectivity of found materials, much of the work discussed here would seem to implicitly support such a stance.

19. Jay Leyda, *Films Beget Films* (New York: Hill and Wang, 1964), 12.

20. A ghettocentric encoding of African American men as an "endangered species" has
surfaced recently in a variety of cultural contexts, including the controversial 1994 "Black Male"

exhibition at the Whitney Museum of American Art. Inexplicably, neither the work of Cokes nor Andrews, nor that of Ulysses Jenkins, Thomas Allen Harris, or Cauleen Smith was included in the exhibition's four separate film and video series.

21. The perspective elaborated by Riggs echoes that of other black cultural commentators; see, for example, Henry Louis Gates Jr., "The Blackness of Blackness: A Critique of the Sign and the Signifying Monkey," in *Black Literature and Literary Theory,* ed. Henry Louis Gates Jr. (New York: Methuen, 1984), esp. 285–93.

22. James Snead, "Repetition as a Figure of Black Culture," in *Black Literature and Literary Theory,* 67–68.

23. In *Tongues Untied,* Riggs renounces the dire historical consequences of silence, as summarized in this anthem spoken by the late poet Essex Hemphill: "Silence is my shield/Silence is my sword/Let's end the silence." The interweaving of disparate modalities of black speech is a prominent feature of not only Riggs's work but that of Andrews and other artists.

24. P. Adams Sitney provides the most lucid account of psychodrama in his seminal history of the American avant-garde, *Visionary Film: The American Avant-Garde, 1943–2000* (New York: Oxford University Press, 1974/2002), esp. 3–19 and 86–90. Although Sitney tends to periodize the form as a stepping-stone in the development of post–World War II filmmakers, a wider perspective suggests that the psychodrama has served as initial vehicle through which various emerging artistic cadres—Beats, women, gays, Asian Americans—have asserted the primacy of visual subjectivity.

25. Isaac Julien's *Looking for Langston* (1990), a seminal film in the development of black experimental cinema, is quite explicit in its debt to the psychodramatic trance films of Deren and Anger. Not only does its elliptical structure recall the earlier works' subjective shattering of time, but individual shots and techniques pay tribute to the liberatory promise of the postwar avant-garde. Manthia Diawara's grudging acknowledgment of Julien's relation to American avant-garde traditions is offered in "The Absent One: The Avant-Garde and the Black Imaginary in *Looking for Langston,*" *Wide Angle* 13, nos. 3/4 (July 1991): 96–109. Regrettably, Diawara oversimplifies the history of this movement as "concerned solely with the process of filmic production itself" (101), failing to recognize the avant-garde's persistent mobilization of outcast sexualities. This leads to a muddled opposition of "avant-garde" and "blackness." I see no merit to his claim that *Langston* and other films "parody the avant-garde in order to reveal its racism"(103). My preference for demarginalizing black experimentalism, positioning it in a broader film-historical flow, is arguably less condescending to both the white avant-garde and to the political and aesthetic goals of black media artists.

26. Alexandra Juhasz discusses Dunye's video, along with the work of Sadie Benning and others, as an example of a new wave of feminist art that challenges outmoded prohibitions against exhibiting women's bodies: "Our Auto-Bodies, Ourselves: Representing Real Women in Feminist Video," *Afterimage* 21, no. 7 (February 1994): 10–14.

27. In 1997, Greaves was still anticipating the film's belated theatrical release and was putting together funding to complete a "sequel" using unedited footage from the original shoot. I wish to acknowledge his generosity in allowing me access to a revised print and for answering assorted questions with great good humor and enough spicy anecdotes to fill a separate essay.

28. Quoted in Scott MacDonald, *A Critical Cinema 3: Interviews with Independent Filmmakers* (Berkeley: University of California Press, 1998), 53. A selection of Greaves's notes, before and during production, and a transcription of a brief scene from *Take One* have been published

in MacDonald's *Screen Writings: Scripts and Texts by Independent Filmmakers* (Berkeley: University of California Press, 1995), 31–48.

29. See McDonald, *Screen Writings,* 32, 34.

30. Not coincidentally, the important avant-garde filmmaker Peggy Ahwesh programmed *Take One* as part of a 1997 retrospective of her work at the Whitney Museum of American Art, implicitly claiming Greaves's film as a precedent for the recent reemergence of reflexive performance in majority avant-garde practice.

8. Bodies, Language, and the Impeachment of Vision

1. I address Warhol's oral fixation in "Flesh of Absence: Resighting the Warhol Catechism," in *Andy Warhol Film Factory,* ed. Michael O'Pray (London: British Film Institute, 1989), 147–48. Much of what I understand about the Warholian drama of presence and absence, and what I will suggest about it later on, derives from Stephen Koch's seminal *Star-Gazer* (New York: Praeger, 1973).

2. It should be noted that most of what follows concerns what I take to be the ongoing tradition of the North American movement since its "official" inauguration in 1943 with Maya Deren's *Meshes of the Afternoon.* There are many points of intersection in the European avant-garde and in American video art, and I recognize that the boundary separating these precincts is not always clear, but a combination of less-than-comprehensive knowledge and limitations of space prevents me from considering them here. Arguing the meaning or validity of the term "avant-garde" at this juncture strikes me as ridiculous, and while sensitive to the dangers of periodization, my focus on salient issues of the last fifteen years is not intended to circumscribe a unified period or aesthetic program but instead loose braids of family resemblance.

3. Robert Kelly, "The Image of the Body," reprinted in *Film Culture Reader,* ed. P. Adams Sitney (New York: Praeger, 1970), 393–96.

4. Clearly, there were segments of the avant-garde for which the body never lost its centrality, even during the period of structural film's dominance. For a cogent discussion of structural dynamics, see David E. James, *Allegories of Cinema* (Princeton: Princeton University Press, 1989), 237–80. See also Nöel Carroll, "Film," in *The Postmodern Moment,* ed. Stanley Trachtenberg (Westport, Conn.: Greenwood Press, 1985), 101–3.

5. Snow makes the humorous claim that the temporal scope of *Wavelength* is the equivalent of a "long fuck," and the visual pulse of Ernie Gehr's celebrated *Serene Velocity* (1970) has been referred to as "masturbatory," but neither these nor similar comments vitiate the prolonged avoidance of "organic" shaping in the corpus of structural film.

6. Alexandra Juhasz traces a cognate twenty-year trajectory of feminist representations of the body in documentary film and video in "Our Auto-Bodies, Ourselves: Representing Real Women in Feminist Video," *Afterimage* 21, no. 7 (February 1994): 10–14. Some of her conclusions about recent work are directly pertinent to the avant-garde: "films and videos about bodies aren't bodies, they are images. In the terrain of body-footage, women can play with their bodies—their color, age, HIV-status, fantasies and desires—in a way often unavailable in 'real' life. Body images allow us to see the mutability, not the essential nature, of our bodies and the identities they signify . . . Instead of deconstruction, the body must be specified back into existence, acknowledging the material affects of race, class, gender, weight, disease, and other body-rooted indices of privilege." (14)

7. Ivone Margulies, "After the Fall: Peggy Ahwesh's Verité," *Motion Picture* 3, nos. 1/2 (winter 1989–90): 31.

8. For a detailed reading of *Peggy and Fred*, see Linda Peckam's "Total Indiscriminate Recall: *Peggy and Fred in Hell*," *Motion Picture* 3, nos. 1/2 (winter 1989–90): 16–18.

9. A cogent precedent for recent doll-play, albeit with a more prominent bite of sadistic regression, is Jack Smith's frightening manipulations in Ken Jacobs's *Little Stabs at Happiness* (1959–63).

10. R. Bruce Elder has offered an interesting, thematically organized overview of the avant-garde's invocation of the body in the catalogue *The Body in Film* (Toronto: Art Gallery of Ontario, 1989).

11. *Star-Gazer,* 118.

12. Obviously, there has been a considerable amount of discursive, as well as political, energy devoted to the arena of pornography in recent years. For an assessment that I take to be more or less consistent with the underpinnings of the avant-garde fascination, see Andrew Ross, "The Popularity of Pornography," in *No Respect: Intellectuals and Popular Culture* (New York: Routledge, 1989), 171–208. David James charts a dynamics of cultural resistance in amateur erotic video, which he claims as an extension of the avant-garde's "oppositional" sexual practices of the 1960s: "Hardcore: Cultural Resistance in the Postmodern," *Film Quarterly* 42, no. 2 (winter 1988–89): 31–38.

13. A locus classicus of apparatus theory is Jean-Louis Baudry's "Ideological Effects of the Basic Cinematic Apparatus," reprinted in *Movies and Methods, Volume* 2, ed. Bill Nichols (Berkeley: University of California Press, 1985), 531–42. An especially interesting precursor for the recent wave of "disturbances" to the strip, albeit laden with a high Dada irony, is Tony Conrad's "film cooking" experiments of the early 1970s, in which deep-fried, pickled, electrocuted, and otherwise unprojectable rolls were dished up to movie audiences as visual artifacts. The longstanding centrality of the body in Austrian avant-garde film is recalled in a 1995 traveling exhibition curated by Steve Anker, "Austrian Avant-Garde Cinema, 1955–1993."

14. Jacobs, program notes to *XCXHXEXRXRXIXEXSX*, Anthology Film Archives, 16 January 1993. For more on the "Nervous System" performances, see my "Creating Spectacle from Dross: The Chimeric Cinema of Ken Jacobs," *Film Comment* (March–April 1997): 53–58.

15. See, for instance, "For a Metahistory of Film: Commonplace Notes and Hypotheses," reprinted in *Circles of Confusion* (Rochester: Visual Studies Workshop Press, 1983), 107–16. Nöel Carroll provides a helpful gloss of Frampton's revisionist history in "A Brief Comment on Frampton's Notion of Metahistory," *Millennium Film Journal* 16/17/18 (fall/winter 1986–87): 200–05.

16. See the special issue of *Frame/Work* 2, no. 3 (1989) for a spectrum of views on the essayistic in avant-garde film and video.

17. Barthes, *Image-Music-Text*, trans. Stephen Heath (New York: Hill and Wang, 1977), 146.

18. Leyda, *Films Beget Films* (New York: Hill and Wang, 1964), 13.

19. Two recent studies expand on the relationship between avant-garde and pre-Hollywood cinema: Scott MacDonald, *Avant-Garde Film: Motion Studies* (New York: Cambridge University Press, 1993); and Bart Testa, *Back and Forth: Early Cinema and the Avant-Garde* (Toronto: Art Gallery of Ontario, 1992).

20. Here, as in the following section, I am responding to P. Adams Sitney's assertion that "modernist literary and cinematic works stress vision as a privileged mode of perception, even of revelation, while at the same time cultivating opacity and questioning the primacy of the

visible world," *Modernist Montage: The Obscurity of Vision in Cinema and Literature* (New York: Columbia University Press, 1990), 2. A defining characteristic of the postmodern is its abandonment of the first half of this antinomy.

21. Quoted in *Found Footage Film*, ed. Cecelia Hausheer and Christoph Settele (Lucerne, Switzerland: VIPER/zyclop verlag, 1992), 131. Along with short essays by Yann Beauvais, Peter Tscherkassky, and others, this useful catalogue contains a section of highly informative statements by filmmakers about the aesthetic functions of found footage; of special note is an analysis by Standish Lawder of the terms of appropriation that is similar to my own, 113–14. Another recent catalogue by William C. Wees explores similar territory and includes more expansive filmmaker interviews: *Recycled Images* (New York: Anthology Film Archives, 1993).

22. The type-token relationship in art has been most forcefully and convincingly articulated by Richard Wollheim in *Art and Its Objects* (Cambridge: Cambridge University Press, 1980), 199–202. I am indebted to Larry Schwartz for pointing out this aspect of the found-footage dynamic.

23. See my "History and Crass Consciousness: George Kuchar's Fantasies of Un-Power," *Millennium Film Journal* 20 (fall/winter 1988–89): 151–58.

24. Carroll, "Film," 112.

25. The historical background for an "oppositional" use of found footage includes European as well as American sources. Distinct from the strategies of, say, Conner or Kenneth Anger, Maurice Lemaitre's chance operations in *Pellicule* (1968) or the matched-cutting interpolations of banal Hollywood footage in Gianfranco Barucello's and Alberto Griffi's *Veritus in Certu* (1965) function as signifiers of both resistance and psychic detachment from the materials they treat. Among younger European avant-garde filmmakers, Martin Arnold (e.g., *Piece Touche*, 1989) and Matthias Muller (e.g., *Home Stories*, 1991) evince a distanced attitude parallel to that of their American cohort and, in both cases, television may be the decisive influence rather than avant-garde or New Wave legacies.

26. Arthur Danto discusses the politics of collage in a review of Heartfield's work at the Museum of Modern Art: *The Nation* (28 June 1993): 918–29. For filmmakers' recent statements concerning found footage's social program, see Wees, *Recycled Images*, especially the sections by Craig Baldwin, Abigail Child, Keith Sanborn, and Leslie Thornton.

27. Baldwin, in *Recycled Images*, 68.

28. Sharon Sandusky, "The Archeology of Redemption: Toward Archival Film," *Millennium Film Journal* 26 (fall 1992): 11.

29. Fredric Jameson, "Postmodernism, or the Cultural Logic of Late Capitalism," *New Left Review* 146 (March/April 1984): 72.

30. My interest here is almost exclusively with isolated, visually bracketed and industrially produced "representations" of language. Instances of profilmic texts, as in Frampton's *Zorns Lemma* (1970), shots of typewritten words and sentences, as in Mekas's *Lost Lost Lost* (1976), and words scratched or painted directly onto the film surface, as in Friedrich's *Gently Down the Stream* (1983), constitute techniques that often overlap yet remain somewhat separate from the conceptual issues tackled here.

31. See Eikhenbaum's 1927 essay, "Problems of Film Stylistics," *Screen* 14, no. 4 (winter 1974–75): 7–34. See also Paul Willemen, "Cinematic Discourse: The Problem of Inner Speech," in *Cinema and Language*, ed. Stephen Heath and Patricia Mellencamp (Los Angeles: American Film Institute, 1983), 141–67. Willemen explicitly rehearses the avant-garde's challenge to this concept, albeit in somewhat different terms.

32. For instance, the didactic "lesson" inscribed by the structural development of *Zorns Lemma* is that of a substitution of visual acuity and sensuality for language-based, "rote" comprehension. Similarly, the Beatles provide a diegetic motto for the heightened state of attention in *Wavelength* as they intone, "Living is easy with eyes closed/Misunderstanding all you see." Brakhage's call for an "adventure in perception"—"Imagine a world 'before the beginning was the word'"—is most powerfully stated in "Metaphors on Vision," *Film Culture* 30 (fall 1963): n.p.

33. W. J. T. Mitchell, *Iconology* (Chicago: University of Chicago Press, 1986), 21.

34. For reasons of length as well as cohesion, I cannot adequately comment on linguistic developments in the art world or television advertising of the 1980s. Suffice it to say that several large-scale New York gallery shows, "Text and Image: The Wording of American Art" at Holly Solomon in 1986 and "Words" at Tony Shafrazi in 1987, highlighted the critical appropriation of painted and photographed language. Fully one-quarter of all the gallery artists represented in the Whitney Biennials of 1987 and 1989 incorporated words in their work. As for TV, media critic Leslie Savan maintained in 1989 that three of every ten commercials employed running intertitles or superimposed text (presumably as a way of hooking consumers who tune out spoken messages): "Titular Head," *Village Voice* (21 February 1989): 56.

35. Cited in *Film-Makers' Cooperative Catalogue No. 7* (New York: New American Cinema Group, 1989), 492.

36. P. Adams Sitney makes a rather different but related reading of Land's film in *Modernist Montage*, 213–19.

37. Scott MacDonald offers a useful survey of language-images in "Text as Image in Some Recent Avant-Garde Films," *Afterimage* 13, no. 8 (March 1986): 9–20.

38. Cited in Sitney, *Modernist Montage*, 22.

39. Cited in Mitchell, *Iconology*, 79.

40. I adapt this insight from Emile Benveniste's writings on the linguistic sign. See, for example, "Subjectivity in Language," in *Critical Theory since 1965*, ed. Hazard Adams and Leroy Searle (Tallahassee: Florida State University Press, 1986), 725–32.

9. "I Just Pass My Hands over the Surface of Things"

1. See P. Adams Sitney, "Rear-Garde," *American Film* (July–August 1985): 13, 61; Fred Camper, "The End of Avant-Garde Film," *Millennium Film Journal* 16/17/18 (fall/winter 1986–87): 99–125. Nöel Carroll's essay on "Film," in *The Postmodern Moment*, ed. Stanley Trachtenberg (Westport, Conn.: Greenwood Press, 1985), 101–33, is more descriptive than evaluative but concludes on a distinct note of pessimism: "The dominant movements of the last two decades appear to have either exhausted themselves or ground to a halt" (127); likewise, J. Hoberman uses a rhetoric of "crisis" but also notes a series of promising developments: "After Avant-Garde Film," in *Art after Modernism: Rethinking Representation*, ed. Brian Wallis (New York: New Museum of Contemporary Art, 1984), 59–74. I participated in the chorus of naysaying by descrying the impact of narrative feature filmmaking on established avant-garde practices; see chapter 5, "The Last of the Last Machine?" A very different version of this essay was presented as a talk at Karlstad University, Sweden, for the 2002 conference "Gunvor Nelson and the Avant-Garde." I am grateful for the useful feedback given on that occasion by Steve Anker, Chris Holmlund, and Malcolm Le Grice.

2. The specific animosities and charges surrounding this event are not worth annotating here. I participated in the Congress and filed a report that is accompanied by an "Open Letter"

from dissident filmmakers and a response by a prime organizer: "No More Causes? The International Experimental Film Congress," *The Independent* 12, no. 8 (October 1989): 22–26.

3. It can reasonably be argued that I am judging the movement's ebbs and flows through a distorted New York–centric critical lens. Surely it is no accident that most proponents of the "crisis" hypothesis were based in and around New York, although other negative voices, including that of Stan Brakhage and several scholars in Toronto, arose from independent precincts. Thus my sense of events or films that signaled a renewal is also undoubtedly skewed. For early insights into the new wave, see the special issue of *Motion Picture* 3, nos. 1, 2 (winter 1989–90) edited by me and Ivone Margulies. Tom Gunning's contribution to that collection, "Towards a Minor Cinema: Fonoroff, Herwitz, Ahwesh, Klahr, and Solomon" (2–6), is particularly prescient. Several large-scale exhibitions also lent credence to fresh avant-garde tendencies, including "Independent America: New Film, 1978–1988" at the American Museum of the Moving Image, organized by David Schwartz. I am aware that different signposts are germane to different cities; for instance, an upheaval around the administration and programming of the San Francisco Cinematheque took place in 1981–82, one result of which was to focus more attention on younger, local filmmakers.

4. During the last decade or so, there has also been increased attention to the American avant-garde, including books and journal essays, in European film circles. I do not have comparable figures for non-English publications, but for a fairly recent sample, see the bibliography attached to the catalogue *L'art du mouvement: Collection cinematographique du Musee national d'art moderne, 1916–1996* (Paris: Editions du Centre Pompidou, 1996).

5. A small contingent of filmmakers, upholding an honorable but tattered tradition of disaffected vanguardism, have occasionally attacked what they claim as a *contraction* in discursive interest and support. For an example, see Chris Robbins and Jeffrey Skoller, "The X Factor," *MAIN: National Alliance for Media Arts and Culture* (June 1993): 1, 9. They assert: "it has become clear that those we assumed to be our most supportive 'allies' [media arts organizations and academia] have proven to be the most disingenuous and insidious of antagonists" (1).

6. Telephone interview with MM Serra: 8 June 2002. Subsequent information about Co-op finances is taken from this conversation. The workings of the (mostly) artist-run Canadian Filmmakers Distribution Centre in Toronto are somewhat peripheral to my concerns here since, although a substantial portion of their holdings—over 2,800 titles—come from the avant-garde sector, they also distribute numerous documentaries, animations, and narrative features. And not surprisingly, their paid staff and operating budget are both considerably larger than those of their U.S. counterparts due to higher levels of government subsidy. For further information on the three major distributors, see www.film-makerscoop.com; www.canyoncinema.com; www.cfmdc.org. In addition, it should be said that many individual filmmakers privately distribute their work and/or have placed their films in multiple outlets. Finally, several smaller, adventurous distributors have halted operations since the mid-nineties. The American Federation of the Arts, which had pioneered in the curating of thematic and regional avant-garde shows, transferred their collection of prints to the Museum of Modern Art in 1997. Two New York–based artist-run ventures, Drift and Parabola Arts Foundation, like similar projects in other cities, lost financial backing.

7. The New York Co-op, for instance, has had only three directors since 1965, of which one left after less than a year under a cloud of scandal. A similar situation exists at Canyon.

8. At the opposite end of the distribution spectrum, filmmaker Bruce Posner put together two impressive touring shows of experimental films made in 35mm that played educational,

museum, and art venues: "Spirit Stream Storm" (1995) and "White Heat/White Light" (1997). Posner's ambitions here recall the illustrious Genesis programs of the late sixties, featuring short works by Pat O'Neill and Scott Bartlett, among others—perhaps the first truly commercial attempt to bring the avant-garde to average moviegoers. Although discontinued after Genesis II, it was reported that these shows had over 300 bookings.

9. Not unexpectedly, the social and material histories of the avant-garde have been less compelling to scholars than issues of aesthetic innovation. There are, however, piecemeal accounts that address distribution along with other institutional functions and often include video art or other nonfiction genres besides avant-garde film. See Grant Kester, "Rhetorical Questions: The Alternative Arts Sector and the Imaginary Public," *Afterimage*, 20, no. 6 (January 1993): 10–16; also Julie Zando, "Recipe for Radical Engagement," *MAIN: National Alliance for Media Arts and Culture* (June 1993): 3, 11–12. Another important source of information is the "Media Clips" section of *The Independent* in the early nineties.

10. The number of veteran and younger filmmakers who have curated individual programs or film series is quite extensive: Peggy Ahwesh, Bradley Eros, Brian Frye, Joe Gibbons, David Sherman, and others. They of course follow the lead of Jonas Mekas and the participation of Brakhage, Peter Kubelka, and James Broughton on the selection committee for Anthology Film Archives in the early seventies. Interestingly, the intervening generation of makers that came of age between, say, 1972 and 1985 were far less involved in curatorial or, for that matter, institutional activities in general.

11. Several brief caveats are necessary here. I base my information on what has opened in New York, on anecdotal reports from colleagues, and on movie-review search engines. A larger number of feature-length (one hour or longer) works have played at festivals, and I have not counted films made directly for cable TV, nor have I counted relatively conventional narratives made by artists formerly within the avant-garde network (e.g., Cheryl Dunye's 2001 HBO production, *Stranger Inside*). It is probable that a number of the filmmakers would reject the label of "experimental" or "avant-garde" for what they are currently making, but my criteria, as previously noted, have to do with institutional protocols and affiliations, not stylistic choices. Tangentially, there have been theatrical showings of feature-length documentaries on the careers of Brakhage, Snow, Warhol, Mekas, and Maya Deren.

12. In the early nineties, some of us felt that the sheer volume of product needed by emerging cable channels to fill their schedules, especially the odd gaps between films, would result in an economic, if not an aesthetic, bonanza for avant-garde makers. Although nothing remotely like the dream of televisual "discovery" has taken place, channels such as Sundance and IFC have occasionally run collections of short experimental works or programs combining experimental with documentary films (e.g., a 2002 tribute to New York City on Sundance included films by Hilary Harris, Jem Cohen, and Jeffrey Scher). PBS and affiliates such as WNET in New York have also sponsored programs or series containing recent films (e.g., WNET's "Reel NY" series).

13. I am grateful to Saul Levine, Adam Hyman, and Steve Anker for sharing their substantial knowledge of institutions and practices in Boston, Los Angeles, and San Francisco, respectively.

14. For more on exhibition patterns in LA, see Rita Gonzalez, "Screen Scene," *Release Print* 25, no. 6 (June/July 2002): 29–33.

15. For more on the Cinematheque, see Steve Anker's essay "A Brief History," in the pamphlet published in 2001 by the San Francisco Museum of Modern Art in honor of the organization's fortieth anniversary (www.sfmoma.org).

16. Information about the microcinema movement is available at www.microcinema.com. The Web site lists do-it-yourself screening spaces in, among other cities, Pittsburgh, Albuquerque, Atlanta, and Washington, D.C.

17. The mention of installations raises a tricky question that, unfortunately, goes outside the purview of this essay: the relationship of avant-garde cinema to the vogue for film and video pieces by gallery artists. There are, to be sure, distinct affinities between, say, the films of Shirin Neshat and those of Maya Deren, those of Pippilotti Rist and Owen Land, or the installations of Douglas Gordon and structural films of the seventies. Yet there is little or no crossover or collaboration between these realms. An instructive correspondence, however, exists between the anticorporate, low-tech, antimastery practices of avant-garde film and a variety of art *collectives* that use moving images in combination with assemblage and other media: recent groups include Bureau of Inverse Technology, Dearraindrop, and Forcefield. A well-received historical exhibition in 2001 at the Whitney Museum of American Art, "Into the Light," traced the origins of gallery artists' use of film/video images; of the eighteen artists represented, five are or were associated with the avant-garde (Snow, Warhol, Paul Sharits, Anthony McCall, and Yoko Ono). One indication of the chasm separating artworld and avant-garde is that the reported five-million-dollar budget for Matthew Barney's *Cremaster 3*—the last in a five-part series that his gallery, Barbara Gladstone, sold as a DVD edition of ten at $400,000 each—would probably have financed Stan Brakhage's entire 400-film output, to say nothing of Barney's poverty-ridden aesthetic touchstone, Jack Smith. For a useful discussion of gallery "movies" by leading theorists and practitioners, see Round Table, "The Projected Image in Contemporary Art," *October* 104 (spring 2003): 71–96.

18. Film was added to the display of painting, sculpture, and photography in 1979, four years after the first exhibits of video, avant-garde film's "artier" younger sibling. Although the physical context for projected images has varied—with occasional forays from the central theater into gallery spaces to accommodate installations and other nontraditional formats—my figures are derived from the programs curated and exhibited separately from the bulk of Biennial art. It is worth recalling that Sitney's 1985 gloomy prognosis for the movement was triggered by observations on the Biennial. I criticized certain aspects of the Biennial ethos in "Desire for Allegory: The Whitney Biennials," *Motion Picture* 2, no. 1 (fall 1987): 1, 6–7, 15.

19. "Andy Warhol Speaks," *Cahiers du Cinéma in English* 10 (May 1967): 39.

20. Dollar amounts of grants, along with exact production costs, are notoriously hard to pin down, for understandable reasons. Interviews with filmmakers rarely delve into this area, but an important exception is a collection of seventeen conversations conducted by fellow makers published in *Cinematograph* 2 (1986): 56–110. Another useful source of concrete information about production exigencies is the portfolio of responses to a questionnaire created for a special issue of *Millennium Film Journal* that I guest-edited: *MFJ* 35/36 (fall 2000): 4–60.

21. Sitney, *Visionary Film: The American Avant-Garde, 1943–2000* (New York: Oxford University Press, 1974/2000), 409.

22. Rainer, "Thoughts on Women's Cinema: Eating Words, Voicing Struggles," in *Blasted Allegories*, ed. Brian Wallis (New York: New Museum of Contemporary Art, 1987), 380.

23. Sitney, *Visionary Film*, 418.

24. I disagree with Sitney both that this is a "new" genre and that it is "dominant"; see *Visionary Film*, 410–14.

25. For an informative and theoretically nuanced discussion of this thread of activity, see

Catherine Russell, *Experimental Ethnography: The Work of Film in the Age of Video* (Durham: Duke University Press, 1999). Unfortunately, Russell does not treat exciting recent makers such as LaPore and Fenz.

26. Gunning, "Towards a Minor Cinema," 2, 3.

27. I have adapted the idea of bodily displacement from human image to apparatus in recent avant-garde history from Annette Michelson, "Gnosis and Iconoclasm: A Case Study of Cine-philia," *October* 83 (winter 1998): 11–15.

28. Ray Privett and James Krul, "A Cinema of Possibilities: An Interview with Brian Frye," *Millennium Film Journal* 37 (fall 2001): 40.

29. Critical accounts and documentation of this short-lived phenomenon are somewhat scattered; the earliest and most comprehensive study is Gene Youngblood, *Expanded Cinema* (New York: Dutton, 1970); see also David E. James, *Allegories of Cinema: American Film in the Sixties* (Princeton: Princeton University Press, 1989), 133–40. David Gerstein provides a brief overview of the issues at stake in the performance ideas of a younger generation in "Perforated Spaces: Breaking Out from Darkness," *Cinematograph* 1 (1985): 132–36. For a look at the inter-face between gallery performance and film, see Carolee Schneeman, *More than Meat Joy* (New Paltz, N.Y.: Documentext, 1979). Chrissie Iles offers an overview of the history of projected installations in "Between the Still and Moving Image." See *Into the Light: The Projected Image in American Art, 1964–1977,* ed. Chrissie Iles (New York: Whitney Museum of American Art, 2001), 32–69.

30. "Structural Film," *Film Culture* 47 (summer 1969): 1.

31. Sitney provides robust analyses of the films of Menken and Smith; see *Visionary Film,* 160–61, 326–27, and 235–58.

32. Privett and Krul, "Interview with Brian Frye," 37.

Permissions

An earlier version of "The Western Edge: Oil of LA and the Machined Image" appeared in *Millennium Film Journal* 12 (fall/winter 1982–83). Reprinted by permission of *Millennium Film Journal*.

"Springing Tired Chains: African American Experimental Film and Video" was first published in Phyllis R. Klotman and Janet K. Cutler, eds., *Struggles for Representation: African American Documentary Film and Video* (Bloomington: Indiana University Press, 1999). Copyright 1999 Indiana University Press. Reprinted by permission.

An earlier version of "Bodies, Language, and the Impeachment of Vision: The Avant-Garde at Fifty" appeared in *Persistence of Vision* 11 (1995). Reprinted by permission of the City University of New York.

"Appendix: Lines of Sight (A Travelogue)" was published as "Lines of Sight: A Travelogue" in *Millennium Film Journal* 35/36 (fall 2000). Reprinted by permission of *Millennium Film Journal*.

Index

Absolute films, 63

Acceleration (Stark), 52

Adynata (Thornton), 68, 139

Agee, James, 54

Ahwesh, Peggy, xv, 38, 40–41, 124, 134, 137, 150, 160, 162, 164, 187n5, 197n30

Airshaft (Jacobs), 54

Akerman, Chantal, 57

Albee, Edward, 130

Alien, 99

Allen's Last Three Days on Earth as a Spirit (Mekas), 40

Almereyda, Michael, 161

Altered States, 99, 101

Alter Kinder, 167

Althusser, Louis, 119, 120

American Dreams (Benning), 68, 69, 71, 72, 73, 139

American Werewolf in London, 99

Amerika (Razutis), 149

Andrews, Lawrence, 120, 122, 127, 130, 196n20

and they came riding into town on BLACK AND SILVER HORSES (Andrews), 127

Andy Warhol (Menken), 36

Anemic Cinema (Duchamp), 149

Angela Davis: Portrait of a Revolutionary, 40

Angell, Callie, 29

Anger, Kenneth, 28, 63, 84, 95, 101, 124, 161, 196n25, 199n25

An I for an I (Andrews), 120

Anker, Steve, 198n13, 200n1, 202n13

Annie Hall, 193n14

Anthology Film Archives, 7, 23, 154, 155, 156

Anticipation of the Night (Brakhage), 84

Antonio: A Portrait of the Woman, 184n4

Apropos of San Francisco (Levine), 43

Arnulf Rainer (Kubelka), 187n2

Aronowitz, Stanley, 16

Art for Teachers of Children (Montgomery), 156–57

Art Gallery of Ontario, 154, 156, 159

Art of Vision, The (Brakhage), 63, 64

Ashur, Geri, 40

Auden, W. H., 36

Auster, Paul, 46, 57

Autobiography, 35, 63, 75, 98, 114, 115, 142

Avocada (Vehr), xi, xii, xv, xvi
Award Presentation to Andy Warhol (Mekas),
    xi, 185n30

B, Beth, 157
Babobilicons (Krumins), 99
Bad and the Beautiful, The (Sonbert), 36
Baillie, Bruce, 11, 28, 36, 46, 80, 145, 160, 162,
    167, 171–73
Baldwin, Craig, 68, 117, 141, 143, 156, 158, 162
Ballet Mecanique (Leger), 105
Barney, Matthew, 203n17
Bartel, Paul, 157, 190n24
Barthes, Roland, 140
Bartlett, Scott, 101, 192n11, 202n8
Barton, Peter, 40
Barton, Rebecca, 158
Barucello, Gianfranco, 199n25
Bataille, Georges, 136
Baudelaire, Charles, 45, 46
Baudry, Jean-Louis, 137
Bazin, André, 27, 80
Bearden, Romare, 112
Beats, xi, 21, 50, 114, 183n43, 196n24
Beauty Becomes the Beast (Dick), 101
Beauty #2 (Warhol), 34
Beavers, Robert, 153, 161
Beck, Julian, 11
Beckman, Ericka, 101
Bedtime Story (Shatavsky), 140
Bell, Larry, 96, 107, 108, 192n6
Beloff, Zoe, 165
Belson, Jordan, 63, 101, 192n11
Benning, James, 68, 69, 71–75, 139, 162
Benning, Sadie, 124, 196n26
Berliner, Alan, 67, 157, 161
Berlin: Symphony of a Great City (Ruttman),
    57
Berman, Marshall, 46
Bertolucci, 62
Beydler, Gary, 95
Bierman, Gregg, 165
Birth of a Nation, The (Mekas), 40
Black Arts Movement, 112, 127, 194n2
Black Audio collective, 194n6
Black Celebration (Cokes), 118–19

Black Is . . . Black Ain't (Riggs), 120, 121, 122,
    124
Blake, William, 15
Bland, Edward, 11, 18
Bleu Shut (Nelson and Wiley), 76
Blow Job (Warhol), 28, 42
Blue Moses (Brakhage), 84
Bogawa, Roddy, 149
Bopping the Great Wall of China Blue
    (Levine), 38
Borden, Lizzie, 81, 89
Bordowitz, Gregg, 42
Bordwell, David, 154
Born in Flames (Borden), 81, 88, 89
Brakhage, Jane, 35
Brakhage, Stan, xii, xiii, xv, 12, 63, 77, 80,
    81, 84, 123, 133, 135, 145, 162, 166, 167,
    174–76, 179n3, 189n5, 200n32, 201n3;
    abstract films and, 38; aftering and, xiv;
    Co-op and, 15–16; domestic consumption
    and, 155; Metaphors on Vision and, 137;
    portraits by, 37–38; Snow and, 61; work of,
    28, 34, 36, 37, 46, 47, 48, 64, 139
Brecht, Bertolt, 92
Bremer, Arthur, 68–69, 70, 71
Bridges-Go-Round (Clarke), 48
Brig, The (Mekas), 7
Brinckman, Christine Noll, 193n18
Bromberg, Betzy, 96, 99, 100, 101, 102
Bronx Morning, A (Leyda), 47, 54
Broomfield, Nick, 115
Broughton, James, 42, 80, 190n24, 202n10
Brustein, Robert, 2
Burckhardt, Rudy, 52
Bureau of Inverse Technology, 203n17
Bursell, Cade, 165
By Twos and Threes: Women (Keller), 38

Caligari's Cure (Palazzolo), 81
Callenbach, Ernest, 183n37
Camper, Fred, 151
Campus, Peter, 195n13
Canyon Cinema, 155, 170, 182n20, 189n7,
    201n7
Carroll, Noël, 143, 151, 190n16, 195n11, 198n15
Cartwright, Lisa, 191n27

Cassavetes, John, 112, 180n2
Castro Street (Baillie), 171–73
Cather, Willa, 123
Césaire, Aimé, 127
Cézanne, Paul, 50
Chambers, Jack, 57, 163, 187n5
Chandler, Raymond, 95
Chelsea Girls, The (Warhol), 28, 50
Child, Abigail, 66, 67, 117, 160, 164, 199n26
Childs, Lucinda, 31
Chomsky, Noam, 65
Chuck D, 127
Ciao Bella (Bromberg), 99
Cinema of Surface, 168
Cinéma vérité, 18, 26, 27, 31, 101, 126, 130, 134, 145
Citizen Kane, 94
City films, 47, 50, 55, 57, 59–60, 83, 108–10
Clair, Rene, 46
Clancy (Brakhage), 37
Clarke, Shirley, 12, 26, 48, 50, 56, 86, 95
Cleaver, Eldridge, 128
Climate of New York, The (Burckhardt), 52
Close Encounters of the Third Kind, 102
Cohen, Jem, 57, 161, 202n11
Cokes, Tony, 118–19, 127, 160, 196n20
Collective for Living Cinema, 193n1
Color Adjustment (Riggs), 120
Color of Love, The (Ahwesh), 137
Coltrane, John, xii
Come Back Africa, 18
Communists are Comfortable, The (Kobland), 68
Comolli, Jean-Louis, 137
Conner, Bruce, 43–44, 117, 139, 142, 143, 163
Conrad, Tony, 63, 165, 166, 198n13
Conscious (Murray), 144
Cooperation of Parts (Eisenberg), 150
Corman, Roger, xi, 142
Cornell, Joseph, 43, 47, 141, 163, 184n6
*Corpus Callosum (Snow), 157
Couch (Warhol), 187n9
Covert Action (Child), 67
Creeley, Robert, 35, 108
Cremaster 3 (Barney), 203n17
Critical Mass (Frampton), 133

Cry of Jazz (Bland), 18
Cycles (Davis), 125

Dash, Julie, 125, 161
Daughters of Chaos (Keller), 38, 66, 140
David Holzman's Diary, 130
Davis, Angela, 121, 128
Davis, Zeinabu Irene, 125
Deadman, The (Ahwesh and Sanborn), 136, 150
Decasia (Morrison), 157
De Certeau, Michel, 56
De Hirsch, Storm, 190n24
De Landa, Manuel, 66
De Lauretis, Teresa, 190n23
De Laurot, Eduardo, 17
DeLillo, Don, 46, 180n1
De Mille, Cecil B., 109
Demon Seed, The, 101
Departure (Levine), 38
Deren, Maya, xv, 28, 80, 86, 101, 124, 144–45, 161, 197n2, 202n11, 203n17
De Rochemont, Louis, 128
Detour, 142
DeWitt, Tom, 192n11
Diaries, Notes, and Sketches (Mekas), 36, 185n30
Diary films, 4, 5, 7, 13, 38, 139, 162
Dick, Vivienne, 50, 101
Diploteratology (Land), 83
Disderi, André, 31
Displaced Person (Eisenberg), 68
Doberman, Gary, 81, 83, 190n17
Documentary, 10, 83, 109, 161; avant-garde and, 3, 11, 25, 37–38, 72, 115; cinéma vérité, 35, 128, 136
Dog Star Man (Brakhage), xiv, 61, 80, 146
Dominance, 20, 77, 126
Doppelganger (Ahwesh), 41
Dorn, Ed, 35
Dorsky, Nathaniel, 153, 161
Do the Right Thing, 119
Doublier, Francis, 118, 140
Downey, Robert, 157, 180n2
Driver, Sara, 81
Du Luart, Yolande, 40

Dunye, Cheryl, 124, 125–26, 130, 157, 196n26, 202n11

Dwoskin, Steven, 190n24

Dykstra, John, 101, 193n15

Easyout (O'Neill), 105, 106

Easy Rider, 2, 145

Eat (Warhol), 32, 33

Ehrenstein, David, 182n23

Eikhenbaum, Boris, 145

Eisenberg, Daniel, 68, 150

Eisenstein, Sergei, 54

Elder, R. Bruce, 149, 162, 198n10

Emerson, Ralph Waldo, 7, 16, 108

Empire (Warhol), 49, 50

Empire Strikes Back, The, 96

Emshwiller, Ed, 36, 95

End, The (MacLaine), 63

End Credits (Kobland), 42

Engel, Jules, 95

Epstein, Jean, 1, 149

Eros, Bradley, 164, 165, 202n10

Essay film, 57, 65, 66, 72, 139, 188n7

E.T., 99, 193n14

Eureka (Gehr), 52, 66, 140

Evans, Walker, 48, 141

Ewig, Laura, 96, 99, 100, 101

Expanded cinema, 18, 165

Export, Valie, 190n16

Fade to Black (Cokes), 119

Fall (DeWitt), 192n11

Fallen World, The (Keller), 38

Family Album (Berliner), 67

Farber, Manny, 83

Fassbinder, W. R., 84

Fast Trip, Long Drop (Bordowitz), 42

Faulkner, William, 92

Fejos, Paul, 94

Fenz, Robert, 162, 204n25

Filippo, Mary, 41, 149

Film-makers (Iimura), 36

Film-Makers' Cooperative, xvi, 6, 7, 8, 11, 14, 19, 155, 169, 179n3, 181n10, 189n7, 194n3, 201nn6–7

Film Portrait (Hill), 184n4

Firestone, Shulamith, 41

First Comes Love (Friedrich), 150

Fischinger, Oscar, 94, 192n5

Fisher, Morgan, 68, 141, 142, 148, 191n26

Five Bad Elements, The (LaPore), 162

Flag (Gibson), 124

Flaming Creatures (J. Smith), 7, 10, 11, 14, 15, 19

Fleischner, Bob, 138

Flicker, The (Conrad), 63, 101

Florey, Robert, 94, 187n7

Fluxus, 152, 165

Fonorof, Nina, 140, 162

Footprints (Morrison), 149

Foregrounds (O'Neill), 104, 105

Foucault, Michel, 65, 73

Fragments Project, The (Ahwesh), 41

Frampton, Hollis, 56–57, 63, 67, 75, 80, 81, 83, 133, 139, 142, 146, 176–77, 190n16, 199n30

Frank, Robert, 47, 50

Freud, Sigmund, 147

Friedrich, Su, 135, 148, 150, 157, 162, 199n30

Frye, Brian, xv, 164, 168, 202n10

Fuses (Schneeman), 167, 173–74

Futility (Snider), 144

Galaxie (Markopolous), 36

Gatten, David, 162

Gehr, Ernie, 52, 54–57, 58, 59, 63, 66, 83, 140, 145, 153, 160, 197n5

Geiser, Janie, 161

Geldzahler, Henry, 32

Generations (Gerson), 54

Genet, Jean, 10

Gently Down the Stream (Friedrich), 148, 199n30

George (Hills), 43

George Dumpson's Place (Emshwiller), 36

Geritz, Kathy, 158

Gerry, Lyn, 99

Gershfield, Burton, 95

Gerson, Barry, 54, 83, 164

Gibbons, Joe, 135, 162, 164, 202n10

Gibson, Linda, 124

Gidal, Peter, 83, 97, 190n19

Gilliam, Leah, 122, 123, 127

Gimme Shelter, 130

Ginsberg, Allen, xii, 11, 180n1
Gitlin, Todd, 6, 22, 182n28
Gloria! (Frampton), 43, 67, 140
Godard, 72, 84, 130, 142
Godmilow, Jill, 184n4
Goffman, Erving, 187n10
Go! Go! Go! (Menken), 48, 167
Goldin, Nan, 82, 186n31
Goldman, Peter Emanuel, 47
Gombrich, Ernst, 149, 185n16
Gordon, Bette, 66, 81, 82, 190n23
Gordon, Douglas, 203n17
Gorin, Jean-Pierre, 68
Gottheim, Larry, 46, 162
Governor, The (Brakhage), 37
Gratuitous Facts (Leeser), 96, 97–98, 99
Greaves, William, 128–29, 196n27, 196–97n28, 197n30
Greenaway, Peter, 157
Grenier, Vincent, 160
Griffi, Alberto, 199n25
Griffith, D. W., 40, 79
Grosz, George, 143
Guccione, Michael, 101
Gunning, Tom, 163, 193n16
Guns of the Trees (Mekas), 11, 17, 112
Gutman, Walter, 190n24
Guttenplan, Howard, 56, 57

Hammer, Barbara, 42, 160, 161
Hapax Legomena (Frampton), 80
Harrington, Curtis, 28, 95, 157, 161, 180n2
Harris, Hilary, 48, 202n11
Harris, Thomas Allen, 125, 161, 196n20
Hart of London, The (Chambers), 57, 163
Haynes, Todd, 135, 161
Heartfield, John, 143
Heaven, Earth and Hell (Harris), 125
Hebdige, Dick, 21
Heller, Eve, 161
Henry Geldzahler (Warhol), 32
Her Fragrant Emulsion (Klahr), 43, 137, 138
Herwitz, Peter, 168
Hide and Seek (Friedrich), 157
Highway (Harris), 48
Hill, Jerome, 8, 184n4

Hills, Henry, 43
History (Gehr), 63
Hitchcock, Alfred, 102, 142
Hold Me While I'm Naked (Kuchar), 50
Home Stories (Muller), 199n25
Hudina, Chuck, 165
Hughes, Langston, 216
Huillet, Danielle, 72
Hutton, Peter, 56, 57, 160, 162

I An Actress (Kuchar), 42
Iimura, Takahiko, 36
Illuminated Texts (Elder), 149
In Between: 1964–68 (Mekas), 8
Indeterminate Focus (McClure), 168
Institutional Quality (Land), 76, 83, 146
In the Bag (Taubin), 41
In the Street (Levitt, Loeb, and Agee), 54
Introduction to Arnold Schoenberg's Accompaniment to a Cinematographic Scene, 72
Is/Land, The (Goldberg and Oblowitz), 149

Jacobs, Ken, xv, 14, 15, 47, 55–56, 59, 63, 133, 137–38, 139, 153, 160, 163, 164, 170–71
Jacoby, Roger, 137, 167
James, David, 4, 31, 102, 116, 180n4, 183n43, 198n12
Jameson, Fredric, 20, 60, 144, 193n17
Jane (Brakhage), 37
Janie's Janie (Ashur and Barton), 40
Janine (Dunye), 124
Jarman, Derek, 157
Jarmusch, Jim, 87, 191n29
Jennifer, Where Are You? (Thornton), 40–41
Jennings, Jim, 48
Jones, Art, 127, 128
Journeys from Berlin/1971 (Rainer), 57, 67–68, 139
Julien, Isaac, 117, 157

Keller, Marjorie, 38, 66, 140, 179n3
Kelly, Robert, xii, 34, 35, 133, 179n1
Kino Da! (Hills), 43
Kiss (Warhol), 28, 187n9
Kitch's Last Meal (Schneeman), 165
Klahr, Lewis, 43, 136, 137, 138, 161, 162

Knowledge Reigns Supreme (Jones), 127, 128
Knowledge They Cannot Lose, A (Fonoroff), 140
Know Your Enemy (Jones), 127
Kobland, Ken, 42, 68, 149
Koyaanisqatsi, 109
Kren, Kurt, 162
Krumins, Diana, 99
Kubelka, Peter, 40, 81, 162, 187n2, 202n10
Kuchar, George, xiv, 42, 50, 84, 88, 124, 130, 153, 164

La Chinoise, 142
Laitala, Kerry, 162
Landscape and Desire (Kobland), 149
Lang, Fritz, 46
LaPore, Mark, 56, 162, 163, 204n25
La Raison avant la passion (Wieland), 83, 146
Larcher, David, 167
La Region Centrale (Snow), 63
Lawder, Standish, 52, 83, 199n21
Lee, Spike, 119, 184n1
Leeser, Tom, 96, 97, 98
Léger, Fernand, 105
Legions (Guccione), 101
LeGrice, Malcolm, 83, 97, 164, 200n1
Lemaitre, Maurice, 199n25
Le Maîtres fous, 65
Let's Make a Sandwich (O'Neill), 103
Let's Play Prisoners (Zando), 135
Letter from Siberia, 65–66
Levine, Charles, 43
Levine, Naomi, 10, 11
Levine, Saul, xii, 38, 39, 179n3, 183n36, 187n5, 202n13
Lewis, Brady, 149
Leyda, Jay, 54, 118
Life and Death of 9413—A Hollywood Extra, The (Vorkapich, Florey, and Toland), 94
Life Dances On (Frank), 47
Liotta, Jeanne, 165
Lipsett, Arthur, 163
Lipzin, Janis Crystal, 149
Little Stabs at Happiness (Jacobs), 170–71, 198n9
Lives of Performers (Rainer), 133
Lost Book Found (Cohen), 57

Lost Boundaries, 128
Lost, Lost, Lost (Mekas), 4, 6, 11, 30, 56, 199n30
Lowe, Pelle, 136, 164, 187n5
Ludlum, Charles, xv
Luma Nocturna (Pies), 192n11
Lumière brothers, xvi, 24–27, 29
Lye, Len, 166

MacLaine, Christopher, 63
Macunius, George, 152
Magellan (Frampton), 63, 67
Mahagonny (H. Smith), 63
Makavejev, Dusan, 72, 130
Malanga, Gerard, 31
Malina, Judith, 11
Manhatta (Strand and Sheeler), 47, 50
Manual of Arms (Frampton), 36, 43, 83
Manupelli, George, 85
Man Who Envied Women, The (Rainer), 66, 140
Man with a Movie Camera, 46, 57
Marasmus (Bromberg and Ewig), 96, 99, 100, 101
Marcuse, Herbert, 1, 2, 20
Margulies, Ivone, 134
Marilyn Times Five (Conner), 43–44
Marker, Chris, 65, 72, 130
Markopoulos, Gregory, 10, 12, 36, 41–42, 95
Martina's Playhouse (Ahwesh), 134
Mayhem (Child), 66
McCall, Anthony, 164, 203n17
McClure, Bruce, 165, 168
McClure, Michael, 35
McElwee, Ross, 115, 122
McLaughlin, Sheila, 81
McLuhan, Marshall, 97, 180n3
Mekas, Adolfas, 4, 6, 11
Mekas, Jonas, xi, 1, 6, 8, 14, 20, 21, 23, 35, 36, 56, 112, 130, 160; activism of, 3, 10, 12, 19; avant-garde and, 11, 134, 182–83n35; career of, 3, 4–5, 15, 153, 161
Menken, Marie, 36, 48, 50, 51, 52, 56, 86, 167
Merhige, Elias, 161
Meshes of the Afternoon (Deren), xv, 95, 197n2
Micheaux, Oscar, 130, 193n1
Michelson, Annette, 83, 189n11
Mills, C. Wright, 9, 181n14

Mitchell, W. J. T., 146

Montgomery, Jennifer, 156–57

Morrison, Bill, 149, 157

Mosholu Holiday (Kuchar), 50

Mothlight (Brakhage), 167

Movie, A (Conner), 117, 139, 142, 193n13

Mr. Hayashi (Baillie), 28

Muller, Matthias, 167, 199n25

MURDER and murder (Rainer), 157

Murder Psalm (Brakhage), 139

Murnau, F. W., 46

Murray, Julie, 136, 144

Nares, James, 38

Nauman, Bruce, 186n31, 195n13

Near Sight (Levine), 38

Necrology (Lawder), 52, 83

Nelson, Gunvor, 85, 153, 160

Nelson, Robert, 76

News from Home (Akerman), 57

Newsreel of Dreams (Vanderbeek), 193n13

New York Ghetto Fishmarket 1903 (Jacobs), 59

New York Newsreel, 13

New York Portrait (Hutton), 56

Nicholson, Annabel, 164

Night and Fog, 65

Nobody's Business (Berliner), 157

Non, Je Ne Regrette Rien (No Regret) (Riggs), 42, 120

Noren, Andrew, 160

Normal Love (J. Smith), 12

(nostalgia) (Frampton), 142

Notebook (Menken), 48, 51, 52, 167

Notes for Jerome (Mekas), 38

Notes on the Port of St. Francis (Stauffacher), 47

Now That the Buffalo's Gone (Gershfield), 95

#15: Untitled Seminole Patchwork Film (H. Smith), 167

N.Y.C. Diary '74 (Guttenplan), 56

NY NY (Thompson), 47, 48

Oblowitz, Michael, 149

Ode to the New Pre-History (Ahwesh), 134

Offon (Bartlett and DeWitt), 192n11

100 Views of New York (LaPore), 56

O'Neill, Pat, 93, 95, 102, 103–4, 108–10, 145, 187n5, 191n26, 193n18, 202n8

Ono, Yoko, 86, 203n17

On the Bowery (Rogosin), 47

On the Marriage Broker Joke as Cited by Sigmund Freud in Wit and its Relation to the Unconscious, *or Can the Avant-Garde Artist be Wholed?* (Land), 63, 76, 146, 147

Opposing Views (Leeser), 96, 97

Other Reckless Things (Lipzin), 149

Our Lady of the Sphere (Jordan), 192n11

Outer and Inner Space (Warhol), 28, 34

Out of Hand (Beckman), 101

Pacific Film Archive, 158

Paik, Nam June, 152, 195n13

Painting the Town (Jennings), 48

Palazzolo, Tom, 81, 85, 187n5

Paris qui dort (Clair), 46

Peggy and Fred in Hell (Thornton), 135, 140, 160–61

Pellicule (Lemaitre), 199n25

Pestilent City (Goldman), 47

Peterson, Vickie Z., 86

Picasso, Pablo, 26, 27, 34, 141

Piece Touche (Arnold), 199n25

Pierre Vallières (Wieland), 146

Pittsburgh Trilogy (Ahwesh), 41

Political Portraits (Markopolous), 36

Pollock, Jackson, 165

Polta, Steve, 165

Portrait of Jason (Clarke), 26

Portraits, 34, 38, 43, 50, 184n6; AIDS, 42; avant-garde, 27, 36, 37; emergence of, 27, 28; gay/lesbian, 41–42; self-, 26, 37, 164

Positiv (Hoolboom), 42

Posner, Bruce, 157, 201–2n8

Potluck and the Passion, The (Dunye), 126

Potter, Sally, 157, 190n16

Praise House (Dash), 125

Price, Luther, 135, 136, 164

Projection Instructions (Fisher), 148

Psychodrama, xiv, 25, 94–95, 101, 110, 122–28, 136, 164

Pull My Daisy (Frank and Leslie), 50, 55

Pynchon, Thomas, 46

Quarternion (Frampton), 43
Quixote (Baillie), 193n13

Rainer, Yvonne, xiv, 57, 66, 67–68, 72, 75, 81,
     133–34, 140, 149, 157, 162, 187n3, 190n16;
     narrative and, 88, 120
*Rameau's Nephew by Diderot (Thanx to Dennis
     Young) by Wilma Schoen* (Snow), 63, 133
Raps and Chants, Part II (Levine), 38
Raw Nerves (de Landa), 66
Razutis, Al, 149
Real Italian Pizza (Rimmer), 54, 83
Reble, Jurgen, 167
Recorder, Luis, 165
Reeves, Jennifer, 168
Regarding Penelope's Wake (M. Smith), 163
Reggio, Godfrey, 109–10
Remains to be Seen (Solomon), 137
Reminiscences of a Journey to Lithuania
     (Mekas), 5
Renee Walking/TV Talking (Leeser), 96
Resnais, Alain, 65
Rice, Ron, xi, 10, 130, 133
Riggs, Marlon, 42, 113, 115, 118, 120–21, 127,
     130, 195n12, 196nn21, 23
Rimmer, David, 54, 83
Robertson, Anne, 162
RocketKitKongoKit (Baldwin), 68, 143
Rodriguez, Jose, 162
Roger and Me, 114
Rogosin, Lionel, 18
Rome '78 (Nares), 38
Rose, Peter, 150, 160
Rose for Red (Wilson), 99
Rose Hobart (Cornell), 43, 44, 141, 184n6
Rosenquist, James, 32, 43
Rossellini, Roberto, 71, 72
Roszak, Theodore, 185n25
Rothschild, Amalie, 40
Rouch, Jean, 65
Routine Pleasures (Gorin), 68
Rubin, Barbara, 7, 10, 11, 12, 15
Rubin, Jerry, 20
Runs Good (O'Neill), 104, 106
Ruscha, Ed, 107
Ruttman, Walter, 57, 109

Sachs, Lynne, 149, 161
Sailboat, 1933 (Wieland), 146
Saks, Erin, 162
Sanborn, Keith, 136, 150, 160, 199n26
Sandusky, Sharon, 143
San Francisco Cinematheque, 154, 156, 158,
     159, 165, 194n5, 201n3
Sans Soleil, 72
Sapphire and the Slave Girl (Gilliam), 122, 123
Sapphire Tape #1: The Message (C. Smith), 126
Saugus Series (O'Neill), 105, 106
Scary Movie (Ahwesh), 134, 136
Scenes from the Life of Andy Warhol (Mekas), 40
Scenes from under Childhood (Brakhage), 35
Schneeman, Carolee, 133, 164, 165, 167, 173–74
Screen Test (Warhol), 29, 31, 42, 184n14, 187n9
Secondary Currents (Rose), 150
Sedgwick, Edie, 34
Sennett, Richard, 60, 133
Serene Velocity (Gehr), 43, 76, 80, 197n5
Serra, MM, 136, 155, 161
Serra, Richard, 78
7362 (O'Neill), 105–6
Shadows (Cassavetes), 112
Sharits, Paul, 43, 81, 137, 164, 203n17
Shatavsky, Esther, 140
She Don't Fade (Dunye), 125–26
Sheeler, Charles, 50
She Had Her Gun Already (Dick), 50
Shulie (Subrin), 41
Sidewinder's Delta (O'Neill), 104, 105, 106
Signal—Germany on the Air (Gehr), 57, 58, 59
silt, 165, 168
Silvercup (Jennings), 48
Single Wing Turquoise Bird, 95
Sink or Swim (Friedrich), 135
Sitney, P. Adams, xii, xiv, 7, 38, 40, 65, 67, 76,
     147, 151, 161, 166
Skyscraper (Clarke), 48
Smith, Cauleen, 126, 196n20
Smith, Harry, 32, 40, 167
Smith, Jack, xi, xv, 10, 14–15, 19, 41, 59, 84, 130,
     133, 136, 138, 152, 164, 182n23, 184n14,
     198n9
Smith, Michelle, 163, 164
Snider, Greta, 136, 144

Snow, Michael, 54, 61, 63, 81, 83, 84, 104, 133, 146, 153, 160, 202n11, 203n17
Snyder, Gary, 21–22
Sogo, Stom, 168
So Is This (Snow), 146, 148, 150
Solomon, Phil, 137, 141
Sonbert, Warren, 36, 42, 191n26
Song 15: Fifteen Song Traits (Brakhage), 34, 35–36
Songs (Brakhage), 34
Sonic Outlaws (Baldwin), 156
Sontag, Susan, 14, 36
Soothing the Bruise (Bromberg), 99
Sparkle's Tavern (McDowell), 81
Spiral, 154
Standard Gauge (Fisher), 68, 141, 142
Stark, Scott, 52, 160, 165
Stein, Gertrude, 34
Steiner, Wendy, 26
Still (Gehr), 54, 55, 83
Strand, Chick, 95, 162, 179n3
Strand, Paul, 50
Stranger Inside (Dunye), 202n11
Stranger than Paradise, 87
Straub, Jean-Marie, 72, 84
S:TREAM:S.S.ECTION:S.ECTION:S:S: ECTIQNED (Sharits), 137
Street, Mark, 168
Structural film, xiv, 37, 62, 76, 77, 79, 81, 83, 86, 119, 142, 147; body and, 133; critical underpinnings of, 190n15
Students for a Democratic Society (SDS), 8, 12, 13, 17, 19, 21–22
Subrin, Elizabeth, 41
Suicide Squeeze, The (Lewis), 149
Surface Tension (Frampton), 52
Symbiopsychotaxiplasm: Take One (Greaves), 128–29, 130, 131

Tambellini, Aldo, 164
Taubin, Amy, 41
Taylor, Cecil, 111, 127
Text of Light, The (Brakhage), 63
Thank You Jesus for the Eternal Present (Land), 81
Thigh Line Lyre Triangular (Brakhage), 84

Thirteen Most Beautiful Women (Warhol), 187n9
Thompson, Francis, 48
Thompson, Kristen, 154
Thoreau, Henry David, 16, 108, 186n4
Thornton, Leslie, 40–41, 68, 75, 135, 136, 139, 160–62, 199n26
Through a Lens Brightly: Mark Turbyfill (Markopoulos), 36
Tillman, Lynn, 81
Together (Broughton), 42
Toland, Gregg, 94
Tomb of Ligeia, The, xi
Tom, Tom, the Piper's Son (Jacobs), 76, 138, 163
Tongues Untied (Riggs), 117, 118, 120, 121, 124
Trance films, 28, 153
Tribulation 99: Alien Anomalies under America (Baldwin), 141, 143
Trilling, Diana, 2
Trinh Minh-ha, 162
Trumbull, Leslie, 169
Tscherkassky, Peter, 199n21
Tung (Baillie), 36
Turner, Victor, 22–23
23rd Psalm Branch (Brakhage), 189n5
2001, 101
Two Wrenching Departures (Jacobs), 137, 138

Un Chant d'amour (Genet), 10
Un chien andalou (Dali and Bunuel), 149
Under the Brooklyn Bridge (Burckhardt), 47
Untitled 1981 (Gehr), 55

Valentin de las Sierras (Baillie), 36
Vanderbeek, Stan, 11, 189n5, 193n13
Van Meter, Ben, 43
Van Sant, Gus, 161
Variety (Gordon), 66, 81, 82, 83, 191n29
Vawter, Ron, 42
Vehr, Bill, xi, xv, xvi
Veritus in Certu (Barudello and Griffi), 199n25
Vertigo, 94, 119
Vertov, Dziga, 1, 46, 54, 57, 109
Visit, The (Katz), 66
Visiting Desire (Beth B), 157
Vogel, Amos, 9, 14, 181n17

Von Praunheim, Rosa, 190n16
Von Sternberg, Joseph, 109
Vorkapich, Slavko, 94

Wait (Gehr), 83
Wallin, Michael, 143
Walsh, Jack, 161
Warhol, Andy, xv, 28, 34, 37, 41, 49, 56, 124,
  130, 157, 160, 180n2; critical literature on,
  185n18; documentary and, 185n17; por-
  traiture and, 28, 42; screen tests by, 132;
  structural film and, 80
Water and Power (O'Neill), 57, 103, 107, 108,
  109, 110
Watermelon Woman (Dunye), 157
Wavelength (Snow), 43, 54, 61, 76, 80, 83, 133,
  197n5, 200n32
Wedlock House: An Intercourse (Brakhage), 84
White, Hayden, 65, 71–72, 188n7
White, William H., 60
Whitman, Robert, 164
Whitman, Walt, 16
Whitney, James, 94
Whitney, John, 94, 189n6
Who Do You Think You Are? (Filippo), 41, 149
Wieland, Joyce, 83, 86, 146
Wiley, William T., 76
Williams, Spencer, 130, 193n1

Williams, William Appleman, 65
Wilson, Diana, 99
Window Water Baby Moving (Brakhage),
  174–76
Winter Footage, The (Jacobs), 55–56
Wolfe, Tom, 180n1
Wolfen, 101
Wollen, Peter, 157, 190n16
Women I Love (Hammer), 42
Women Make Movies, 155, 194n5
Wonder Ring (Brakhage), 47, 50
Woo Who? May Wilson, 40
WR: Mysteries of Organism, 72

XCXHXEXRXRXIXEXSX (Jacobs), 137–38,
  139

Yalkut, Jud, 164
Yellow Springs (Sharits), 43
You Are Not I (Driver), 81

Zando, Julie, 135
Zavattini, Cesare, 27, 28
*Zefiro Torna or Scenes from the Life of George
  Macunius* (Mekas), 40
Zinn, Howard, 65, 68
Zorns Lemma (Frampton), 52, 53, 76, 83,
  176–77, 199n30, 200n32

Paul Arthur is professor of English and film studies at Montclair State University. He is coeditor of *Millennium Film Journal* and a regular contributor to *Film Comment* and *Cineaste*. His essays on avant-garde cinema, documentary, and Hollywood genres have appeared in more than two dozen book anthologies and catalogs. He is a past president of the board of directors of the Film-Makers' Cooperative in New York and has been active in experimental filmmaking since 1971.